DATE DUE		
OCT 4 1999			

The
Rise of
Experimentation
in American
Psychology

Edited by

Jill G.

Morawski

The

Rise of

DISCARDED

Experimentation

in American

Psychology

YALE

UNIVERSITY

PRESS

NEW HAVEN

AND LONDON

Published with assistance from the foundation established in memory of Philip Hamilton Mc-
Millan of the Class of 1894, Yale College.

Designed by Jo Aerne and set in Electra type with
Helvetica Condensed for display by David E. Seham
Associates, Inc., Metuchen, N.J. Printed in the
United States of America by Vail-Ballou Press,
Binghamton, N.Y.

Library of Congress Cataloging-in-Publication Data
The Rise of experimentation in American
psychology / edited by Jill G. Morawski.
p.   cm.
Includes index.
ISBN 0–300–04153–5
1. Psychology, Experimental—United States—
History.
I. Morawski, Jill Gladys.
[DNLM: 1. Psychology, Experimental—history—
United States.   BF 181 R595]   BF181.R57
1988   150′.724—dc19
DNLM/DLC
for Library of Congress   87–18154   CIP

The paper in this book meets the guidelines for
permanence and durability of the Committee on
Production Guidelines for Book Longevity of the
Council on Library Resources.

10 9 8 7 6 5 4 3 2 1

CONTENTS

INTRODUCTION

At the end of the last century American psychologists moved to establish the laboratory, a well-marked territory, as a means to explore that other, less readily identifiable world of human experiences and their behavioral manifestations. The massive project to implement experimentation on mental processes necessitated the scrutiny and rejection of some deep cultural beliefs about personal experience and the extent to which they are accessible to others. The project also required substantial alterations in scientific work practices, since the laboratory had to accommodate human subjects, rather than gases, minerals, cells, molecules, and drosophila. Few of the instruments and procedures from the biological or physical sciences could be adopted directly. Instead, researchers had to construct ways of observing psychological events, often redefining the very phenomena along the way. They likewise had to devise entirely new work procedures that could meet the practical problems encountered when the experimenters' subjects were fellow humans.

Viewed in terms of its proper subject matter and work practices, experimental psychology can be seen as a transformative enterprise. Through the creation of laboratory instruments and techniques, the reeling, cacophonous world of human experiences was transformed into discrete, feasible problems that could be analyzed in controlled settings. Human experiences were translated into a shared scientific language and increasingly sophisticated inscriptions (both numeric and graphic) of that language. This was necessary for the growth of a professional community defined by a common language and skills.

But psychological experimentation has also had broader implications for society. Techniques of isolating, controlling, and describing human variables can ultimately serve technological ends, and such techniques have been extended to foster scientific social reform. When they have been used outside the laboratory, the presumed boundaries between researchers' scientific efforts and social interests have become further blurred. As a consequence, human experimentation has raised ethical and legal concerns, which have been especially salient whenever experimentation has been extended to natural environments or has utilized instruments (such as computers) for unobtrusive assessment or surveillance.

The design of new work practices to study humans has also required fundamental changes in social relations. Existing social and moral constraints have limited researchers' latitude to design relations between experimenters and their subjects. Yet, even within such confines, there have emerged distinctly new social arrangements, whose power is evident in the extent to which they have been maintained under a variety of conditions. Regulated "experimental" interactions have been attained even outside the geographical space of the laboratory proper: experimenters successfully induced them in schools, work places, and homes. In these projects, researchers have been allowed to impose assorted controls on the surrounding environment. New forms of conduct have been expected of the subject and experimenter alike. It comes as no surprise, then, that another major consequence of human experimentation has been the need for a new level of psychological analysis: the creation of a psychology of the psychology experiment and even a psychology of the psychologist.

The transformative nature of psychological experimentation illustrates how scientific work involves social and interpretive practices. It suggests various social consequences that can ensue from the implementation and reproduction of experimental procedures. New ways of perceiving, acting, speaking, and knowing were introduced with the invention of the "naive" subject, who supposedly knew nothing about the experimental conditions and could not interfere with them, and his or her counterpart, the knowing but detached "experimenter," who had masterful control of the testing situation. With the acceptance of these practices each participant acquires a particular role vis-à-vis the maintenance and ultimate evaluation of the situation. The roles are further structured whenever standardized tests and behavioral (usually nonverbal) tasks are substituted for the normal form of communication, ordinary conversation. Experimental techniques replace certain practices with other practices and, in so doing, generate new ways of imagining and treating human beings. In other words, experimental practices themselves modify our knowledge of human nature. They provide a new language of psychical events, and interpretations of these events, in a reflexive and dialectic manner, influence the course of subsequent conduct, including experimentation.

This volume aims at a better historical understanding of the psychology experiment and how it has structured both social relations and our knowledge of human conduct. Historians of psychology have only recently begun to study the archaeology of the experiment. Until the late 1960s, most historians simply saw experimentation as the *sine qua non* of psychology's scientific status. So important was the symbolic status of experimentation that historians invested substantial energies in debating, for instance, which was the first psychological laboratory and which lab had the more sophisticated equipment.[1] Most of psychology's textbook histories, following a prototype established by E. G. Boring's text, herald experimentation as the key to the scientific ascendancy of psychological knowledge.[2]

For most of this century, histories of psychology, buttressed by conventional philosophies of science, have focused on "crucial" experiments, "clever" designers, or on otherwise notable experimental procedures and results. In part as a reaction to this reification of experimentation and idolatry of science-like activities and in part as a rejection of strictly internalist accounts, historians in the 1960s began investigating the broader social context in which American psychology developed. There thus emerged a new scholarship focusing on other factors that shaped the science. Studies documented the way in which economics, politics, and metaphysics were constitutive of psychological knowledge. They demonstrated that, although fashioned as a positive science, American experimental psychology, even avowedly atheoretical behaviorism, has been built on firm moral, often religious, foundations. The political influences on psychology have been diverse, and there is now ample evidence of the political ideology that undergirds mental testing, eugenics, immigration, and education.[3]

Tracing these political underpinnings has also indicated how practical problems, more or less connected with larger ideological commitments, have fostered certain *styles* of work and *attitudes* toward the objects of inquiry. For example, psychologists specializing in mental tests worked jointly to standardize test formats, thereby relieving interpersonal conflict, disunity, and internal competition among test-designers. Problems surrounding the distribution of tests for commercial use and the control of who would do the testing had to be resolved, one solution being the creation of corporations for marketing and administering various forms of tests. In fact, the corporate model, complete with management hierarchies, division of labor, and the image of the devoted company man was adopted more than once as a solution to the theoretical disunity and inadequate research styles that many psychologists found threatening in the 1920s. The interdependence of work situations and intellectual developments is likewise illustrated in the response of psychologists to unemployment during the depression. In this instance the crises led some psychologists to form a society that simultaneously promised to improve employment opportunities within the profession while promoting a somewhat radical commitment to political and social action.[4]

Recent studies go further in suggesting the need to examine more closely not just psychologists' actions and beliefs, but also their accounts of these actions and beliefs. Psychologists' designations of "discovery," "facts," "data," "genius," and the like are verbal strategies for giving symbolic meaning to ongoing events. Through such socially constructed accounts, researchers tally the success or failure of work and reach consensus over the meaning of particular actions. In giving symbolic form to work practices, this accounting also provides a disciplinary lore, a repertoire of community myths.[5] As a result of such mythmaking, August Comte came to be named the father of social psychology, at once equipping social psychologists with signifiers of proper epistemology, absolving them from accusations of metaphysical leanings, and enhancing their status as positive scientists (not social reformers). Researchers' accounts of their work and heritage are not fixed, however, and the meaning that is attached to scientific events may change. In the case of John Watson's famous conditioning of Little Albert, the interpretation of the experiment altered with the periodic modifications in learning theory.[6]

Toward Studies of Laboratory Life

These investigations have sparked an interest in psychologists' day-to-day practices. This interest leads to the experiment and frequently to the laboratory setting in which most experimental work is conducted. Studies of the ideology of psychological knowledge have not delineated fully the connections between particular personal desires or class needs and the elaborate symbol systems that have constituted psychological knowledge. By analyzing work practices like experimentation, however, it is possible to locate some of the means by which personal ambitions, social interests, and the like are transformed into action and eventually into a symbolic system of knowledge claims.

It seems that studies of experimentation must proceed with a less restricting sense of the distinction between the laboratory (the place where science is done) and the outside world (society). Just as recent historians have uncovered the significance of ideology and everyday work practices, so sociologists of science are uncovering ways in which laboratory activities resemble ordinary social conduct. Bruno Latour has convincingly argued that studies of science have wrongly perceived boundaries between the laboratory (as microcosm) and society (as macrocosm). He has suggested, instead, that laboratory work begins by reproducing events that are occurring outside the lab and, in so doing, actively transforms such events. At the end of this process "societies are displaced and reformed with and through the very contents of science."[7] Scientific investigation then, requires attention to such dynamic displacements in our sense of the world. Taking Latour's argument seriously means seeing the laboratory, that geographically confined inner space, as being confected in much the same way as the boundaries of the inner space of the mind.

Social-Historical Understandings of Experimentation

Extending these understandings of science to psychology makes obvious the need to examine the experiment. Before all else it is important to recognize the real sense in which experimentation has comprised psychologists' work skills and has been critical to the identity of early American psychologists. This identity was complicated by the fact that psychologists, unlike other scientists, could not simply set out to find an interesting event and then relocate it within the laboratory. First, psychologists had to gain confidence in their laboratory skills, which, among other things, led them to emulate the higher sciences. In a preface to his 1892 outline of a psychology course, Edmund C. Sanford reminded potential instructors that "the student of psychology must have its facts and principles brought home to him in a way not inferior to the best in other sciences, if psychology is to have the infusion of new vigor that they have had, and afford the healthy and virile training that they afford."[8] Some researchers, however, were skeptical about this identification: the Chicago-trained psychologist Harvey Carr referred to this attitude as psychologists' "inferiority complex."[9] Not surprisingly, laboratory training received high priority in the newly established psychology departments and programs. The first generation of American psychologists, those who received graduate training in Germany, often embellished their memoirs with detailed accounts of innumerable hours spent in dark chambers or fixating on colorful stimuli as part of a proper psychological training. A plethora of painstakingly prepared textbooks, articles, and manuals were developed for experimental training. Apparatuses were ingeniously designed specifically for use in classroom demonstrations of experimental procedures or effects. Proof of experimental skills was a requirement for calling oneself a psychologist, or at least for gaining entry into most professional organizations.

The centrality and intensity of experimental training fostered particular styles of work, but this training also had symbolic functions. Many psychologists saw the mastery of experimental technique as preparation for manhood, truthfulness, and rationality. Experimental skills qualified one not just to be a scientist but to become more selfless, unprejudiced, honest, and reasonable—in other words, to attain the highest qualities of humanity and citizenship. When Sanford wrote that training in experimentation is a means to infuse "new vigor" and provide "healthy and virile" exercise, he was referring to a correct scientific attitude *and* a desirable psychological character. In Victorian culture, the vision of science as a noble activity—as a way to discipline the mind to be rational and pure—was not only a professional ideology but also a means to reduce the tensions between science and religious traditions.[10]

Psychologists elaborated on and ultimately exaggerated these metaphors of citizenship and scientific work, used them in private as well as public accounts, and conscientiously instilled them in their students. Edward Titchener referred to the necessity of "long training" to overcome the "ignorance" that he observed in the untrained. In his autobiography, E. W. Scripture, founder of the labs at Yale, lamented that the psychologist of his later years was no longer "a fully trained man." Almost forty years earlier Scripture had recommended training in experimentation, claiming that it would heighten cognitive and physical abilities and thus prepare not just "earnest scientific workers" but also typesetters, sign-painters, and the Harvard crew. He encouraged the "education of men, instead of bookworms and mummies." In making such claims, he concurred with G. Stanley Hall, another founder of labs and graduate programs, in believing that research "emanicipates the mind from error and superstition," reinvests the adult with childlike "wonder and curiosity," and above all, "gets the mind into independent action, so that men become authorities and not echoes." To Scripture, experimental training, along with mathematical skills, was essential if the psychologist were to understand the workings even of his wife's mind.[11]

Whether guided by metaphors of religion, manhood, or combat, or later by corporate models, discourse on experimenters and the experimental method gave meaning to work activities. This talk of the noble character and exceptional duties of the experimenter intimates the same American archetype associated with the explorer, the hero, and the astronaut. In locating rationality and truthfulness in experimentation, such talk also accorded power and prestige to experimenters. It ultimately underscored an image of expertise that was to help psychologists participate in social reform and commercial ventures and to gain financial support for their research.

Analysis of the actual evolution of laboratory practices and the participants' accounts of such practices reveals the social structure of psychological work. Other facets of this structure are seen in the ways in which experimentation changed social interactions and conceptions of psychological phenomena. As suggested earlier, the interactional changes included the creation of special roles for experimenters and participants alike. The subject matter of research, psychological experiences, also underwent transformation. Debates over what was to count as a "reaction," a "sensation," a "distraction," or an "idea" were frequent. More complicated were decisions about what was to count as "intelligence," "anger," "creativity," "masculinity," "neurosis," or "genius." During the first half of this century researchers wrestled with various techniques for making psychological phenomena amenable to experimentation. A popular mode of reformulation was the direct translation of a phenomenon into quantitative form, such as the Intelligence Quotient (IQ) or the description of Greek and English verse through "indicator numbers." Another mode of redefining phenomena entailed the use of behavioral definitions: for instance, a "distractor" was any stimulus that altered the behavior of an individual exposed to it. Most exemplary of translation modes was "operationalism," the logical positivist reduction of problems to their logical, empirical (behavioral), and mathematical forms.[12]

The (re)interpretive tasks of translating ordinary experiences and events into a specialized scientific language were held to be absolutely essential for the production of valid knowledge. Even the ideas of Freud, used often in American psychology, had to be redefined in experimental language before their veridicality could be appraised. Such reinterpretation was essential to establishing a massive enterprise for producing knowledge.

The alterations both in the phenomena under study and in the performance roles of all experimental participants have had unintended consequences. First, the new identities, social relations, and specialized language have resulted in knowledge claims that in the end may be more relevant to laboratory life than to ordinary life outside the lab. In addition, the knowledge acquired through these alterations and displacements affects future relations in experimental settings and hence can influence the content of future knowledge claims. Finally, the recent emergence of a more political self-consciousness—what Michael Foucault called a sense of "subjectivity"—has produced a critical attitude toward aspects of human experimentation and social control.[13] Recognition of these and other consequences has threatened the validity of the psychology experiment, and during the last two decades a number of psychologists have proposed new research techniques to accommodate these consequences. Some have suggested that the social relations of the experiment become more like those of a partnership, a dramatic skit, an anthropological field study, or mutual storytelling.

The rise of cognitive psychology has displaced many of the threatening consequences of experimentation, however. Cognitive theories tend to neglect what are taken to be "social" features, including those in experimental settings. Further, the study of internal, often unconscious, cognitive functioning makes it more difficult for nonpsychologists to question laboratory findings, and the use of computers makes the subject matter even less accessible to them. At present, the significant, if sometimes disturbing, consequences of experimental arrangements are receiving little attention, and the authority of experimentation is not being seriously challenged.

The chapters in this volume exemplify the diversity among the emerging studies of laboratory culture. They are not intended to provide a comprehensive picture of the genesis of psychological experimentation. Rather, they illustrate the multiple paths to understanding psychological science in terms of work practices, social relations, and the ongoing task of interpreting experiences and events.

The first chapter illuminates the process of redefining psychic phenomena in quantitative terms. Using the cases of psychophysics and mental testing, Gail Hornstein analyzes this radical translation. The introduction of quantification posed serious conceptual, as well as practical, problems, which had to be either resolved or denied if psychology were to serve the institutional control of practical social problems. Once adopted, quantitative methods enabled researchers to advance forceful scientific claims and, more important, to extend their techniques to situations outside the laboratory. Chapters 6 and 7 examine the extension of such methods to the industrial work place and to the lifelong experiences of individuals.

Just as psychologists had to construct definitions of their subject matter, so they had to negotiate new social relations in experimental situations. In chapter 2, Kurt Danziger traces the shifting social status and identity of the "subjects" of psychology experiments. He examines scientific language to determine how psychologists identified the people who participated in experiments. Karl Scheibe considers the other major social role in experimentation, that of the psychologist. Inside and outside laboratory situations psychologists have held special advantages in negotiating social relations. Scheibe's chapter locates these advantages and suggests their mutability over time. Despite the experimenter's privileged position, the social relations that could be established in experiments have been constrained by both material conditions and cultural norms. These constraints, or scientific "impossibilities," are considered in chapter 4, which takes case studies to illustrate limitations of laboratory conduct and the strategies that researchers have employed to circumvent them and so continue their work. Like the previous chapter, this analysis shows the psychologists' advantage to be central to the strategical handling of constraints.

Psychologists' styles of work have also been influenced by conditions outside the local work place. Psychologists have had to communicate with one another to exchange information and to reach agreement about contesting views. Professional societies have provided such communication opportunities, and Laurel Furumoto traces the genesis of one such organization, the Experimentalists. Her investigation reveals how this professional society and the resultant science were guided by larger social factors, as well as by scientific aims, and how the group's rules excluding women had real consequences both for women and for psychology. Prevailing cultural conditions influence even the experiments themselves, and in his study of the classic Hawthorne experiments, Richard Gillespie documents the social and political dynamics of industrial research at the Hawthorne plant. His chapter outlines the manifestations of these dynamics in the experiment and discloses the real power scientists have to control and give public meaning to workers' behavior. In the following chapter, Henry Minton's analysis of Lewis Terman's studies of the gifted illustrates other social dynamics of experimenting in the real world. As a major figure in the development of tests and assessment measures, Terman exemplifies the psychologist's ability to maintain his advantage by controlling the interpretation of psychological experiences (through psychometric tests) and extending his authority to create an influential relationship (often paternal) with participants.

Experimental settings and their unique social relations have influenced the knowledge ultimately produced. However, this has not always been recognized, and even when it has been, it has sometimes been regarded as unproblematic. Experimental "artifacts" are one such case where certain consequences of experiments were recognized and deemed undesirable, and attempts were eventually made to eradicate them. Unlike its archaeological counterpart, the psychological artifact is not considered a "found object" of value, but rather, an accidental one that should be eliminated. Jerry Suls and Ralph Rosnow reconstruct the history of experimental artifacts and document psychologists' continued reluctance to confront one of the most revealing implications of experimentation. The final chapter concerns not a consequence of experimentation, but an attempt to remedy such consequences. Subjects are frequently not aware of what is happening in an experiment, and a "debriefing" process has been introduced to inform them of what actually occurred. As Benjamin Harris has found, the language and practice of debriefing have surplus meanings which, when unpacked, reveal ambiguities and contradictions in this experimental procedure. Once analyzed, the discourse on debriefing confirms connections between scientific practice and social structure.

These chapters offer an entry into the historical and social study of psychological experimentation in the twentieth century. Much more work remains to be done; but an initial understanding of the social relations and styles of work associated with the human psychology experiment will facilitate analyses of its material bases—from instrumentation and other devices for recording psychic experience to the economic support systems of universities, foundations, and governments. Training procedures and scientific language, verbal and written, can also be analyzed, and their local and cultural variations recorded. Such studies uncover the inherently social nature of the experiment. The psychological laboratory will then come to be seen not as a place admitting those who have faith, to borrow a famous expression in the natural sciences, but as a place where we can begin to understand the nature and consequences of this faith.

Notes

1. Sigmund Koch aptly describes such historical exercises as illustrating a " 'science' legislated into existence by fiat" ("Wundt's Creature at Age Zero—and as Centenarian: Some Aspects of the Institutionalization of the 'New Psychology'," in *A Century of Psychology as Science,* ca. Sigmund Koch and David E. Leary (New York: McGraw-Hill, 1985), p. 10.
2. E. G. Boring, *A History of Experimental Psychology* (New York: Century, 1929). On the politics of Boring's historiography, see John M. O'Donnell, "The Crisis of Experimentalism in the Twenties: E. G. Boring and his Uses of Historiography," *American Psychologist* 34 (1979):289–95.
3. On the religious and moral foundations of modern American psychology, see Clarence J. Karier, *Scientists of the Mind: Intellecutal Foundations of Modern*

Psychology (Urbana: University of Illinois Press, 1986); David E. Leary, "The Intentions and Heritage of Descartes and Locke: Toward a Recognition of the Moral Basis of Modern Psychology," *Journal of General Psychology* 10, no. 2 (1980):283–310; J. G. Morawski, "Assessing Psychology's Moral Heritage through our Neglected Utopias," *American Psychologist* 37 (1982):1082–95. On behaviorism, see Franz Samelson, "Organizing for the Kingdom of Behavior: Academic Battles and Organizational Policies in the Twenties," *Journal of the History of the Behavioral Sciences* 21 (1985):33–47; John M. O'Donnell, *The Origins of Behaviorism: American Psychology, 1870–1920* (New York: New York University Press, 1985). On psychology and World War I, see Thomas M. Camfield, "Psychologists at War: The History of American Psychology and the First World War" (Ph.D. diss., University of Texas at Austin, 1969); Franz Samelson, "Putting Psychology on the Map: Ideology and Intelligence Testing," in *Psychology in Social Context*, ed. A. R. Buss (New York: Irvington, 1979). On ideology, see also, A. R. Buss, ed. *Psychology in Social Context*; Nicholas Pastore, *The Nature-Nurture Controversy* (New York: King's Crown Press, 1949); Clarence J. Karier, "Testing for Order and Control in the Corporate Liberal State," in *The IQ Controversy*, ed. N. J. Block and G. Dworkin (New York: Pantheon, 1976), pp. 339–73. M. M. Sokal, ed. *Psychological Testing and American Society, 1890–1930* (New Brunswick: Rutgers University Press, 1987).

4. Gail Hornstein, "Intelligence Testing and the Quantification of Psychology" (Paper presented at the annual meeting of the American Psychological Association, Toronto, 1984); Lorenz Finison, "Unemployment, Politics and the History of Organized Psychology," *American Psychologist* 31 (1976):747–55; J. G. Morawski, "Organizing Knowledge and Behavior at Yale's Institute of Human Relations," *Isis* 77 (1985):219–42; Michael Sokal, "The Origins of the Psychological Corporation," *Journal of the History of the Behavioral Sciences* 17 (1981):54–67.

5. Barry Barnes and Steven Shapin, eds., *Natural Order: Historical Studies of Scientific Culture* (Beverly Hills, Calif.: Sage, 1979); Augustine Brannigan, *The Social Basis of Scientific Discoveries* (Cambridge: Cambridge University Press, 1981); Karin Knorr-Cetina and Michael Mulkay, eds., *Science Observed: Perspectives on the Social Study of Science* (Beverly Hills, Calif.: Sage, 1983); Henrika Kuklick, "The Sociology of Knowledge: Retrospect and Prospect," *Annual Review of Sociology* 9 (1983):287–310; Bruno Latour and Steve Woolgar, *Laboratory Life: The Social Construction of Scientific Facts* (Beverly Hills, Calif.: Sage, 1979); Steven Shapin, "History of Science and its Sociological Reconstructions," *History of Science* 20 (1982):157–207.

6. Franz Samelson, "History, Origin, Myth and Ideology: Comte's Discovery of Social Psychology," *Journal for the Theory of Social Behavior* 4 (1974):217–31; Benjamin Harris, "What Ever Happened to Little Albert?", *American Psychologist* 34 (1979):151–60.

7. Bruno Latour, "Give Me a Laboratory and I Will Raise the World," in *Science Observed*, p. 154.

8. E. C. Sanford, "A Laboratory Course in Physiological Psychology," *American Journal of Psychology* 4 (1892):141.

9. Harvey A. Carr, in *The History of Psychology in Autobiography*, vol. 3, ed. Carl Murchison (Worcester, Mass.: Clark University Press, 1936), p. 80.

10. Sanford, "a Laboratory Course in Physiological Psychology," p. 141; David Hollinger, "Inquiry and Uplift: Late Nineteenth-Century American Academics and Moral Efficacy of Scientific Practice," in *The Authority of Experts*, ed. Thomas L. Haskell (Bloomington: Indiana University Press, 1984), pp. 142–56.

11. Edward B. Titchener, *A Text-book of Psychology* (New York: MacMillan, 1910), p. 350; E. W. Scripture, in *A History of Psychology in Autobiography*, vol. 3, pp. 231–62; (1936); idem, "Methods of Laboratory Mind-Study," *Forum*, 17 (1894):558–70.

12. On "indicator numbers," see Scripture, in *Autobiography*, p. 239. On "distractors," see Stanley Dulsky, "What is a Distractor?" *Psychological Review* 39 (1932):590–92.

13. Michael Foucault, "The Subject and Power," *Critical Inquiry* 8 (1982): 777–95.

The
Rise of
Experimentation
in American
Psychology

1

Quantifying
Psychological
Phenomena:
Debates,
Dilemmas,
and Implications

Gail A. Hornstein*

Mount Holyoke

College

Throughout the history of science, quantification has been taken to be one of the key elements in the characterization of a discipline as scientific. Since few phenomena are quantitative per se, every scientific discipline has had to create a conceptual and methodological apparatus by which to render its phenomena quantifiable. However, disciplines differ from one another with respect to the difficulty of this task.[1] One reason why the scientific status of psychology has always been problematic is that a long tradition, dating at least from the work of Kant, has maintained that psychological phenomena

*Portions of this chapter were presented in somewhat different versions in papers entitled "Methodological Change in Science: A Case Study from the History of Perceptual Psychology," given at a meeting of the Sigma Xi Society, Mount Holyoke College, March 1985, and "The Quantity Objection in Psychophysics: A Neglected Chapter in the Institutionalization of a Quantitative Perspective in Psychology," given at the June 1985 meeting of Cheiron, The International Society for the History of the Behavioral and Social Sciences, in Philadelphia. I acknowledge with gratitude the extremely helpful comments and criticism of my colleagues at Tremont Research Institute, especially Elihu M. Gerson, Susan Leigh Star, and Adele Clarke, during the period when I was first formulating many of these ideas. I also thank Rand B. Evans, Evelyn Fox Keller, Jill G. Morawski, Michael M. Sokal, Susan Leigh Star, and William R. Woodward for their careful reading and cogent critique of an earlier draft of this chapter. Some of the research reported here was supported by NSF grant SES-8409068. Support during the preparation of this chapter was provided by the National Endowment for the Humanities and by Mount Holyoke College.

are *in principle* not capable of quantification; hence, no effort at transforming its phenomena can make psychology a science. Nevertheless, in spite of the persistence of this view, late nineteenth-century psychologists undertook as their main task the creation of a scientific psychology. The difficulty inherent in the effort to make psychology a science when its phenomena were seen as being inherently nonquantitative created a major dilemma for the discipline, and attempts at resolving this dilemma have been crucial to the construction of a coherent framework for psychological research.

If we start by accepting the assumption that it was in fact desirable to make psychology a science,[2] we can identify two possible strategies for resolving this dilemma. On the one hand, psychology could have been defined as a science on grounds other than its being quantitative, which would have meant advancing a conceptualization of science that differed from the standard natural science model. On the other hand, an attempt could have been made to transform or redefine psychological phenomena so as to render them capable of quantification, thereby making it possible to define psychology as a science on traditional grounds.

Nineteenth-century American psychologists chose to adopt the latter strategy.[3] During the period roughly spanning the years 1860–1940, two distinct transformations took place. First, a wide range of psychological phenomena (for example, perception, intelligence, personality, and learning) were fundamentally *redefined* to make their basic properties quantifiable. Second, psychological phenomena that resisted quantitative treatment (for example, forms of consciousness, spirituality, and will) were *jettisoned* from the domain of legitimate empirical psychology. As a consequence, psychology shifted in the American context from being a discipline which seemed inherently nonquantitative to one that relied almost exclusively on quantitative approaches.

This shift toward a quantitative perspective did not occur simultaneously across all lines of research; initially, it centered on two areas—psychophysics and mental testing—and then spread from these to the rest of the discipline. The fact that these areas were the first to adopt quantitative methods meant, among other things, that psychophysicists and mental testers became the arbiters of what constituted appropriate forms of measurement for the discipline as a whole.

In this chapter, I analyze the complex social and historical processes underlying the movement toward a quantitative perspective, as well as the means by which the move was accomplished, the functions it served, and the consequences it has had for the nature of research practice in psychology. In contrast to the standard histories, which present the shift toward quantification as if it were an uncomplicated linear process toward "increasing maturity of the field,"[4] I devote considerable attention to the difficulties that faced psychologists as they attempted to quantify psychological phenomena, and the repeated reformulations, debates, and negotiations that took place regarding the conceptualization of quantification and the general possibility of mental measurement.

The fact that these debates and negotiations have typically been omitted from the standard histories illustrates the general process, discussed in detail by Mendelsohn, Star, and others, by which scientific perspectives become stripped of the social, political, and economic contexts in which they were created.[5] This process of deletion renders scientific approaches static and ahistorical, thereby obscuring the ways in which they represent attempts at solving particular technical or definitional problems facing a discipline at a given moment in its development. This general problem is particularly acute with respect to methodologies, which are typically presented as mere sets of techniques, lacking any social or political component, with methodological change regarded simply as technical "progress."

By contrast, I start from the assumption that the designation of a particular method as an "advance" over others and the general determination of which methods are "scientific" depend on complex negotiations and debates within a particular scientific community. Thus, in examining the development and institutionalization of a quantitative perspective in psychology, I focus on the inherently social nature of the process by which this transformation came about. I begin with the effort to quantify sensation, in the area of psychophysics, the first major battlefield on which the possibility of a quantitative perspective was fought out.

Psychophysics: The Quantification of Sensation

As a line of research, psychophysics began in the mid-1800s in response to the by then well-known finding that the perception of changes in the strength of a stimulus is not isomorphic with changes in stimulus intensity as measured by a physical measuring instrument. For example, if the luminosity of a visual stimulus is increased by a factor of two, the perceived brightness of that stimulus does not change to the same degree—that is, it does not appear to be twice as bright. However, although it could clearly be said that one stimulus appeared brighter than another, one pitch sounded higher than another, and so forth, these were qualitative distinctions. The question that arose was whether there was any meaningful way of *measuring* these differences, of saying precisely *how much* brighter one stimulus appeared than another.

The solution that the German physicist Gustav Fechner proposed to this problem in the 1860s was predicated upon a key assumption: that although psychological dimensions could not be measured in the same ways that physical dimensions could, they could nevertheless be measured using special psychological procedures.[6]

One such procedure employed an empirical psychological unit as the measure of psychological magnitude. When the difference in brightness between two stimuli was so small that an observer could just barely see it as a difference, it was said to be a "just noticeable difference," or jnd. Originally introduced by the physiologist E. H. Weber as an observational unit, Fechner converted it into a theoretical unit, making the assumption that all jnds were equal in subjective magnitude and could thus be used as unit intervals. This meant that numerals could be assigned to stimuli so as to represent the number of brightness jnds they lay above brightness zero (either an arbitrary zero or the lower threshold for brightness). Using this logic, Fechner proposed the following law:

$$\psi = k\log\phi,$$

where ψ is a psychological magnitude expressed in jnd units, ϕ is a physical magnitude expressed in the appropriate physical units, and k is a constant that varies for different perceptual modalities. Fechner went on to outline a set of methods that could be used to gather empirical data in accordance with the general logic of this psychophysical law. The three main methods were:

> 1. The method of limits. *The subject was presented with a standard stimulus and a variable stimulus, which, on different trials, was made equal to or larger than the standard. The value of the variable stimulus was increased in systematic steps, so that the experimenter could determine at exactly what value it was perceptibly larger than the standard.*
> 2. The method of average error. *The subject was required to adjust a variable stimulus so that it seemed subjectively equal to a given standard stimulus. This was done a large number of times, and the arithmetic mean of all the obtained values was calculated.*
> 3. The method of constant stimuli. *Values for the variable stimulus were fixed at the beginning of the experiment, and each of these values was presented to the subject a large number of times in random order, either alone or in comparison with a standard stimulus.*

During the sixty to seventy years following the publication of Fechner's work, innumerable objections and criticisms were made of his assumptions, his mathematics, and the specifics of the law he had proposed.[7] Interestingly, however, there seemed to be few substantive criticisms of the psychophysical methods per se, a fact of crucial significance to which I shall return in some detail.

The most basic of the theoretical objections to Fechner's work came to be termed "the quantity objection." Unlike objections that focused on the details of his mathematics or his specific claims (most notably, that all jnds can be assumed to be equal), this objection was directed at the underlying assumption entailed by Fechner's law and his methods—namely, that sensations can be measured. In other words, the quantity objection had to do with the fundamental issue of whether it is possible to quantify psychological phenomena. As the first major debate about "mental measurement," this dispute is of considerable significance for understanding how a quantitative perspective came to be established in psychology.

As the historian of psychology E. G. Boring summarized it, the quantity objection "denied the possibility of a quantitative correlation between [mind and body] on the ground that mind was not possessed of magnitude and that mental measurement was an impossibility." Raised in various forms by the psychologists James, Ebbinghaus, Külpe, Müller, Stumpf, and Münsterberg and the physicist von Kries, the objection was that introspection reveals no quantitative distinction between sensations, and thus that it makes no sense to say that sensations can be measured. James, for example, in what has come to be the most famous statement of the argument, put it this way: "To introspection, our feeling of pink is surely not a portion of our feeling of scarlet; nor does the light of an electric arc seem to contain that of a tallow-candle in itself." Others made the same point in various ways during the last few decades of the nineteenth century.[8]

What was the fate of the quantity objection once it had been made? Advocates of psychophysics responded by putting forth their experimental measurements as a demonstration that sensations did in fact vary in magnitude. But those who raised the quantity objection argued that these "mental magnitudes" were artificially constructed and resulted from a confusion between sensation and stimulus. They charged, in other words, that psychophysicists had committed the "stimulus error," by measuring the stimulus under the guise of measuring the sensation produced by that stimulus. As Brentano put it even before the quantity objection was formally raised, "If one measures, as Fechner did, the intensities of colors, tones, etc., then one is measuring the intensities of physical phenomena. The color is not the seeing, the tone is not the hearing, the warmth is not the sensing of warmth."[9] Since Fechner's whole psychophysics rested on the assumption that a distinction between the stimulus and the sensation could in fact be made and that measurements of the magnitude of a sensation were possible, this critique constituted a challenge to the core assumptions of the psychophysical enterprise.

Given the seriousness of the criticism and the fact that it was being made by some of the leading theorists of the period, we might have expected that this debate would cast doubt on the results of psychophysical studies and thereby slowed the rate of progress in this area. At least we would expect the debate to occupy a prominent place in historical accounts of the development of quantification. What is interesting is that neither of these things happened.

In their historical reviews of perceptual psychology, the psychologists Boring and Newman each mention the quantity objection only in passing, mainly to point out that it was largely ignored by psychophysicists at the time, who went on with their research as if the results of their studies could be unambiguously interpreted. So, in Star's terms, what we have here are two concurrent forms of deletion: one at the level of research practice, the other at the level of historical accounts within perceptual psychology.[10]

I suggest that the fate of the quantity objection can best be understood in the context of the larger political issues facing the discipline at the time. Chief among these was the increasingly problematic status of the introspective method. In setting forth their position, advocates of the quantity objection relied primarily on introspective data, arguing that such data were not in accord with Fechner's claims. To say, for example, that "our feeling of pink is surely not a portion of our feeling of scarlet" is to assume that introspective data are so obvious, so valid, and so consistent among observers that no further evidence or argument is needed. However, during this period, introspective data were increasingly being discredited in psychology, on the grounds that they were often unreliable and could not therefore be used as the basis for scientific theorizing.[11] As psychologists moved toward establishing their discipline as a science independent of philosophy, the need to ground psychological research in reliable, publicly verifiable procedures became paramount.

Thus, the debate about the quantification of perceptual phenomena became part of the larger battle regarding the possibility of a scientific psychology. To take the quantity objection seriously implied retaining introspective data and ties with metaphysical philosophy.[12] The problem, however, was that there seemed to be no clear theoretical grounds on which to argue against it. The solution to these essentially political problems turned out to lie in methodology, rather than theory: by adopting Fechner's methods, psychologists could turn their attention to collecting data, rather than searching for theoretical grounds on which to support the notion that perceptual processes could indeed be quantified.

What seems to have occurred in the development of psychophysics, therefore, is a striking disjunction between theory and methodological practice. At the theoretical level, a major debate was going on as to whether perceptual phenomena could be said to differ from one another quantitatively or whether differences between sensations could really be described only in qualitative terms. But although this debate was far from being resolved, the quantitative methods that Fechner introduced began to be used widely.[13] Employment of these methods presupposed an answer to the theoretical question but did not address it directly. Because the methods seemed useful in collecting perceptual data, they gained widespread acceptance. The nature of our assumptions about perceptual phenomena eventually became transformed, since the methods presupposed a quantitative view and produced data in support of it.

Indeed, it may even be the case that the raising of the quantity objection had the inadvertent effect of strengthening Fechner's theoretical position, since under some conditions, protracted opposition renders an original scientific claim more robust.[14] As Fechner himself put it: "The tower of Babel was never finished because the workers could not reach an understanding on how they should build it; my psychophysical edifice will stand because the workers will never agree on how to tear it down."[15]

How does the fate of the quantity objection in psychophysics shed light on the more general question of how a quantitative perspective in psychology became institutionalized? First, it illustrates the use of an important debating tactic, which we might describe as "ignoring the opposition." The fact that psychophysicists went on with their research despite the ongoing debate about what they were really measuring merely strengthened their position. In other words, the theoretical ambiguities surrounding their work became buried in the profusion of empirical findings that emerged from their laboratories. This was clearly a successful tactic: what we need to understand, however, is what allowed it to be used in the first place. The answer may lie in the disjunction between theory and method noted earlier. The strategy of splitting theoretical issues from methodological practice was an enormously profitable one, because it made it seem possible to proceed with the work despite the ongoing debates about what it meant. As we shall see, this same tactic was used even more successfully in the area of mental testing, where theoretical debates about the nature of intelligence were split off from the development and widespread use of empirical measures of mental ability. In both these lines of work, the methods themselves presupposed an answer to the theoretical debate, yet the link was systematically ignored. As a consequence, the foundation was laid for the later view that methods are theoretically neutral, that they are simply techniques by which to collect data and do not carry with them any implications regarding the nature of the phenomena that they are used to investigate.[16]

What made it possible to effect this disjunction between theory and research practice? I suggest that it was a consequence of differences in the criteria governing the adoption of methods versus the acceptance of theories. Methods are adopted on primarily practical grounds—Are they easy to use? Do they provide clear results? Can they be taught easily to research assistants? Are they expensive?—or for what might be termed "political" reasons—Are they like the methods of a highly regarded discipline? Do the leading scientists use them? And so on. By contrast, the acceptance of theories seems to involve a complex relation between dominant modes of thought in a discipline at a particular time and the personal commitments of individual scientists. To the extent that methodological choices are governed by the exigencies of the work situation, these local factors may serve to mask the fact that such choices necessarily imply theoretical commitments. For example, Fechner's methods were inexpensive, required little apparatus, were easy to use and to teach, and produced what appeared to be clear-cut results. These characteristics made them attractive to researchers, and, in the face of these practical benefits, the theoretical debates surrounding the meaning of the data could well have appeared to be of little relevance to individual researchers.

The discussion thus far has suggested that psychophysics dealt in a complex way with the question of whether mental measurement was possible. On the one hand, Fechner's law appeared to provide a way to conceptualize perceptual phenomena in quantitative terms, and his methods allowed data to be collected in support of such a view. On the other hand, this law did not directly resolve the question of whether perceptions themselves can be quantified; it simply stated that changes in perception were a function of changes in stimulus intensity. The indirectness of the approach meant that a number of fundamental questions about the possibility of mental measurement remained below the surface, ready to reemerge any time the quantitative status of psychological phenomena was directly challenged.[17] As we shall see, these questions have yet to be fully resolved, although the form in which they are posed is reframed somewhat each time they emerge.

Mental Testing: The Quantification of Intelligence

After psychophysics, the line of work most important in the development of a quantitative perspective in psychology has been mental testing. The history of mental testing has been traced in detail by a number of writers;[18] rather than attempt to summarize this work, I will concentrate on the question of how testing affected the conceptualization of quantification. Although the label "mental tests" was later applied to measures of personality, vocational interests, aptitudes, and so on, the quantification of these "higher mental processes" derived from models developed for testing intelligence. Thus, in considering the question of what role mental testing played in the development of quantification, we can limit ourselves to the case of intelligence testing.

It is important to appreciate at the outset that unlike the move toward quantifying perception, the move toward the quantification of intelligence did not receive its main impetus from theoretical disputes or the desire to place psychology on a more secure scientific footing. Rather, it emerged in the context of certain educational and social needs that lay far outside the boundaries of academic psychology. One such need concerned the problem of how to allocate the limited spaces available in schools for the "feeble-minded." Despite the opening of many such schools during the period 1850–70, the number of applicants far exceeded the number of places, and there was no clear way to determine which individuals were likely to benefit from such an environment or from remedial treatment once placed in such a school.[19] Another need concerned the problem of distinguishing between "normal" children whose failure at school was due to retardation and those who might more properly be considered delinquent. The increasing numbers of immigrant children pouring into the schools during the first decade of this century created enormous problems for teachers and administrators, especially in the primary grades, where a classroom might have children whose ages ranged from six to sixteen. Since it was unclear which of these children were in need of special help and which were delinquent, it was difficult for teachers to respond to the problem of overcrowding in an effective way.[20]

Other factors more explicitly political than these also played a part in creating a context for mental testing. In particular, the assumption that "feeble-mindedness" was associated with crime, delinquency, and a general "weakening of the race" led to a variety of attempts to identify feeble-minded individuals so that they could be monitored, sterilized, or refused admission to the country as immigrants.[21] The solution to each of these educational and political problems seemed to lie in finding a way to evaluate an individual's mental ability objectively, so that he or she could be classified in relation to others and either placed in an appropriate setting or removed from society at large.

We have seen some of the controversy that arose in response to the claim of psychophysicists that a generalized aspect of human mind like perception could be made amenable to quantitative treatment. To go further and argue that the idiosyncratic features of an *individual* mind could be quantified seemed to many at the turn of the century to be absurd; such an attempt appeared to defy any existing meaning of the concept of measurement.

It was the British biometrician Francis Galton who broke through this conceptual barrier and led the way toward "reducing the mass of chaotic impressions derived from observation of human beings to [create] systematic order." Impressed by the work of the Belgian astronomer Adolph Quetelet, Galton decided that an individual measurement could be expressed quantitatively "in terms of the frequency with which it may be expected to occur in a given population."[22] In other words, what Galton did was to focus attention on the relative standing of an individual within a group, rather than on the absolute measurement of his or her characteristics.

The tests that Galton pioneered relied primarily on perceptual and motor abilities, and responses were scored in terms of the amount of time it took to complete a given task or the number of tasks completed in a given time. Thus, in a general sense, it can be said that these early tests quantified intelligence in the same way that Fechner's law quantified perception—namely, by relating a psychological ability that was not itself quantitative (perception, intelligence) to a physical measurement that was (stimulus intensity, time).

It was the French psychologist Alfred Binet who took the further step and introduced a concept that could do for intelligence what the jnd had done for perception—namely, provide a psychological magnitude. Having discarded sensory and motor tests of the sort that Galton used, Binet's work began to center on the use of memory, imagination, and comprehension tasks, with which he measured not the amount of time taken to complete the task, but rather, the percentage of children of a given age who reached a given solution. This new measure provided a set of age norms for each task, which meant that a given child could be compared with others, either of the same age or of a different age. The use of this procedure, coupled with Galton's notions of variability, led Binet to introduce the concept of *intellectual level*, which represented the child's mental ability in relation to the distribution of responses made by others of his or her age.[23]

The translation of Binet's tests into English by the American psychologist Henry Goddard in 1910 and their subsequent revision by his Stanford colleague Lewis Terman in 1916 paved the way for their immediate and widespread use in the United States. What is striking about this period is that although there were numerous disagreements among American psychologists about the precise scoring method that was most useful,[24] there was essentially no argument about the basic notion that mental ability could be quantified using tests of this sort. When Terman popularized the German psychologist William Stern's notion of the "intelligence quotient" (defined as the ratio of "mental age" to chronological age), various technical problems that had plagued the intellectual level concept were resolved, and it then became possible to represent a child's mental ability by a single score.[25] Given that thirty years before it had seemed impossible to quantify something as subjective and idiosyncratic as an individual person's mind, the notion of IQ appeared to constitute a major breakthrough in bringing even recalcitrant phenomena like intelligence into the domain of an increasingly quantitative psychology.

There were debates about the tests themselves, of course, as well as about the explicitly political uses to which the results were being put.[26] The dispute between Terman and the journalist Walter Lippmann in the pages of *The New Republic* was the most visible of these debates;[27] but within psychology itself there was also considerable disagreement about what it was that the tests actually measured. A 1921 symposium in which the leading figures in the testing movement expressed their views as to the nature of intelligence and intelligence testing revealed a wide divergence of perspectives and no obvious way of reaching a common ground.[28] The central problem was the old issue of validity that had confounded efforts to quantify perception and was now reemerging with respect to intelligence—namely, the inherent difficulty of constructing *any* measuring technique in view of the fact that there was no objective metric against which it could be compared. When the question was raised as to whether intelligence tests were really measuring intelligence, there was no clear response, since there was no standard to use in validating the tests.

We can imagine the relief, therefore, that met Boring's claim, now famous as a pithy summary of operationism, that "intelligence is what the tests test."[29] In one swift move, this claim swept away the whole argument about validity and the more general question of whether intelligence could be measured. If the tests claimed to be measuring intelligence, then intelligence could be measured. Such a view was really no different, Boring argued, from the view of measurement taken by the physical sciences. When physicists ask what *weight* means, for example, they answer by saying that "weight is the amount of gravitational pull upon a given mass which is registered on an instrument especially designed for measuring this pull."[30] Thus, in Boring's view, if physicists can define *weight* as what their scales measure, then why shouldn't psychologists define intelligence as what their tests measure?

With the validity question apparently set aside, mental testing developed apace. By 1937, the reviewer South could cite "5005 articles, most of them reports of new tests, which [had] appeared during the fifteen year period between 1921 and 1936."[31] But as the tests multiplied, the question of what was actually being measured arose in a new form. If intelligence was what the tests measured and there were hundreds of different kinds of tests, then did this mean that there were hundreds of different kinds of intelligence, or that intelligence had hundreds of different aspects or components? Clearly, if psychology were to adhere to the canon of parsimony taken to be characteristic of science, such a conclusion would be untenable. Further, developments in statistical technique had made it possible to assess the degree of correlation that existed between various tests, and it was clear that there was typically some degree of statistical agreement between them. As early as 1904, the British psychologist Charles Spearman had attempted to resolve the question of what was being measured by proposing what later came to be known as his "two factor theory." Simply put, this theory asserted that some degree of correlation between tests was an indication that they were measuring a common factor; the fact that such correlations were never perfect meant that each test was also measuring some additional specific factor or factors. Spearman's claims were subject to considerable criticism on a variety of theoretical and mathematical grounds, and a major debate arose as to whether there was a general factor, as Spearman argued; some small number of "group factors" as the Chicago psychologist L. L. Thurstone and others asserted; or simply a large number of specific factors, as his Columbia colleague E. L. Thorndike claimed.[32]

What is striking about these arguments concerning the nature of intelligence is the form they took. In attempting to support his theory, Spearman had

introduced a powerful new statistical technique—factor analysis—which came
to play a crucially important role in the continuing battle to quantify intelligence. By mathematically reducing a complex set of correlations to a small
number of dimensions, or factors, factor analysis provided a statistical means
of determining what it was that intelligence tests were measuring. In so doing,
factor analysis enabled the basic theoretical question underlying mental testing
to be reduced to a technical difficulty. In other words, instead of focusing on
the question of whether intelligence could in fact be measured, psychologists
could now take that assumption for granted and argue instead about how
many factors comprised it. And instead of having to propose an answer to
this question on theoretical grounds, they could use the statistical means provided by factor analysis to do so. The fact that different psychologists arrived
at different answers by introducing different mathematical procedures for their
analyses was, in the end, unimportant; if anything, these disagreements had
the indirect effect of strengthening the basic quantitative view underlying factor
analysis.

The struggle to quantify intelligence was essentially over by the 1930s. Like
the earlier effort to quantify perception, this battle was won by effecting a
sharp disjunction between theory and research practice. Once mental tests
were introduced, their tremendous utility to education, industry, and the military ensured a level of support sufficient to fund their continued development.[33] By the 1920s, the rapid proliferation of tests and their application in
an increasingly wide variety of contexts enabled testers to transform questions
about validity into technical problems and to argue that the introduction of
more sophisticated statistical techniques would resolve the remaining difficulties. Like the psychophysicists who simply pointed to their empirical findings
as evidence that it must be possible to quantify perception, the testers could
use the existence and widespread use of tests to support their claim that intelligence could likewise be quantified. The fact that no one had answered
the basic theoretical question of whether the phenomenon of intelligence was
comprised of quantitative units came, by the 1920s, to be seen as irrelevant.
When operationism swept the discipline during the next decade, it became
a silly sort of question even to pose. And it is a mark of the success of the
testing movement that such questions have not resurfaced, even though the
tests themselves continue to be the object of considerable debate.

Contrasting Concepts of Measurement in Psychophysics
and Mental Testing

Although they had a similar commitment to the value of quantification, psychophysicists and mental testers did not have the same conception of measurement. This divergence in views is especially interesting in light of the fact,

noted earlier, that Galton's initial approach to the measurement of intelligence was analogous to that used in psychophysics—namely, establishing a relation between a psychological magnitude and a physical measurement like speed of response. But whereas psychophysicists retained the assumption that psychological magnitudes derive their quantitative status from their relation to physical measures, testers after Galton took a different view. Beginning with Binet's work, a relativist view of measurement emerged, which defined psychological magnitudes through comparison with one another. Thus, an individual's score on a mental test represented his or her ability relative to the abilities of others who took the same test. The quantitative status of such scores depended not on some link to a physical measurement, but on the underlying assumption that variability among individuals is distributed normally. In a general sense we can say that the quantitative approach in psychophysics derives from natural science research on the physical measurement of the stimulus, whereas that in mental testing is based on probability theory and statistics.

Despite these differences, both areas were confronted with the same set of conceptual problems. There was no clear evidence to support Fechner's assumption that all jnds were equal, yet this assumption was essential to his law. If jnds were not equal, they could not be added in a straightforward way; if they could not be added, then the notion of relating arithmetical increases in psychological magnitude to logarithmic increases in stimulus intensity appeared to fall apart. Similarly, there was no evidence to support the testers' assumption that increases in an individual's score on easy items were equivalent to increases on more difficult items (indeed, such an assumption appeared illogical). Yet if all such increases were not equivalent, then it made no sense to compare one score with another.[34] In both areas there persisted the general problem that without an objective metric against which to compare psychological magnitudes, it was difficult to see how unit intervals could be equalized so as to permit true measurement.

Psychological Scaling as an Integrative Rubric

A crucial conceptual step in the overall development of a quantitative perspective in psychology was taken when the disparate conceptions of measurement that emerged in psychophysics and mental testing were brought together within the rubric of psychological scaling, and the core problems were reconceptualized in light of this new framework.

Thurstone took the first step toward the integration of the two views in a series of papers published between 1925 and 1929.[35] Although these papers focused on certain problems concerning the representation of variability in mental test scores, Thurstone argued that these problems were instances of a larger set of issues in psychological measurement, which applied equally to the problem of determining psychophysical thresholds. Specifically, his claim was that this whole range of problems could be conceptualized in terms of the notion of a psychological scale. In his 1926 paper, for example, he wrote: "In every form of mental measurement, whether it be the determination of a psychophysical [threshold], a mental age, or the relative standing of an individual with reference to a group, we always have a more or less definitely graded series of tasks which ranges from easy to difficult levels."[36] This notion, that mental testing essentially involves locating subjects at different points along a continuous dimension of abilities, just as psychophysical measurement involves locating perceptual magnitudes along a continuous dimension of stimulus intensities, was implicit in Binet's notion of intellectual level. But it was Thurstone who made the conceptual link between the two forms of measurement explicit.

This integration of the two areas under the rubric of scaling was advanced considerably by the Nebraska psychologist J. P. Guilford, who argued in his influential 1936 textbook on psychometric methods that the concept of psychological scaling underlies both psychophysical and testing methods and therefore provides a way of "bridging the gap that has too long existed between them."[37] By discussing both sets of methods in the same text, by repeatedly drawing attention to various parallels between them, and by devoting considerable attention to scaling techniques themselves, Guilford's work paved the way for a range of subsequent developments.

But these discussions of scaling served to highlight the fact that the problems which had plagued psychological measurement from the beginning were still present, even though they were being debated in more technical ways. The key stumbling block was the lack of an absolute zero point on psychological scales. Unlike measuring scales in the physical sciences which start at such a point (for example, zero length, zero weight, zero time), psychological scales defined points of origin arbitrarily. As a consequence, the intervals on such scales were not necessarily equal to one another, and this created conceptual problems when comparing scales which purportedly assessed the same thing.[38]

Thurstone addressed this problem directly in a series of papers written in the late 1920s.[39] In one of these papers, he argued that a "rational origin" for intelligence scales could be specified mathematically. Having plotted the relation between mean test performance and the standard deviation for each age, he had noticed that the relation was linear. "Extrapolating the linear relation until it reached a base line of zero dispersion," Thurstone reasoned, would give a point that constituted a "rational origin because the dispersion cannot be negative." When repeated use of this procedure revealed that "the age at which the rational origin is located turns out to be several months before birth," he concluded that his mathematically derived value fitted with neurological data and was therefore valid.[40] Despite some criticism, this conclusion was generally accepted and provided a starting point for resolving the absolute zero point problem.[41]

But Thurstone's most important contribution was his formulation of a new psychophysical law termed the "law of comparative judgment." Using the method of paired comparisons, in which every stimulus is compared with every other stimulus rather than with only one standard, Thurstone established a subjective continuum on which each stimulus could be located.[42] Since repeated presentations of the same stimulus did not produce an identical response each time, but rather, a distribution of responses, he assigned two kinds of values, based on the central tendency and the dispersion (variability) of this distribution. According to Thurstone's law, the standard deviation of the dispersion for a given stimulus constituted a subjective unit of measurement that was operationally defined and internally consistent. Thus, for example, the "sum of the subjective separations between the stimulus pairs AB and BC [were shown to] be equal to the experimentally independent determination of the separation AC."[43]

The law of comparative judgment provided a solution to the problem of scale intervals by establishing an empirical means for equalizing them. What was especially striking about Thurstone's law was that it resolved the interval problem without recourse to physical measurements. Rather than relying on physical stimuli to provide psychological measures with a quantitative status, as Fechner had done, Thurstone created a subjective metric with its own mathematical foundation.

The significance of this accomplishment is that it made it possible to expand the scope of quantification to include phenomena such as attitudes, opinions, and judgments which had long seemed incapable of being quantified. In an article triumphantly entitled "Attitudes can be Measured," Thurstone demonstrated how his approach could be used to construct a scale of attitude statements which could yield a score for each individual, as well as a frequency distribution for any specified group. In Thurstone's method, each attitude statement was assumed to occupy a certain position on the scale, with an individual's score being determined by the scale values of the statements he or she endorsed.[44] Likert's introduction of a simpler calculation procedure placed attitude scaling on an even firmer basis and demonstrated that social phenomena were no less amenable to quantification than, for example, perceptions.[45]

Meanwhile, similar problems were emerging in perceptual psychophysics. By the 1930s, it had become clear that different varieties of Fechner's methods produced conflicting data. In other words, the value of the psychological magnitude derived from different procedures did not always turn out to be the same. Since the theoretical issues surrounding the measurement of sensation had never been adequately resolved, there was no way of choosing among the various results. The old question of whether it was possible to add sensations arose once again, because all Fechner's methods rested on the assumption that the units of psychological magnitude (jnds) could be combined to comprise a linear scale.

The Harvard psychologist S. S. Stevens, who emerged in the 1930s as the major figure in psychophysics, popularized a new method that attempted to overcome these problems.[46] Part of the difficulty with Fechner's methods was that they yielded quantitative data only through an indirect procedure: the subject gave a series of comparative judgments about which stimuli were louder than which others, for example, but he or she did not indicate in quantitative terms exactly how much louder. This had to be determined by the experimenter, through mathematical transformation of the data. Stevens argued that a more direct method could be used, in which subjects would be asked to assign numbers to stimuli in such a way as to indicate how much louder a given stimulus was than a standard. For example, if a given stimulus sounded twice as loud as the standard and the standard were given the arbitrary value of 10, then the subject would say that the value of the new stimulus was 20. This method, now termed the "method of magnitude estimation," yielded data that did not fit Fechner's psychophysical law, especially at the extremes of the scale. Stevens argued that a better description of the overall relation between stimulus intensity and psychological magnitude is given by a power function, of the form

$$\psi = k\phi^n,$$

where ψ is a psychological magnitude, ϕ is a stimulus intensity, and n is an exponent which varies for different perceptual modalities.[47]

Despite the fact that Stevens's power law and his method of magnitude estimation became widely accepted, the old debate about whether any psychophysical method actually allowed sensations to be measured continued. A committee of the British Association for the Advancement of Science considered the issue for eight years during the 1930s and, being unable to reach any resolution, was finally discharged. In the early 1940s, Stevens argued that the fundamental problem really had to do with the meaning of measurement. If measurement were not taken to be synonymous with addition, then, he argued, one could distinguish different forms of measurement, utilizing different mathematical operations. Starting from the definition that measurement "is the assignment of numerals to objects or events according to rules," Stevens claimed that "the fact that numerals can be assigned under different rules leads to different kinds of scales and different kinds of measurement." He went on to describe four such scales, the so-called nominal, ordinal, interval, and ratio scales, outlining the transformations under which each was invariant.[48]

What Stevens did in proposing these four scales of measurement was to recast the basic issue which had been debated for so long. Instead of asking "Can sensations be measured?" (or, by extension, "Is psychological measurement possible?"), he asked, "What do we mean by measurement?" His definition was broad enough that the question of whether sensations can be measured could be answered in the affirmative. However, although the introduction of this broad view of measurement had the potential for resolving the issue, the actuality depended on others agreeing with Stevens's definition. This turned out not to be the case. Although Stevens's distinction among the four scales of measurement has been widely accepted, there continues to be considerable disagreement as to whether nominal or ordinal scales constitute appropriately sophisticated forms of measurement for scientific work. A number of psychologists have argued that if psychology is to be scientific in the usual sense of that term, its methods must produce data that fit ratio, or at least interval, scales. However, there is considerable controversy about whether even psychophysical data conform to this criterion. Stevens claimed that his method of magnitude estimation produced ratio data, but recent critiques have disputed this.[49] And it seems clear that most studies in mental testing and social psychology produce interval data at best. As a consequence, although we have a new terminology with which to debate the issue, the question of whether psychological phenomena can actually be measured persists, since if such phenomena are not being measured on a ratio scale, some critics would argue that they are not really being measured at all.

The basic question that first emerged at the time of the quantity objection thus remains with us today: Does it make sense to say that psychological phenomena vary along quantitative dimensions? On the methodological level, this issue has been decided, in that quantitative methods have become the established methods of the discipline. But on the theoretical level, the debates continue, which means that the rationale for the adoption of quantitative methods has yet to be clearly established.[50]

Consequences of Institutionalizing a Quantitative Perspective

Even though its conceptual grounding may be problematic, the development and institutionalization of a quantitative perspective has had a number of consequences for the structure of psychology as a discipline and for the nature of the research process. These consequences help to explain how the perspective was adopted in spite of the persistent difficulties that surrounded it. In the discussion that follows, I review a number of these consequences.

First, quantification aided in the resolution of certain definitional and boundary problems that plagued psychology at the end of the nineteenth century. By allowing the discipline to define itself as a science according to a criterion used by the natural sciences, quantification enabled psychology to complete its differentiation from philosophy, a crucial step in the process of establishing itself as an independent discipline.[51] Since the types of problems addressed by late nineteenth-century psychologists (for example, the nature of consciousness, the structure of the mind, the relation of mind and body, and so on) were indistinguishable from the types of problems with which philosophers were concerned, psychology had to differentiate itself from philosophy on grounds other than the nature of its content. Methodology in general and quantification in particular aided in effecting this separation in several ways.[52] First, by providing a set of techniques that were fundamentally different from those used by philosophers, quantification allowed psychologists to assert that the results of psychological research were clearly different from those of philosophical work. Second, because the phenomena of interest had to be redefined to make them amenable to quantitative treatment, psychologists were increasingly able to argue that they were not in fact studying the same things as philosophers.

This differentiation of psychology from philosophy was not merely an abstract exercise. For psychologists to secure university positions and thereby provide an institutional base for their work, they had to be able to convince university administrators that their enterprise was sufficiently different from philosophy to warrant the allocation of separate resources.[53] Although such efforts were aided in a general way by the introduction of laboratory practice, the specific use of quantitative analysis conferred an additional aura of scientific respectability and helped to make its continued development possible.

But even as it fought to secure its status as an independent academic discipline, psychology had to protect its other flank—namely, its apparent connection with pseudo-scientific movements like phrenology, palmistry, fortune-telling, and so on. A crucial aspect of the legitimation work that faced psychologists at the turn of the century centered on creating an alliance with the professions and constructing a separate conceptual category of "pseudo" or "amateur" psychology from which they could differentiate themselves.[54] The development of a quantitative approach to psychological issues, especially the introduction of arcane statistical techniques and mathematical formulations, was extremely helpful in creating a sharp distinction between academic and popular psychology and in providing a means by which to protect the professional status of academic psychologists. By translating psychological discourse into a technical, abstruse language that only professionals could speak or comprehend, quantification created a category of knowledge for which special training was required. It was then possible to require such training as a necessary qualification for the status of professional psychologist. In a report of the American Psychological Association committee entrusted in 1918 with proposing standardized credentials for psychological examiners, for example, one of the specific requirements listed is a minimum of 70 classroom hours of instruction in statistical analysis. Clearly the intent of this and other requirements was to restrict the ranks of examiners and to prevent amateur testers from passing themselves off as psychologists.[55]

Creation of Products and Markets

A second general consequence of the development of a quantitative perspective was that it facilitated the creation of various products which, by being marketed to diverse client groups, helped to increase the visibility and prestige of psychology as an independent discipline. Some of these products were the direct result of quantitative work itself (for example, statistical tests and scaling procedures); others were more indirect and resulted from the application of quantitative approaches to particular lines of research (for example, intelligence, personality, and vocational tests derived from testing research and signal-detection procedures and hearing devices derived from psychophysical research). In addition to the financial benefits accruing from widespread marketing of such products, the connections with clients in education, business, government, and the military that developed in the course of marketing increased psychology's visibility outside the academic context and further legitimated it as a discipline important to the larger society.[56]

Two brief examples illustrate this point. The small group of psychologists who had worked together on the development of group intelligence tests during World War I decided immediately after the war to adapt tests of this sort for use in schools. This effort was phenomenally successful: by 1922, three million children a year were being tested with one or another of the resulting tests.[57] By the mid-1920s, the use of tests in systems of tracking by ability was widespread. Such tests provided educational administrators with "an efficient way to divide students into homogeneous ability groups and thereby to meet the problems of size in postwar schools."[58] In other words, part of the reason why psychologists were so successful in marketing intelligence tests to schools was that they had created a product that was especially well suited to school administrators' needs.

Psychophysicists were similarly successful in a later period. On the basis of their previous research, Stevens and his associates were able to invent a number of hearing devices that proved to be of considerable use to the military during World War II. For example, one such device, the "ear warden," could be fitted into a soldier's helmet, affording him some protection against temporary hearing loss produced by nearby explosions, while still allowing him to hear the spoken commands of his superiors.[59] Such products provided so-lutions to a variety of urgent problems faced by the military, and their success ensured continued funding and increased recognition of psychophysical re-search. After the war, many of these devices were marketed commercially, thereby creating additional contacts, new client groups, and further visibility for psychophysical research, a line of work whose most salient characteristic was its firm quantitative foundation.

Increased Communication and Cooperation within the Research Community

The development of quantitative methods also had important consequences for the structure of research practice within the discipline. In the late nineteenth century, individual psychologists established their own laboratories, each fo-cusing on certain types of problems. While collaborative work clearly went on within each laboratory during this initial period, it was not until consid-erably later that lines of research were sufficiently organized for researchers in different laboratories to work on the same problems in the mode of col-laborative "puzzle-solving" that Kuhn describes as characteristic of "normal science." The development of a quantitative perspective facilitated this or-ganizational structuring of research in certain key respects. By providing a common methodology, language, and set of rules by which to conceptualize psychological phenomena, quantitative methods allowed researchers to com-municate with one another, to work together, and to combine and contrast their individual results more directly. In particular, the use of such methods increased the efficiency of the research process by enabling researchers to focus their attention on the research problem itself, rather than deflecting their energies to debates about the criteria for what would constitute an ad-equate solution.[60] Thus, researchers could take a complex phenomenon, de-compose it into its constituent elements on the basis of quantitative transformation of its basic properties, and then divide up the work in a coherent and systematic way.

A clear example of how quantification facilitated cooperative work among psychologists engaged in similar kinds of research can be seen in the con-struction of testing as an organized line of work.[61] Prior to 1917, a number of researchers were involved in the effort to develop intelligence tests for use with different populations (for example, elementary schoolchildren, college students, non-English-speaking adults, and so on). Each of these psychologists worked independently, then published the test he or she developed, often in a paper which attempted to demonstrate that it was somehow "better" than others in the area.[62] Thus, during this prewar phase, testing research was decentralized, with each investigator working separately and to some extent in competition with others. This was also the period in which intelligence tests were seen primarily as having the narrow purpose of identifying so-called feeble-minded children. Although widely used in schools for this purpose, typically, the tests were still administered individually, rather than to groups, and were not seen as appropriate for use with "normal" children.[63] Given the decentralized, competitive way in which the work was carried out, this narrow focus is not surprising; it is difficult to see how a broader purpose could have been envisioned, let alone realized, within such an organizational structure.

The profound effect of the wartime testing effort on the widespread use of intelligence tests in American society has been discussed at length.[64] But what has not been emphasized in previous accounts is how this effort led to the reorganization of the structure of testing research. The challenge of trying to organize a massive testing program for army recruits (without much support from the army) put psychologists in the position of having to produce tangible results in very little time. These pressures required them to coordinate their efforts, to set aside most of their major differences, and to standardize their procedures. The use of statistical techniques aided this process enormously, and statisticians such as Truman L. Kelley, who played a minor role in the beginning stages of the war work, emerged as key figures in the postwar testing movement.

In the years immediately following the war, the small group of psychologists who had led the war effort consolidated their leadership role by working together to develop a group test that could be used in the schools. Whenever differences arose among them about what items to include on the test, they were resolved by appealing to statistical criteria. This meant that the group could effectively avoid having to deal with such thorny and divisive theoretical questions as what constitutes intelligence, how many factors comprise it, and so forth.[65] I suggest that these changes in the organization of testing research, especially the extent to which it became centralized and cooperative, are part of what led this field to assume such dominance in postwar psychology. Specifically, we can see here how the use of quantitative methods—in this case, statistical analysis—made cooperation possible, thereby allowing this area to move forward in a systematic and organized manner, something that previously was not feasible.

Shift toward Methodological Criteria for Evaluating Research Practice

Prior to the institutionalization of a quantitative perspective, psychologists used criteria like logical coherence, plausibility, correspondence with introspection, and so on as means by which to evaluate each other's theories and findings. Given that these criteria were subjective and could vary considerably from person to person, there were widespread disagreements about which theories or findings ought to be treated seriously and which discounted. For example, by 1894, there were a number of different textbooks by American psychologists, each of which presented a different view of psychological phenomena, the relation of mind and body, and so on.[66] Each view had its followers and its detractors, but there was no one, generally accepted set of criteria by which to decide among them. If the discipline were to develop beyond this somewhat anarchistic stage, a set of general criteria had to emerge. In principle, such criteria could have taken any form as long as there was general agreement concerning their use—for example, correspondence with introspection could have been taken to be the deciding factor in evaluating competing theories.

What happened, however, was that the development of a quantitative perspective created conditions under which a methodological, rather than a theoretical or logical, criterion emerged. For a set of findings to be treated seriously, they had to be seen to be methodologically adequate, which increasingly came to mean that they must conform to quantitative criteria, defined first in terms of precise measurement and mathematical transformation of data and later in terms of adequate sample size, statistical significance, and so forth. Eventually, it became possible to discount empirical findings simply because they had not been collected in a sufficiently "scientific" way, even if they appeared to be plausible on other grounds.[67] By the 1930s, when the appeal of operationism swept over the discipline, criteria of methodological adequacy had spread to the level of theory. Theories seen as generating the greatest number of "testable propositions"—that is, statements that could be quantified easily—came to be taken most seriously, and theories that appeared difficult to translate into such terms were discounted.[68]

Thus, methodological adequacy (typically defined in terms of quantitative sophistication) became the criterion according to which an argument, a set of findings, or a theory was evaluated.[69] To some extent, this meant that quantification became a technique of persuasion, as well as a methodology, in that one could strengthen the basis for one's claims by demonstrating that they were grounded on a firmer quantitative base than those of one's competitors.[70] A hierarchy of plausibility was thereby established, such that the more quantitative a line of research, the more plausible its results were seen to be.

Whatever other consequences the establishment of this methodological criterion had for psychology as a discipline, it clearly improved the efficiency of research practice by providing a consensually agreed-upon basis for evaluating competing findings or alternative theories. Thus, by allowing for the creation of a generalized criterion defining what constituted good work, quantification restructured the conduct of research, the form in which arguments were made, and the means by which disagreements were adjudicated.

Transformation of Subjectivity into Objectivity

The most general consequence of the institutionalization of a quantitative perspective for the nature of research practice was that it created a means by which subjective phenomena could be objectified. The mere fact that complex phenomena could now be represented in some kind of numerical form conferred a degree of objectivity on the results of psychological research that qualitative findings appeared to lack.[71] But beyond the use of numbers in and of themselves, quantification made it possible to objectify aspects of decision making that would otherwise be seen as clearly subjective. The conduct of research requires that one make a whole variety of choices: which groups to compare and how to compare them, how to measure the phenomenon of interest, what to count, how to count it, what data to include and what to ignore as error or artifact, which statistical test to use, how to represent the findings graphically, which findings to stress and which to discount, and so on. By providing ways to "package" these choices, quantification transformed the experience of the researcher into one of merely applying various standardized techniques, rather than having to make a series of complex choices. In this connection, we can glimpse part of the reason why operationism would seem appealing during a period in which a quantitative perspective was being institutionalized. By defining the phenomenon of interest in terms of the operations used to measure it, operationism buried the choice of what to count and how to count it within the process of formulating an operational definition, thereby making it appear as if such choices did not really have to be made.[72]

Statistical techniques provided a way of deleting other steps, in that choices about how groups should be compared, what scores should be used, what constituted a meaningful result, and so forth no longer had to be made once the general choice of which statistical test to use had been made. The considerable debate among those engaged in developing the statistical tests does not seem to have been apparent to the psychologists who increasingly came to rely on them. As statistical textbooks specifically for psychologists began to be written in the 1920s, "the edifice of statistical technique . . . [was presented in such a way as to] look monolithic and cohesive." This was accomplished by describing statistical ideas without reference to the individuals who developed them, by omitting discussion of the mathematical and philosophical bases of a given procedure, and by deleting debates and disagreements among statistical theorists.[73] Thus statistics texts became "cookbooks," with the process of using a particular statistical test reduced to following a recipe that is supposedly guaranteed to yield an unambiguous, objective result. This packaging of research procedure can be considered a form of industrial efficiency, similar in many ways to the mechanization of production in other work settings.

The Social Construction of Methodology

At the most general level, the development and institutionalization of a quantitative perspective in psychology illustrates the process whereby methodologies are socially constructed to serve both the needs of particular scientific communities and those of the larger society in which they are embedded.[74] It is not simply a historical coincidence that quantitative methods were introduced at a time when psychology was struggling to transform itself into a science and American society was engaged in developing new means of controlling its increasingly heterogeneous population. Rather, the quantification of psychological phenomena has to be understood as a response to both these situations, as well as to the internal needs of psychology, which required a way of organizing the process of research more efficiently. On this view, the success of quantification may have been as much a function of the urgency with which these needs were felt as it was a technical accomplishment in its own right.

Unlike the natural sciences, whose objects of investigation have no theory about their own workings, psychology has to deal with the fact that its conceptions of human behavior often differ in fundamental ways from those of the human beings it seeks to study. As a consequence, psychology has of necessity been required to form alliances with such agents of social control as government, education, and the military, in order to ensure that its perspective will gain credence over competing popular notions of human behavior. But the success of such alliances has depended on psychology's being able to formulate a view of human nature that coincides at least in part with the views of the institutions from which it seeks support. It is not surprising, therefore, that American psychology has increasingly advanced a view which has emphasized control, prediction, and classification, rather than personal freedom, spontaneity, and individuality.[75] It was in the attempt to formulate such a view and to convince its institutional clientele that it was in that clientele's own interest to support it that psychology came to rely increasingly on quantitative methods. Quantification provided a clear way of meeting the needs of a growing bureaucracy, and the seeming impartiality of quantitative statements matched the democratic ideology of American institutions. At the same time, quantification reduced the marginal status of psychology among the sciences and allowed it to expand the range of phenomena to which its methods could be applied.

In this light, we can understand how the theoretical question of whether psychological phenomena are inherently quantitative increasingly came to seem irrelevant to the conduct of psychological research. But the disjunction between theory and method that rendered this question moot has left psychology with an approach to measurement that remains problematic. As Block and Dworkin have noted in a recent critique, in most cases "if one can measure a quantity, one has some sort of theory of it . . . . thus measurement usually *presupposes* definition, or at least definability."[76] The fact that this link has been systematically denied in psychology has allowed for the development of highly complex techniques of measurement whose underlying theoretical base is unclear. Thus, although psychology has clearly succeeded in the attempt to measure its phenomena quantitatively, it remains an open question whether it can explain them at a level of sophistication equal to that of the measurements themselves.

Notes

1. For comparative analyses of the role of quantification in different disciplines, see C. W. Churchman and P. Ratoosh, eds., *Measurement: Definitions and Theories* (New York: Wiley, 1959); H. Woolf, ed., *Quantification: A History of the Meaning of Measurement in the Natural and Social Sciences* (New York: Bobbs-Merrill, 1961).

2. I will not debate the merits of this assumption here. Since it was clearly made by almost all the important figures in the discipline at the time, a historical account of the period requires that we accept it as given.

3. It is important to note that psychologists in other countries did not follow the same route. Among the most prominent examples is the German psychologist Wilhelm Dilthey, whose interpretive approach represented a clear alternative to the natural science model. Many other leading figures in German and French psychology maintained the importance of qualitative methods. Certain American psychologists, such as E. B. Titchener, did so as well, but with considerably less success than their European counterparts.

4. As just a few examples of this standard account, see E. G. Boring, *A History of Experimental Psychology*, 2d ed. (New York: Appleton-Century-Crofts, 1950); M. H. Marx and W. A. Hillix, *Systems and Theories in Psychology* (New York: McGraw-Hill, 1963); R. I. Watson, *The Great Psychologists*, 4th ed. (Philadelphia: Lippincott, 1978).

5. E. Mendelsohn, "The Social Construction of Scientific Knowledge," in *The Social Production of Scientific Knowledge*, ed. E. Mendelsohn, P. Weingart, and R. Whitley (Dordrecht: Reidel, 1977), pp. 3–26; S. L. Star, "Simplification in Scientific Work," *Social Studies of Science* 13 (1983): 205–28; J. G. Morawski, "Contextual Discipline: The Unmaking and Remaking of Sociality," in *Contextualism and Understanding in Behavioral Science*, ed. R. L. Rosnow and M. Georgoudi (New York: Praeger, 1986), pp. 47–66.

6. G. T. Fechner, *Elements of Psychophysics* (1860); vol. 1 trans. H. E. Adler (New York: Holt, Rinehart and Winston, 1966).

7. For reviews of these criticisms, see, e.g., C. W. Savage, *The Measurement of Sensation: A Critique of Perceptual Psychophysics* (Berkeley: University of California Press, 1970); L. E. Marks, *Sensory Processes: The New Psychophysics* (New York: Academic Press, 1974).

8. E. G. Boring, "The Stimulus Error" (1921), in *History, Psychology, and Science: Selected Papers of E. G. Boring*, ed. R. I. Watson and D. T. Campbell (New York: Wiley, 1963), p. 258. The quantity objection is discussed in that paper and also in idem, "Beginning and Growth of Measurement in Psychology" (1961),

in *History, Psychology, and Science*, pp. 140–58; and in E. B. Titchener, *Experimental Psychology*, vol. 2, part 2 (New York: Macmillan, 1905), pp. ii, x, lviii–lxiii. See also J. von Kries, "Über die Messung intensiver Grossen und über das sogenannte psychophysische Gesetz," *Vierteljahresschrift für Wissenschaftliche Philosophie und Soziologie* 6 (1882): 257–94. The James quotation is from W. James, *Principles of Psychology*, vol. 1 (New York: Henry Holt, 1890), p. 546.

9. Boring, "The Stimulus Error," describes the arguments here. The Brentano quotation is from F. Brentano, *Psychologie vom empirischen Standpunkt*, vol. 1 (Leipzig: Duncker and Humbolt, 1874), p. 91.

10. Boring, A *History of Experimental Psychology*; E. B. Newman, "On the Origin of 'Scales of Measurement,' " in *Sensation and Measurement: Papers in Honor of S. S. Stevens*, ed. H. R. Moskowitz, B. Scharf, and J. C. Stevens (Dordrecht: Reidel, 1974); S. L. Star, "Simplification in Scientific Work."

11. See R. Dodge, "The Theory and Limitations of Introspection," *American Journal of Psychology* 23 (1912): 214–29; E. G. Boring, "A History of Introspection," *Psychological Bulletin* 50 (1953): 169–89; K. Danziger, "The History of Introspection Reconsidered," *Journal of the History of the Behavioral Sciences* 16 (1980): 241–62.

12. It is interesting to note that when Boring wrote his 1921 paper discussing the quantity objection, he seems to have been motivated by the desire to defend introspection against the attacks of the behaviorists. But the introspection that he embraced, that of Titchener, rested on the assumption that mental measurement was possible; thus Boring could hardly agree with the advocates of the quantity objection who claimed that it was not. What he did, therefore, was to offer a detailed critique of the objection in an effort to show that the use of introspective data per se did not mean having to question the whole psychophysical enterprise. In other words, in contrast to James, who used introspection as a way of refuting Fechner's claims, Boring argued that introspection allows for Fechner's data. Such an argument was clearly to Boring's advantage, given the beleaguered state of the introspective method at the time, because it allied the introspectionists with the psychophysicists, who by then had considerable status as scientific psychologists. And it set them both against the more strident behaviorists, who wanted to deny the possibility, or at least the utility, of "mental" measurement of any kind.

    In his 1953 paper, Boring argued for an even stronger link between introspection and psychophysics, by claiming that psychophysical judgments were essentially introspections (a viewpoint that Titchener would have disputed). By dissolving what had, at an earlier period, been seen as an inherent disparity between the two, Boring was attempting to legitimize at least some forms of introspection and thereby to retain the concept of consciousness within the subject matter of an increasingly behavioristic psychology.

13. Titchener, *Experimental Psychology*, seems to have paved the way for the key transformation here, by questioning the basis of Fechner's quantitative view but accepting and promulgating his methods anyway. Boring continued this strategy.

The widespread use of these methods is described by H. E. Adler, "Vicissitudes of Fechnerian Psychophysics in America," in *Psychology: Theoretical-Historical Perspectives*, ed. R. W. Rieber and K. Salzinger (New York: Academic Press, 1980), pp. 11–23; and W. R. Woodward, "A Case Study in Scientific Revolutions: Kuhn, Popper, Lakatos, and Psychophysics" (Paper presented to the American Psychological Association, Toronto, Canada, August 1978).

14. For a discussion of some of these conditions, see S. L. Star, "Scientific Theories as Going Concerns: The Development of the Localizationist Perspective in Neurophysiology, 1870–1906" (Ph.D. diss., University of California, San Francisco, 1983).

15. Quoted by S. S. Stevens, "On the Psychophysical Law," *Psychological Review* 64 (1957): 153.

16. The assumption that methods are theoretically neutral has been criticized most strongly in relation to operationist methodology. See, e.g., E. Newbury, "Philosophic Assumptions in Operational Psychology," *Journal of Psychology* 35 (1953): 371–78; and T. H. Leahey, "The Myth of Operationism," *Journal of Mind and Behavior* 1 (1980): 127–43. For more general critiques of the assumption of methodological neutrality in psychology, see K. Danziger, "The Social Evolution of the Psychological Experiment" (Paper presented to the Canadian Psychological Association, Ottawa, May 1984), and idem, "The Methodological Imperative in Psychology," *Philosophy of the Social Sciences* 15 (1985): 1–13.

   At its broadest, the notion that methods are theoretically neutral rests on the assumption that observational statements can be distinguished from theoretical statements. This assumption has been subject to considerable criticism among philosophers of science, who have argued that such a distinction cannot be meaningfully supported, on either logical or historical grounds. For reviews of these critiques, see, e.g., F. Suppe, "The Search for Philosophic Understanding of Scientific Theories," and D. Shapere, "Scientific Theories and their Domains," both in *The Structure of Scientific Theories*, ed. F. Suppe (Urbana: University of Illinois Press, 1977), pp. 3–232, 518–65, respectively.

17. For one among many examples of unsuccessful attempts to resolve the ambiguity inherent in psychophysical measurement, see the symposium "Are the Intensity Differences of Sensation Quantitative?", *British Journal of Psychology* 6 (1913): 137–89. See also refs. in n. 49 below.

18. See K. Young, "The History of Mental Testing," *Pedagogical Seminary* 31 (1923): 1–48; J. Peterson, *Early Conceptions and Tests of Intelligence* (Yonkers, N.Y.: World Book Company, 1925); F. L. Goodenough, *Mental Testing: Its History, Principles, and Applications* (New York: Rinehart, 1949); L. J. Kamin, *The Science and Politics of I.Q.* (Potomac, Md.: Erlbaum, 1974); B. Evans and B. Waites, *IQ and Mental Testing* (Atlantic Highlands, N.J.: Humanities Press, 1981); R. Marks, *The Idea of IQ* (Washington, D.C.: University Press of America, 1981); "Historical and Legal Context of Ability Testing," in *Ability Testing: Uses, Consequences, and Controversies. Part 1: Report of the Committee*, ed. A. K. Wigdor and W. R. Garner (Washington, D.C.: National Academy Press, 1982), chap. 3; W. G. Dahlstrom, "The Development of Psychological Testing,"

in *Topics in the History of Psychology*, vol. 2, ed. G. A. Kimble and K. Schlesinger (Hillsdale, N.J.: Erlbaum, 1985); R. E. Fancher, *The Intelligence Men: Makers of the IQ Controversy* (New York: Norton, 1985).

19. Goodenough, *Mental Testing*, pp. 9–11; L. Zenderland, "The Debate over Diagnosis: Henry Herbert Goddard and the Medical Acceptance of Intelligence Testing," in *Psychological Testing and American Society, 1890–1930*, ed. M. M. Sokal (New Brunswick, N.J.: Rutgers University Press, 1987), pp. 46–74.

20. Goodenough, *Mental Testing*, pp. 14–19.

21. Kamin, *The Science and Politics of I.Q.*, discusses these attempts in some detail. But see F. Samelson, "On the Science and Politics of the IQ," *Social Research* 42 (1975): 467–88, for a critique of some of Kamin's claims.

22. Goodenough, *Mental Testing*, pp. 24, 25.

23. Unlike later testers, Binet assumed that intelligence was "quantifiable only to a limited and tentative degree" (Fancher, *The Intelligence Men*, p. 82). He thus used the general term "intellectual level" to describe a child's overall score, rather than the seemingly more precise "mental age," a term substituted by his successors (p. 77).

24. The main disagreement centered on whether Binet's age-based method or the point-scale method proposed by the American psychologist Robert Yerkes provided the most useful measure. See Goodenough, *Mental Testing*, pp. 59–62, for a summary of the issues here.

25. The problem with the "intellectual level" concept as Binet used it was that any child who tested three or more years "below age" was considered "feeble-minded." This criterion implied the use of different standards for older and younger children, which seemed unfair. Terman's solution to this problem is found in L. M. Terman, *The Measurement of Intelligence* (Boston: Houghton Mifflin, 1916). It should be noted that the use of a single, fixed score to represent a child's intellectual level so contradicted Binet's original intention that his collaborator, Theodore Simon, called it "a betrayal" (Fancher, *The Intelligence Men*, p. 104).

26. See, e.g., Kamin, *The Science and Politics of I.Q.*, and Samelson, "On the Science and Politics of the IQ," on the use of test results with regard to limiting the immigration of low-scoring groups.

27. See N. Pastore, "The Army Intelligence Tests and Walter Lippmann," *Journal of the History of the Behavioral Sciences* 14 (1978): 316–27, for references to the numerous articles in this debate and an interpretation of its significance.

28. "Intelligence and its Measurement," *Journal of Educational Psychology* 12 (1921): 123–47, 195–216, 271–75. See also C. G. Regner, "The Measurement Movement and the Man in the Street," *Education* 44 (1924): 571–75.

29. E. G. Boring, "Intelligence as the Tests Test it," *The New Republic* 34 (1923): 34–37. For one of the most detailed critiques of the operationist view of intelligence, see N. J. Block and G. Dworkin, "IQ, Heritability, and Inequality," in *The IQ Controversy*, ed. N. J. Block and G. Dworkin (New York: Pantheon, 1976), pp. 418–19. For a recent general critique of operationist thinking, see Leahey, "The Myth of Operationism."

30. Goodenough, *Mental Testing*, p. 97.
31. Noted in ibid., p. 90. See E. B. South, *An Index of Periodical Literature on Testing, 1921–1936* (New York: The Psychological Corporation, 1937).
32. C. Spearman, " 'General Intelligence' Objectively Determined and Measured," *American Journal of Psychology* 15 (1904): 201–92; idem, "The Theory of Two Factors," *Psychological Review* 21 (1914): 101–15; L. L. Thurstone, *The Vectors of Mind: Multiple Factor Analysis for the Isolation of Primary Traits* (Chicago: University of Chicago Press, 1935); E. L. Thorndike, *The Measurement of Intelligence* (New York: Bureau of Publications, Teachers' College, Columbia University, 1926).
33. For discussions of the applications of testing in diverse contexts, see F. Samelson, "Putting Psychology on the Map: Ideology and Intelligence Testing," in *Psychology in Social Context*, ed. A. R. Buss (New York: Irvington, 1979), pp. 103–68; M. M. Sokal, "The Origins of the Psychological Corporation," *Journal of the History of the Behavioral Sciences* 17 (1981): 54–67; D. S. Napoli, *Architects of Adjustment: The History of the Psychological Profession in the United States* (Port Washington, N.Y.: Kennikat Press, 1981). For a detailed discussion of the "cult of efficiency" in education, which enabled testing to be so readily accepted, see R. E. Callahan, *Education and the Cult of Efficiency* (Chicago: University of Chicago Press, 1962).
34. Binet had described these problems as early as 1898, but his reservations seem to have had little effect on the testing movement. See A. Binet, "La mesure en psychologie individuelle," *Revue Philosophique* 46 (1898): 113–23.
35. L. L. Thurstone, "A Method of Scaling Psychological and Educational Tests," *Journal of Educational Psychology* 16 (1925): 433–51; idem, "The Scoring of Individual Performance," *Journal of Educational Psychology* 17 (1926): 466–57; idem and L. Ackerson, "The Mental Growth Curve for the Binet Tests,"*Journal of Educational Psychology* 20 (1929): 569–83.
36. Thurstone, "Scoring of Individual Performance," p. 446.
37. J. P. Guilford, *Psychometric Methods* (New York: McGraw Hill, 1936), p. 11.
38. In citing the lack of an absolute zero as a basic problem with psychological scales, theorists such as Guilford and Thurstone repeatedly made reference to scales in the physical sciences that had supposedly overcome this problem. But as Keller notes (pers. com., 1986), certain scales in physics (for example, those that measure energy levels) have no absolute zero point, and this has not prevented their widespread adoption. An analysis of the ways in which psychologists have selectively used models and examples from physics as a justification for various methodological changes in psychology is beyond the scope of this discussion. But it is important to note that physicists may not have perceived the absolute zero issue to have been as problematic as psychologists implied.
39. L. L. Thurstone, "Psychological Analysis," *American Journal of Psychology* 38 (1927): 368–89; idem, "The Method of Paired Comparisons for Social Values," *Journal of Abnormal and Social Psychology* 21 (1927): 384–400; idem, "A Law of Comparative Judgment," *Psychological Review* 34 (1927): 273–86; idem, "The Absolute Zero in Intelligence Measurement," *Psychological Review* 35 (1928): 175–97.

40. Thurstone, "Absolute Zero," pp. 181–82, 194.
41. L. L. Thurstone, in *History of Psychology in Autobiography*, vol. 4, ed. E. G. Boring, H. S. Langfeld, H. Werner, and R. M. Yerkes (Worcester, Mass.: Clark University Press, 1952), pp. 304–05. On the acceptance of Thurstone's conclusion, see, e.g., Goodenough, *Mental Testing*, and Guilford, *Psychometric Methods*.
42. According to Guilford (*Psychometric Methods*, p. 223), this method was first suggested by Fechner in his work on aesthetic judgments but was not introduced formally until 1894, when Cohn used it in studying color preferences.
43. L. L. Thurstone, in *Autobiography*, p. 308.
44. L. L. Thurstone, "Attitudes can be Measured," *American Journal of Sociology* 33 (1928): 529–54. See also idem, "Theory of Attitude Measurement," *Psychological Review* 36 (1929): 222–41; idem and E. J. Chave, *The Measurement of Attitude* (Chicago: Univerity of Chicago Press, 1929).
45. R. Likert, "A Technique for the Measurement of Attitudes," *Archives of Psychology* 22 (1932): no. 140, 1–55.
46. Although Stevens is often credited with having developed direct scaling procedures, this is probably incorrect. Such procedures were introduced as early as 1888 and were rediscovered in the late 1920s by Richardson and Ross. See Marks, *Sensory Processes*, for a more detailed review of this history.
47. S. S. Stevens, "On the Psychological Law."
48. S. S. Stevens, "On the Theory of Scales of Measurement," *Science* 103 (1946): 677 (originally presented to the International Congress for the Unity of Science, Cambridge, Mass., 1941). For a widely ignored precursor of Stevens's scales, see H. M. Johnson, "Pseudo-mathematics in the Mental and Social Sciences," *American Journal of Psychology* 48 (1936): 342–51.
49. See R. N. Shepard, "On the Status of 'Direct' Psychophysical Measurement," in *Minnesota Studies in the Philosophy of Science*, vol. 9, *Perception and Cognition Issues in the Foundations of Psychology*, ed. C. W. Savage (Minneapolis: University of Minnesota Press, 1978), pp. 441–90. For other discussions of the appropriate scale for psychological data, see Savage, *The Measurement of Sensation*; Marks, *Sensory Processes*; W. R. Garner, H. W. Hake, and C. W. Eriksen, "Operationism and the Concept of Perception," *Psychological Review* 63 (1956): 149–59; R. M. Warren and R. P. Warren, "A Critique of S. S. Stevens' 'New Psychophysics'," *Perceptual and Motor Skills* 16 (1963): 797–810; N. H. Anderson, "Functional Measurement and Psychophysical Judgment," *Psychological Review* 77 (1970): 153–70; idem, "Cross-task Validation of Functional Measurement," *Perception and Psychophysics* 12 (1972): 389–95; D. H. Krantz, "A Theory of Magnitude Estimation and Cross-modality Matching," *Journal of Mathematical Psychology* 9 (1972): 168–99; idem, "Measurement Structures and Psychological Laws," *Science* 175 (1972): 1427–35; R. D. Luce, "What Sort of Measurement is Psychophysical Measurement?", *American Psychologist* 27 (1972): 96–106; L. E. Marks, "On Scales of Sensation: Prolegomena to any Future Psychophysics that will be able to Come Forth as Science," *Perception and Psychophysics* 16 (1974): 358–76; A. Parducci, "Category Ratings: Still More

Contextual Effects," in *Social Attitudes and Psychophysical Measurement*, ed. B. Wegener (Hillsdale, N.J.: Erlbau, 1982), pp. 89–105.

50. The fact that these debates continue in their most explicit form in psychophysics (see refs. in n. 49 above) is not surprising. Early in his career, Stevens began to think of psychophysics as "the science of psychological measurement" (unpublished notes ca. 1933, S. S. Stevens Papers, Harvard University Archives), and most of the detailed discussions of the mathematical bases for psychological measurement have taken place within the psychophysical literature. In part, this may be due to the fact that, historically, psychophysical research has required the greatest degree of mathematical sophistication of any work in psychology, which has meant that psychophysicists are especially well equipped to debate issues of measurement. But an equally important factor here is that, since the 1930s, psychophysicists have taken the view that an analysis of the process of discrimination among observers is key to all operational work in science. On this view, psychophysics (the study of discriminatory capacities) is uniquely suited to provide the grounding for scientific measurement. See S. S. Stevens, "The Operational Basis of Psychology," *American Journal of Psychology* 47 (1935): 323–30.

51. As Smith has pointed out, however, the differentiation of psychology from philosophy was to some extent reversed in the 1930s, when behaviorist psychologists utilized logical positivism in constructing the bases for their view of science (L. D. Smith, "Psychology and Philosophy: Toward a Realignment, 1905–1935," *Journal of the History of the Behavioral Sciences* 17 [1981]: 28–37).

52. This use of methodology, rather than subject matter, as the basis for establishing psychology as an independent discipline is in marked contrast to the strategy used in sociology, for example. Claiming "the group" as their primary datum, sociologists were able to differentiate their discipline on the basis of a unique subject matter and thereby maintain a far greater plurality of methods than was the case in psychology. See H. Kuklick, "Boundary Maintenance in American Sociology: Limitations to Academic 'Professionalization'," *Journal of the History of the Behavioral Sciences* 16 (1980): 201–19.

53. This was true mainly in the American context. In Germany, where philosophy was a powerful discipline with considerably more prestige than psychology, psychologists stressed their connections with philosophy, rather than their differences from it. For a discussion of the differences in legitimation strategies used by American and German psychologists, see K. Danziger, "The Social Origins of Modern Psychology," in *Psychology in Social Context*, ed. A. R. Buss (New York: Irvington, 1979), pp. 27–45.

54. For examples of legitimation attempts of this sort, see L. M. Terman, "The Mental Test as an Experimental Method," *Psychological Review* 31 (1924): 93–117; M. Freyd, "What is Applied Psychology?", *Psychological Review* 33 (1926): 308–14. For a detailed discussion of the ideological conservatism inherent in attempts to label certain kinds of activities "pseudoscience," see R. Cooter, "Deploying 'pseudoscience': Then and Now," in *Science, Pseudo-science, and Society*, ed. M. P. Hanen, M. J. Osler, and R. G. Weyant (Wilfrid Laurier University

Press, 1980), pp. 237–72. On the general move toward professionalization of psychologists, see T. M. Camfield, "The Professionalization of American Psychology, 1870–1917," *Journal of the History of the Behavioral Sciences* 9 (1973): 66–75. On the use of disciplinary histories (like Boring's text) as legitimation devices, see *Functions and Uses of Disciplinary Histories*, ed. L. Graham, W. Lepenies, and P. Weingart (Dordrecht: Reidel, 1983).

55. Minutes of the meeting of the Committee on Qualifications for Psychological Examiners and Other Psychological Experts, 20 June 1918, p. 4, Box 20, Folder 1, Lewis M. Terman Papers, Stanford University Archives. See also Napoli, *Architects of Adjustment*, pp. 21–22.

56. For an analysis of how psychologists developed a market for quantitative research among educational administrators, see K. Danziger, "Educational Administration and a Critical Shift in Research Practice" (Paper presented at Cheiron, Vassar College, June 1984), and Callahan, *Education and the Cult of Efficiency*. For a discussion of sociology's attempt to profit from psychology's success by adopting quantitative methods of its own, see Kuklick, "Boundary Maintenance in American Sociology." On the use of psychologists in industry, see L. Baritz, *The Servants of Power* (Middletown, Conn.: Wesleyan University Press, 1960).

57. E. L. Thorndike, "Measurement in Education," in *Twenty-first Yearbook of the National Society for the Study of Education*, Part 1, ed. G. M. Whipple (Bloomington, Ind.: Public School Publishing Co., 1923), pp. 1–9.

58. Wigdor and Garner, *Ability Testing*, pp. 89–90.

59. Papers of the Psycho-acoustic Laboratory (S. S. Stevens, director), Box 2, Harvard University Archives.

60. Gerson describes this move from debating criteria to focusing on actual research problems as "downshifting." See E. M. Gerson, "Evaluating Technical Work" (Unpublished paper, 1980).

61. I have discussed this example in more detail in "Intelligence Testing and the Quantification of American Psychology" (Paper presented at the American Psychological Association, Toronto, August 1984).

62. See, e.g., R. P. Jarrett, "A Scale of Intelligence of College Students for the Use of College Appointment Committees," *Journal of Applied Psychology* 2 (1918): 43–51; S. L. Pressey and L. W. Pressey, "A Group Group Point Scale for Measuring General Intelligence, with First Results from 1,000 School Children," *Journal of Applied Psychology* 2 (1918): 250–69. F. Lowell, "A Group Intelligence Scale for Primary Grades," *Journal of Applied Psychology* 3 (1919): 215–47; R. Pintner, "A Non-Language Group Intelligence Test," *Journal of Applied Psychology* 3 (1919): 199–214. Although these papers were published in 1918 and 1919, they report on tests that were developed at least several years earlier. Note that the fact that there was disagreement about the criteria for deciding which test was "best" is itself reflective of the "inefficiency" of testing research during this period.

63. Wigdor and Garner, *Ability Testing*, p. 87. But see M. Adler, "Mental Tests Used as a Basis for the Classification of School Children," *Journal of Educational Psychology* 5 (1914): 22–28, for an early example of testing as a classification device for normal children.

64. See D. J. Kevles, "Testing the Army's Intelligence: Psychologists and the Military in World War I," *Journal of American History* 55 (1968): 565–81; J. H. Spring, "Psychologists and the War: The Meaning of Intelligence in the Alpha and Beta Tests," *History of Education Quarterly* 12 (1972): 3–15; F. Samelson, "World War I Intelligence Testing and the Development of Psychology," *Journal of the History of the Behavioral Sciences* 13 (1977): 274–82; and Wigdor and Garner, *Ability Testing.*

65. This group was comprised of Yerkes (chair), Terman, Haggerty, Thorndike, and Whipple, and the group test they produced and successfully marketed to the schools was called the National Intelligence Test. My conclusions about the workings of this group are based on minutes of their meetings (Minutes of the Board for the School Intelligence Scale, Box 12, Folder 14, Terman Papers. On the general lack of "internecine warfare" among applied psychologists after the war, see Napoli, *Architects of Adjustment*, p. 8.

66. The most important of these texts are J. Dewey, *Psychology* (New York: Harper and Brothers, 1886); W. James, *Principles of Psychology*; G. T. Ladd, *Psychology, Descriptive and Explanatory* (New York: C. Scribner's Sons, 1894); and J. M. Baldwin, *Handbook of Psychology* (New York: Henry Holt, 1889, 1891).

67. There were occasional instances of the reverse, however, where data that were methodologically rigorous were discounted simply because they appeared implausible. See, e.g., the discussion of how Rhine's ESP data were dismissed by psychologists, even though mathematicians judged his statistical analyses to be correct; in S. H. Mauskopf and M. R. McVaugh, "The Controversy over Statistics in Parapsychology, 1934–1938," in *The Reception of Unconventional Science*, ed. S. H. Mauskopf (Boulder, Colo.: Westview Press, 1979), pp. 105–23.

68. The most obvious examples here are the attempts to discount psychoanalysis on the grounds that its propositions cannot be translated into operationalized variables which can be quantified. For a general discussion of this issue, see Leahey, "The Myth of Operationism." For specific examples of such attempts, see H. J. Eysenck and G. D. Wilson, *The Experimental Study of Freudian Theories* (London: Methuen, 1973); S. Fisher and R. Greenberg eds., *The Scientific Evaluation of Freud's Theories and Therapy* (New York: Basic Books, 1978).

69. See Robinson's discussion of methodology as the "metaphysic of psychology" in D. N. Robinson, *An Intellectual History of Psychology*, rev. ed. (New York: Macmillan, 1981), pp. 395–404, and K. Danziger, "The Methodological Imperative in Psychology."

70. Kuklick refers to this as the "propaganda value of a rigorous methodology" ("Boundary maintenance in American sociology," p. 209).

71. It should be noted, however, that the general notion of using numbers to provide an objective means of representation is itself comparatively recent, as Cohen's analysis of the development of "numeracy" clearly demonstrates. See P. C. Cohen, *A Calculating People: The Spread of Numeracy in Early America* (Chicago: University of Chicago Press, 1982).

72. For a recent defense of operationism on the grounds of its practical utility for research purposes, see Kendler's responses to Leahey's critiques: H. H. Kendler, "The Reality of Operationism: A Rejoinder," *Journal of Mind and Behavior* 2

(1981): 331–41; idem, "Operationism: A Recipe for Reducing Confusion and Ambiguity," *Journal of Mind and Behavior* 4 (1983): 91–97.

73. For examples of early statistical texts, see T. L. Kelley, *Statistical Method* (New York: Macmillan, 1924); H. E. Garret, *Statistics in Psychology and Education* (New York: Longmans, Green & Co., 1926); and K. J. Holzinger, *Statistical Methods for Students in Education* (Boston: Ginn and Co., 1928). For detailed discussions of the history of statistics in psychology, see M. C. Acree, "Theories of Statistical Inference in Psychological Research: A Historico-critical Study" (Ph.D. diss., Clark University, 1978), quote from p. 397); D. Stout, "The Social Construction of Experimental and Correlational Psychology" (Ph.D. diss., University of Edinburgh, in preparation). On the use of statistical techniques as a way of deleting choices by the researcher, see J. K. Skipper, A. L. Guenther, and G. Nass, "The Sacredness of .05: A Note Concerning the Uses of Statistical Levels of Significance in Social Science," *American Sociologist* 2 (1967): 16–18.

74. See Mendelsohn, "The Social Construction of Scientific Knowledge"; and K. Knorr-Cetina, *The Manufacture of Knowledge* (Oxford: Pergamon, 1981).

75. See Marks, *The Idea of IQ*, for a more detailed discussion of the link between psychological theory and social control. Danziger, "The Social Origins of Modern Psychology," provides an especially incisive analysis of the connections between American psychology and the needs of social administrators, businessmen, and politicians.

76. Block and Dworkin, "IQ, Heritability, and Inequality," pp. 418–19.

2

A Question of Identity: Who Participated in Psychological Experiments?

Kurt Danziger*

York University

Nature of the Problem

Human experimental psychology involves the setting up of special social situations in which the participants come together for the purpose of generating certain symbolic products that count as psychological knowledge. It is not unreasonable to suspect that there may be some connection between the nature of these social situations and the kind of psychological knowledge that they generate.

In examining this possibility historically, one is limited to documentary evidence and is unable to conduct field studies of experimental situations or experiments on experiments. However, the conventions of experimental science come to the historian's aid. It has been standard practice for as long as experimental psychology has existed to publish formal reports of laboratory procedures. Now while the natural science model, which experimental psychologists imitated, excluded the social interaction among experimenters from the formal report, it did prescribe that some account be given of the experimenter's interaction with the object of his research. In the case of most psychological experiments, that object is a human person or persons. Thus, quite unintentionally, published reports of psychological experiments have always

*The content analysis of psychological journals reported in this chapter was supported by a grant from the Social Sciences and Humanities Research Council of Canada. I wish to thank Cindi Goodfield, Gregory McGuire, James Parker, and Peter Shermer for their assistance with this work.

contained some information relevant to the social interaction between experimenters and the human sources of their data.

Further, the experimental report is itself a social product, whose purpose is the public communication of specific knowledge claims. To achieve this purpose, the human aspects of experimentation are reported in a highly selective manner, following certain conventions. An analysis of historical changes in these conventions throws light on the relationship between psychological knowledge and the social context in which it is generated.

Published experimental reports contain information on various significant features of the experimental situation. In the first place, they contain information on the role structure of the situation, or, more precisely, on the social distribution of experimental tasks. Someone manipulates the experimental apparatus, someone acts as data source, someone records the results, someone authors the report to be published, and so on. One can ask questions about which tasks are generally combined in one role and which tasks are never combined. One can also turn the question around and ask which tasks, if any, are interchangeable among the participants.

When one pursues such questions, one discovers that experimental psychology started out with at least two models for structuring the interaction of the participants in the experimental situation.[1] In one, certain social functions were rigidly segregated from others, and there was no reciprocity between experimenter and subject roles, the power relationship between the two being asymmetrical and there being a sharp distinction between communication with one's fellow investigators and communication with one's human data source. This model of psychological investigation pretty much duplicated the social situation that characterized medical investigation. In the other model, represented by Wilhelm Wundt's original laboratory at Leipzig, there was much more flexibility in the assignment of functions in the experimental situation; experimenter and subject roles were interchangeable (always in principle and frequently in practice), with power relationships being relatively symmetrical and communication between experimenters and subjects often merely a special case of communication within the scientific community. In its social aspect this model of investigative practice had some similarity to an ongoing research seminar.

Although early psychological experiments differed in terms of their structuring of roles, they often shared some other social features. In particular, experimental situations were usually enacted among people who already knew each other, often in professional relationships and sometimes as friends. Moreover, their experimental interaction was often extended over relatively long periods of time. In these respects, early experimentation differed from a type of experimentation that became increasingly popular in the twentieth century. Here participants were essentially strangers to one another, and their interaction was relatively brief.

We will return to this difference in the third section of this chapter. For the moment it is sufficient to note that structural patterns of role relationships are not the only features of the social practice of experimentation that can be discovered by a comparative analysis of research reports. One can raise questions not only about *how* the participants in psychological experiments interacted, but also about *who* participated in the interaction. As long as published experimental reports refer in any way to the human beings who interacted to produce the experimental results, they must identify these individuals in some way, and the manner of identification is not irrelevant to the knowledge claim that the experimental report seeks to establish.

The results communicated in such reports always involve attributions. That is to say, the behavioral measures, verbal reports, and so on, found in them must be attributed to some data source in order for the communication to be meaningful. The "responses" reported are those of seven-year-old children, of a group of undergraduates, of a psychologically trained individual observer, of a clinical population, or whatever. Now the knowledge claim that is involved in the publication of such experimental results depends quite crucially on the identification of the human source to whom the data are attributed. Different ways of identifying the source convey different claims about the kind of knowledge that the data are held to represent. For instance, if the experimental results are explicitly attributed to children, the reader knows that the information is to be taken as pertaining to a specific subsection of humanity, rather than as a universal generalization.

Reporting the results of psychological experiments has always required some rather elaborate rhetorical constructions. The problem facing the reporter is that a psychological experiment is a social situation involving the interaction of certain individuals with particular personal and social identities; yet something resulting from this historically situated interaction has to be presented as having a claim to universal validity. One way of achieving the necessary transformation is to report the results in such a way that they are not attributed to individuals with particular personal and social identities. In this way the report on the outcome of the experimental interaction is very different from everyday reports on most other social situations, and this difference is important in establishing an experimental report's claim to communicate something of general significance.

One therefore has to distinguish between the actual *identity* of the participants and their *identification* in the experimental report. All human participants in experimental situations necessarily have some identity as individuals and as members of certain social categories. But their identification in research reports may or may not coincide with their normal personal or social identities, and what experimental reports omit may be just as significant as what they mention explicitly. Readily available information about the identity of participants may be omitted from the reports because it is considered irrelevant to the scientific status of the knowledge product. Papers in scientific journals also have a very important rhetorical function.[2] The way they present the experimental process and the results of experimentation must conform to prevailing conceptions of scientificity. Hence, differences in the handling of information about the human identity of participants provide clues to differences in conceptions of what establishes the scientific nature of experimental results.

Another necessary conceptual distinction is that between the identity of participants outside the experimental situation and their identity within it. The latter involves two levels: a unique personal identity and an identity conferred by membership in various social categories like those of age, profession, educational status, and so on. If personal identity serves as the basis for identification in experimental reports, this will take the form of mentioning participants' names. In addition, the social identity of participants may also be indicated.

But because experimental situations involve a division of functions, the published reports are also likely to identify the participants in terms of these functions. The persons concerned have a temporary identity within the experimental situation. Thus, some may have the identity of experimenters and others the identity of subjects. These identities begin and end with the experimental situation and are deliberately created in order to construct the situation.

Our framework for analyzing the historical development of the identity problem in psychological research thus utilizes two conceptual distinctions. First, there is the distinction between the actual identity of those participating in psychological investigations and the way in which these participants are identified in published research reports. Second, there is the distinction of personal, social, and experimental identities. This framework is schematically represented in table 2.1.

We can think of any participant in a psychological investigation as having a particular personal, social, and experimental identity while actually participating in the experimental situation, and the published report will also assign certain identities to him or her. These two sets of identities need not coincide; in fact, they seldom do. For example, the experimental report may not assign any individual identities at all, but may treat the participant as an anonymous member of a group (cell E). Or it may treat the participant's social identity as irrelevant and identify him or her solely in terms of functions internal to the experimental situation (cell F). (Discussion of this last issue will be postponed till the final section.)

TABLE 2.1
Schema for an Analysis of the Identity of Participants in Psychological Investigations

	Actual identity of participants	Identification of participants in published reports
Experimental identity	A Data source, investigator, etc.	D Subject, observer, experimenter, etc.
Individual identity	B Specific historical individuals	E By name, code, initials, anonymous
Social identity	C College students, psychologists, children, etc.	F Salience of social identity for data presentation

This analytic scheme allows us to raise two kinds of questions. First, there are what we might call "within cell" questions. Within cell C, for example, we come up against questions such as the following: What was the social status of people who participated in psychological experiments, and how did this change historically? Did most participants always belong to the social category of "college student"? However, some of the most interesting questions are those involving the relationships between the rows and columns of table 2.1, in particular, the relationship between the actual identities of the participants and the way in which these identities are depicted in research reports. As we have seen, research reports are highly selective in the way in which they report the identities of human participants in psychological investigations. If historical changes are detected in the attribution of identities in experimental reports, this would suggest that the normative criteria for making such attributions also changed. Can such changes be related to changes in prevailing conceptions of the nature of psychological knowledge?

In order to address such questions, the published research reports will have to be examined under two aspects: for what they tell us about the actual identities of participants in psychological investigations and for what they reveal about the rhetorical devices employed by their authors in making certain kinds of knowledge claims. We will pursue this dual inquiry as it affects experimental, personal, and social identities and their interrelations.

Experimental Identities

Any psychological investigation of human individuals must involve one or more persons who act as the source of some information that counts as psy-

chological data. In the social situation that constitutes psychological investigation there will necessarily be participants who have the experimental identity
of data source (cell A, table 2.1). The question we now have to address is
how these participants are identified when the data are published in the psychological research literature (cell D). The published report of the research
will reflect certain decisions that were taken about how to refer to the human
source of the data. The author of such a report has the alternative of referring
to such sources by giving either their ordinary social identities—for example,
boys or girls—or their special experimental identities—for example, "subjects"
or "observers." This choice is not made randomly but depends on prevailing
norms and conventions within the community of investigators. It is likely,
too, that these norms reflect prevailing conceptions of psychological knowledge.

One might think that the choice of how one refers to the human sources
of one's data is a relatively trivial matter. This appearance of triviality, however,
is the product of a situation in which the norms governing such matters have
simply become hallowed by long usage, so that the awareness of their implications has been lost. When we look at the historical development of these
norms, we discover issues that are far from trivial.

The history of experimental psychology is marked by a long period of in-
decision about the appropriate way to refer to the experimental identity of
those who function as the source of data. In the very early days of the discipline,
a number of terms were used,[3] but in the English-language literature two
terms quickly overshadowed all the others. These terms were *subject* and *observer*. By the end of the nineteenth century the former was being used in
about half of all published reports in the *Psychological Review* and the *American
Journal of Psychology*, and the latter in about a quarter. But it took another
half-century for the use of *observer* to dwindle to a negligible level. In fact,
in the *American Journal of Psychology* the term *observer* became far more
common than the term *subject* in the early years of the twentieth century (65
percent versus 14 percent of the articles for the period 1909–11). Clearly, the
connotations of these terms were not a matter of indifference at the time, but
presented authors and editors with a real choice.

This choice was prompted by rhetorical considerations, because in opting
for one or the other, one was declaring one's allegiance to a certain conception
of psychological knowledge. Thus, the promotion of the term *observer* by
some psychologists in the early twentieth century appears to be linked with
the emergence of a more self-conscious kind of introspectionism, which presented itself as "systematic experimental introspection."[4] In the United States,
Titchener was the leading figure in this development, and the *American Journal
of Psychology* became its main publication channel. This movement defined
the role of the psychological data source entirely in terms of introspective
observation, whereas earlier practice had been much less restrictive. Not sur-

prisingly, it also favored research areas whose content gave the most scope for working out its methodological program.

It seems that as a result of this development and the subsequent reaction of the behaviorists, the terms *subject* and *observer* came to be part of the rhetoric of rival schools of experimental practice. By 1929 one well-known experimental psychologist considered the time to be ripe to urge the dropping of the term *observer* from psychological discourse. After all, "in many contemporary lines of psychological investigation the so-called 'observer' does no observing!"[5] This led to a prompt reply (in the *American Journal of Psychology*, of course) by Bentley, a prominent representative of a different point of view, who, while no longer defending Tichenerian introspectionism, objected to a "cult of objectivism" that refuses to recognize the special nature of those experiments "where the organism enters the scene as *agent*."[6] Further controversy did not resolve the divergence of perspectives.[7]

While the rhetorical functions of the terms *subject* and *observer* may have been salient for only a minority of experimentalists, the failure of the discipline to establish uniformity of usage even after several decades is probably a reflection of a continuing division of opinion about the essential function of the human data source. There appears to have been a general feeling that the data source should be identified by reference to its essential function in the experimental situation. But what was this essential function? The "objectivists" clearly felt that it consisted in providing material for the experimenter's observation and use, and the term *subject* had by long usage acquired this kind of meaning (the medical prehistory of the term had been forgotten, though it was preserved in practice). The minority who resisted this trend saw the essential function of the human data source as consisting in its competence to comprehend the experimental task and to act appropriately. This latter interpretation was of course quite close to Wundt's original conception of the role of the human data source in psychological experiments.[8] Experimental psychology began life with two very different conceptions of its practice.[9] Although one of these was in retreat almost from the start, complete uniformity of practice does not appear to have been reached during the period under review here.

Individual Identity

All participants in psychological investigations have an individual identity commonly referred to by the use of a personal name, which identifies the person as a specific historical individual. Whether the published research report provides this identification is likely to depend on whether its author feels that the historical identification of individual participants would back up the knowledge claims in the report or whether such an identification would detract from these claims. Where an experimental report provides the names of the participants in the experiment, it draws attention to the fact that specific, historically situated individuals were involved. The persons mentioned in the published account of the experimental scenario then appear as themselves and not simply anonymous instances of intra- or extra-experimental social categories.

Why might it be considered necessary to make this kind of personal identification in experimental reports? Obviously, the identification of the author of the report, who is also likely to have been a participant, is related to questions of scientific proprietorship which go beyond the present context. Here we will restrict ourselves to the personal identification of the experimental data source, which, as we shall see, undergoes considerable historical change. One reason for identifying a data source by name has to do with conceptions of its essential function, as discussed above. If that function is seen in terms of making trustworthy observations, then attaching the name of a reputable observer may be a way of establishing the scientific credibility of the data.

In order to trace changes in reporting practices, sample volumes of psychological journals were subjected to a content analysis. Usually a three-year period was used—for example, 1924–26—though in two cases the period selected was only two years. In all the volumes sampled, only empirical studies with human subjects were considered. Articles that merely described new apparatus or materials and those that were only brief notes, two pages or less, were excluded. As table 2.2 shows, there is a steady general decline in the practice of identifying subjects by name. The *American Journal of Psychology* is relatively resistant to the general trend, and the applied journals are in the lead.

While the trend illustrated in this table can in part be accounted for by a shift in the nature of the task that defines the function of the data source,

TABLE 2.2

Percentage of Empirical Studies in which All or Some of Those Participating as Subjects are Identified by Name*

Name of journal	Time period			
	1894–96	1909–12	1924–26	1934–36
American Journal of Psychology	54	39	39	24
Psychological Review	35	35	—	—
Journal of Educational Psychology	—	4	0	0
Psychological Monographs	—	18	21	5
Journal of Experimental Psychology	—	—	8	8
Journal of Applied Psychology	—	—	4	0

*Blank cells occur before a journal began publication, or, in the case of *Psychological Review*, when the number of empirical studies becomes very small.

there is another aspect of the identification of individuals that has yet to be considered. In the history of experimental psychology there has been a major shift in the way in which research data are reported. For some time it has been common to report only statistical results pertaining to groups of individuals. But this practice emerged only gradually.[10] In the early years of the discipline the common practice was to report the responses of specific individuals. Quantitative data were set out in tables that related the obtained values to specific individuals acting as data source.

Such an organization of experimental results was of course a reflection of what the authors regarded as psychological knowledge—namely, knowledge of actual processes taking place in human minds. Because human minds were individual entities, such processes could be studied and reported only in this form. This did not mean that the phenomena studied were thought to be idiosyncratic. On the contrary, claims were commonly made for the general, or even universal, significance of experimental findings; but such claims were generally based on one or more additional considerations. In the psychology of sensation, for instance, results from even a single subject could be claimed to have general significance because of the presumed similarity of the underlying physiology in all normal human individuals. Further, claims for generality were supported by repeating an experiment with several individuals. Each additional subject then provided material for a replication of the original experiment. Where attempts at replication were not altogether successful, relevant personal information or introspective evidence could be used to provide a rational explanation of the failure; for example, relevant previous learning experiences or reported fluctuations of attention could be used to account for discrepant results.

Thus the early practice of experimental psychology combined a particular conception of psychological knowledge with an appropriate social structuring of the investigative situation. Psychological knowledge pertained to the analysis, the description, or the causal role of specific subjective processes taking place in or characterizing actual psychological individuals. Such processes were investigated by recording and reporting their manifestations in individuals under specified conditions.

It was not long before certain exceptions to these patterns began to appear in the psychological literature. Some American investigators who taught relatively large classes of undergraduates began to conduct group experiments in which simple experimental tasks were administered to a whole class and individual subjects remained anonymous, the results of such experiments being published simply as statistical averages.[11] There were psychological investigations of children in which literally thousands of individuals were inducted as anonymous participants in a single study.[12] These sorts of investigations were supplemented by early forms of mental testing, which were also designed to yield group data from anonymous individuals.[13] In all these cases the results of psychological investigation were attributed to groups, rather than specific individuals, and the latter lacked both identity and individuality in the published reports. There could be no question of identifying individual participants, because the real data source was now a group of anonymous members.

When one examines the reports of these newer, "statistical," studies, as they were often called, it becomes clear that a different kind of psychological knowledge was being sought. These mass methods were hardly suitable for tracing actual psychological processes as they occurred in individuals; nor was that what they were generally employed for. They were intended to answer quite different questions—namely, questions about the *distribution* of psychological characteristics in populations. Age and sex differences were of interest at an early stage, but soon the psychological characteristics of a wide range of socially identified groups became the subject of inquiry. These included criminal and delinquent groups, specially talented groups, subcultural groups, and so on. Above all, the project of studying the distribution of psychological characteristics in the population as a whole became more and more popular. During the first half of the twentieth century this type of psychological research became increasingly dominant within the discipline. The processes involved in this development were quite complex and have been analyzed elsewhere.[14]

During the first half century of its existence, American psychology shows a highly consistent trend in the way it handles the identity of its human data source. In general, the trend is away from an individualized source with a salient social identity, whose essential function is that of careful observation, and toward an anonymous source, with no relevant identity outside the laboratory, whose function is that of an object of experimental manipulation and scrutiny. In other words, there is a shift away from the expert observer, toward the manipulated object of observation. As Thorndike recognized very early, this involves a fundamental switch from a situation in which it is the function of the psychological experiment "to aid the subject to know what he experienced" to a situation in which the experiment functions "to aid the experimenter to know what the subject did."[15] It is clear that changes in the conventions governing the identification of the human sources of psychological data are a reflection of fundamental changes in the kinds of knowledge claims that psychologists want to establish.

Social Identity

Participants in psychology experiments have a social, as well as a personal, identity. They are members of socially defined groups, whatever their function in a particular experimental situation may happen to be. Let us first consider the relevance of social identity for the actual participation in psychological investigations and then discuss the way social identity is handled in the reporting of psychological data (cells C and F in table 2.1).

Broadly speaking, there are two kinds of functions in the experimental situation to which the external social identity of the participants may be highly relevant. The first is that of the subject or data source, to which the participant's social identity may be relevant because the goals of the investigation treat him or her as a representative of a particular socially defined group—male, female, child in the third grade, and so on. But there is also the function of scientific observation, the reporting and recording of what is observed, which traditionally requires someone with an appropriate social identity. Experimental reports emanating from unqualified persons will not be taken seriously and will not appear in recognized scientific publications. By the time experimental psychology made its historical appearance, the social identity of those functioning as experimenters and/or authors of experimental reports was, on the whole, unproblematical within rather narrow limits. The one who vouches for the reliability and accuracy of the observations and for the care with which they have been made must possess appropriate academic qualifications and experience. In other words, he or she must have a particular social identity.

The function of making observations that count as scientific is one which is common to experimental psychology and other areas of experimental natural science. It is the function of the human data source which is peculiar to psychology experiments and which links them with the social sciences. But there is no reason *in principle* why these two functions should not be carried out by the same person. There may be practical difficulties in combining the two roles, and there may be specific reasons for separating them in particular investigations, but many of the classical, pioneering studies in experimental psychology combined them very successfully. One need only think of Fechner's work in psychophysics or Ebbinghaus's original work on memory to appreciate this fact. The reasons which prompted men like Wundt and G. E. Müller to initiate a division of labor in the psychological laboratory appear to have been of an essentially practical nature. In fact, one finds Wundt in 1907, many years after the establishment of his laboratory, still denying that there is anything essential about the division of labor between experimenter and subject.[16]

Thus it is entirely understandable that in a sample of three volumes of Wundt's journal *Philosophische Studien* for the period 1894–96, about 70 percent of the published experimental studies feature academic psychologists in the role of subjects. (In the successor journal *Psychologische Studien* this proportion even reaches 80 percent for the 1909–11 period.) In most of these studies the subject was required to make careful sensory discriminations in the presence of systematically varied external stimuli, and his social status was a guarantee that these difficult and tiring observations would have been made with due care. In this respect experimental psychology was no different from experimental physics or other natural sciences which insisted that only observations made by persons of appropriate background and experience had scientific credibility. The difference lay in the way in which these observational data were *interpreted:* in the latter case in terms of events in the observed object, in the former in terms of events in the observing subject.

In this model of psychological experimentation, which was prominent in the early years of the discipline, the social identity of the experimental subjects was important in the same way that social identity was important in experimental science in general—namely, as a guarantee of the credibility of the observational data. But, as we have seen, other models of psychological investigation were extant at an early stage, and in these the social identity of the participants was affected by additional considerations. The consideration of scientific credibility remained in force, of course, but if experimenter and subject roles were strictly separated, it might be considered relevant only to the former. What circumstances might bring about such a state of affairs?

In the early experimental literature there are two kinds of study which break with the scientific traditions described above. The first involves the investigation of psychological processes in representatives of populations with a social identity that is thought to be interesting psychologically. Investigations of experimental hypnosis in a clinical context provide the standard example. Other early examples involve people with special abilities or deficiencies—somnambulists, blind or intellectually deficient people, as well as those who are gifted musically, are lightning calculators, and so forth. In all these cases the individual functions as a subject of psychological investigation much as someone with an unusual physiological or pathological condition might function as a subject for medical investigation. The difference is that whereas medical science by now selects its cases by imposing its own categories, early experimental psychology essentially adopted culturally established categories and treated them as psychological (or biological) categories. In this model of psychological research, therefore, the social identity of individuals in the subject role is the crucial factor which pushes them into that role and keeps it separate from the investigator's role. Being an appropriate candidate for medical or psychological investigation goes with membership in certain social categories, and the role that the subject plays in the experimental situation is essentially an extension or elaboration of the role that goes with that social identity.

The second early departure from the scientific norm of the psychologist as subject-observer occurs in studies that adopt a kind of natural history approach to mental phenomena. One finds this approach, for example, in studies that attempt to catalogue the frequency of different kinds of association[17] or of phenomena like synesthesia.[18] To begin with, such studies were purely descriptive. Mental phenomena were not studied as processes, but as isolated instances to be counted. They were not related to any context, and the individuals who reported them acted only as a kind of neutral medium through which the phenomena manifested themselves. So for this kind of psychological investigation the social identity of the subject-reporters was essentially irrelevant. Because the phenomena being studied were not treated as processes to be analyzed, no special observational skill or experience was required from the data source. Thus, virtually any unimpaired person with a certain level of literacy could act as a subject. The only requirement was that such persons be available in some numbers, to permit a convincing count of instances. Undergraduate students fitted this role perfectly.

Where the subject in a psychological experiment was a trained psychologist or a member of some psychologically interesting group, his social identity was crucial to the role he played in the experimental situation. But where the subjects were undergraduate students, this reflected the irrelevance of all social identity for the process of psychological investigation. Hardly anyone conducted investigations with undergraduates because of a primary interest in the special psychological characteristics of this group. They were chosen for reasons of practical convenience. But such reasons would never have seemed acceptable if it had not been for a deeply held belief in the irrelevance of social identity for the nature of psychological phenomena. That belief sprang from an image of the mental world as a natural, rather than a social, phenomenon. The categories in which early American investigators thought about the mind were derived from biology, not from sociology or history. This is reflected in their practical methodology as much as in their theorizing. For them there existed a natural order of the mind conceived by analogy with the natural order of living organisms. In both cases the scientist's first job was to catalogue and count specimens.

Two other categories of subjects appear in the psychological literature with some frequency. The first are research students, who function as expert observers, exactly like fully qualified academic psychologists. From the point of view of the present analysis this category presents no additional points of interest. The second category involves schoolchildren, a group that has always furnished large numbers of subjects for psychological research. Most early American research with schoolchildren involved elements of both styles of non-Wundtian research. Certainly, there was a great deal of simple counting of psychological characteristics; but, unlike undergraduates, schoolchildren belonged to a category that was of considerable interest to psychologists. Much of that interest was purely practical in nature. It was among those working in the educational system that psychologists found their earliest, and over many years most important, clients. Knowledge pertaining to schoolchildren provided psychology with its one major field of application during the period under review here. Hence it is appropriate to categorize this group of subjects separately. The use of this and other categories of subject is shown in table 2.3.

The row totals do not add up to 100 because the research student category has not been included, and because a number of studies employ more than one category of subject. Studies which contained insufficient information on the social identity of participating subjects were excluded.

Certain general trends emerge rather clearly. Academic psychologists were at first the most important group of subjects for psychological research but then showed an overall decline. Undergraduate students have always been an important source of subjects in American psychological research but reached a position of absolute predominance in the post–World War I period. Among subjects not drawn from institutions of higher education, schoolchildren have always formed by far the most important group, featuring in more studies than all the other groups combined. This was true for early applied, as well as "pure," research. The category "others" in table 2.3 includes a variety of subjects who have in common the characteristic that they were not drawn from educational institutions. It is clear that, with the exception of the *Journal of Applied Psychology*, the use of such subjects was not widespread in the portion of the American research literature surveyed here.

Social Identity versus Experimental Identity

So far we have focused on the actual social identity of the participants in psychological investigations (cell C in table 2.1). But how are data sources identified in the published reports of these investigations? Apart from identification by name, which was becoming increasingly rare, there remained only the simple alternative of identification by function in the experiment or by ordinary social identity outside the experimental situation. When reporting and discussing data, the author of a report has the choice, then, between identifying the human data sources by terms such as *subjects* or *observers* and identifying them as children, telegraphists, females, and so forth. (In principle, one could jump from one to another set of terms at random, but in practice authors seem to opt for consistency.) Does the psychological literature reveal systematic patterns with respect to such choices, and if so, what is the meaning of such patterns?

A content analysis of the journals enumerated in tables 2.2 and 2.3 indicates that in the major experimental journals—*Journal of Experimental Psychology, American Journal of Psychology,* and *Psychological Review* in its early phase— there is a very strong tendency to discuss data in terms of the experimental, rather than the social, identity of the data source. This tendency is present from the very beginning and does not diminish with time. In the pre–World War I period the social identity of the data source is mentioned in the context

TABLE 2.3
Background of Those Participating as Subjects in Psychological Studies (as percentage of empirical studies with human subjects)

Name of Journal	Years	Academic Psychologists	Undergraduates	School children	Others
American Journal of Psychology	1894–96	59	32	23	5
	1909–11	41	25	13	9
	1924–26	32	62	6	5
	1934–36	31	63	10	12
Psychological Review	1894–96	47	43	7	0
	1909–11	39	52	13	10
Psychological Monographs	1909–11	35	24	26	18
	1924–26	16	29	34	11
	1934–36	6	42	51	21
Journal of Experimental Psychology	1924–26	12	67	22	15
	1934–36	19	78	13	7
Journal of Educational Psychology	1910–12	4	34	53	11
Journal of Applied Psychology	1917–19	8	28	51	44

of data presentation in only 14 percent of the published research articles. By the 1930s this figure has dropped to 10 percent. The journals are quite consistent in this respect. By contrast, the two journals devoted to possible applications of psychological knowledge—*Journal of Educational Psychology* and *Journal of Applied Psychology*—show a pattern of data presentation which provides a social, rather than an experimental, identity for the human data source in about half the published articles.

While it is true that the applied literature contains a somewhat lower proportion of purely experimental studies, the use of the term *subject* was far from being restricted to the laboratory. Under what circumstances do the authors of these research reports assign a social identity to the data source in the context of presenting and discussing their data? The conferral of particular identities in social situations depends on the perceived relevance of those identities to the social situation. There is no reason to suppose that the social situation which we know as a psychological experiment will be any different from other social situations in this respect. Whatever identities are conferred on the participants in the experimental situation will be the ones that are most relevant to the construal of that situation by those who report on it.

The actual social identities of those functioning as data sources are presented in table 2.3 above. But in those sections of the published research reports which present and discuss these data, the source is identified socially only when children or nonacademic populations are involved, and even then only some of the time. Where the data source consists of college students or academic psychologists, the data are presented and discussed only in terms of experimental identities. Most commonly the data were attributed to abstract *subjects*, rather than to the American college students who actually produced them. While many investigations involving children, psychiatric patients, and others were held to provide information specifically about these groups, most investigations involving college students or academics were not regarded as providing information specific to the psychology of college students or academics. This can be seen as an expression of the widespread assumption among experimental psychologists that their work was unrelated to the social identity of their subjects. In the period under review, childhood (like gender) was not generally seen as a social identity, but as a biological category. For a discipline that defined itself as a biological, rather than a social, science, biological categories had a relevance that social identities lacked.

Experimental psychologists were concerned to establish a kind of knowledge about human beings that would be ahistorical and universal. Yet to obtain this knowledge, they had to work with specific, historically defined human data sources, and they had to extract their data from these sources in investigative situations that were also historically specific. To cope with this paradox, psychologists commonly employed certain rhetorical devices when reporting their data. Two of these have been discussed here. First, it became customary to emphasize the experimental identity of human data sources at the expense of their ordinary personal and social identity. Thus, their actions, as reflected in the experimental results, were attributed to them not as historical individuals, but as incumbents of a special experimental role. Where experimental results are attributed to persons who have no identity apart from that of experimental subjects, the implication is that no other identity is relevant in the experimental context. The experiment and its results stand apart from the socio-historical context in which the rest of human life is embedded. It appears to lead straight to human universals, which are not infrequently identified with biological universals.

A further development that enhances this effect involves not attributing the experimental results to specific individuals at all, not even individuals that only have an experimental identity. When such results are presented as the attributes of experimental groups whose anonymous members have no existence in the experimental report, the isolation of laboratory products from the personal and cultural reality that produced them has gone about as far as it can.

The fact that the handling of the attribution problem in the presentation of experimental results involves rhetorical considerations does not mean that the knowledge claims implied in this presentation are necessarily false, only that they have not been secured empirically, and that the issue remains wide open. Reporters of experimental results cannot avoid the task of establishing the claim that what is being reported can justifiably count as "scientific" information. For a discipline that took "scientific" to entail imply reference to some universal truth beyond individuality, history, and local meanings, the establishment of claims to scientificity frequently depended on appropriate manipulation of the identity of the sources to which data were attributed. With few exceptions, claims to universality were not grounded empirically but were established by fiat. The role of the experimental report was, among other things, to create the illusion of empiricism. By the way the experimental results were presented, the illusion was created that they were not really the product of a social interaction among certain human personalities in historical time, but rather, that they were the manifestation of abstract transpersonal and transhistorical processes. It is ironical that as experimental psychology progressed, the "results" sections of its published reports sometimes became the least empirical parts of those reports.

Notes

1. K. Danziger, "The Origins of the Psychological Experiment as a Social Institution," *American Psychologist* 40 (1985):133–40.

2. See C. Bazerman, "Scientific Writing as a Social Act," in *New Essays in Technical and Scientific Communication*, ed. P. Anderson, J. Brockman, and C. Miller (Farmingdale, N.Y.: Baywood, 1983), pp. 156–84; K. Knorr-Cetina, *The Manufacture of Knowledge* (New York: Pergamon, 1981); and G. N. Gilbert and M. Mulkay, *Opening Pandora's Box: A Sociological Analysis of Scientists' Discourse* (Cambridge: Cambridge University Press, 1984).

3. Danziger, "Origins of Psychological Experiment."

4. See K. Danziger, "The History of Introspection Reconsidered," *Journal of the History of the Behavioral Sciences* 16 (1980):241–62.

5. J. F. Dashiell, "Note on Use of the Term 'Observer'," *Psychological Review* 36 (1929):550–51.

6. M. Bentley, " 'Observer' and 'Subject'," *American Journal of Psychology* 41 (1929):682–83.

7. J. F. Dashiell, "A Reply to Professor Bentley," *Psychological Review* 37 (1930):183–85.

8. See, e.g., W. Wundt, "Die Aufgaben der experimentellen Psychologie," in idem, *Essays*, 2d ed. (Leipzig: Engelmann, 1906), pp. 186–212.

9. Danziger, "Origins of Psychological Experiment."

10. K. Danziger, "Statistical Method and the Historical Development of Research Practice in American Psychology," in *The Probabilistic Revolution: Ideas in Modern Science*, vol. 2, ed. G. Gigerenzer, L. Kruger, and M. Morgan (Cambridge, Mass.: MIT Press, 1987), pp. 35–47.

11. See, e.g., J. M. Baldwin, W. J. Shaw, and H. C. Warren, "Memory for Square Size," *Psychological Review* 2 (1895):236–44.

12. See, e.g., E. Barnes, "A Study of Children's Drawings," *Pedagogical Seminary* 2 (1893):455–63.

13. See, e.g., J. M. Cattell and L. Farrand, "Physical and Mental Measurements of the Students of Columbia University," *Psychological Review* 3 (1896):618–48.

14. K. Danziger, "Statistical Method"; and idem, "Social Context and Investigative Practice in Early Twentieth Century Psychology," in *Psychology in Twentieth-Century Thought and Society*, ed. M. G. Ash and W. R. Woodward (New York: Cambridge University Press, in press).

15. E. L. Thorndike, *Animal Intelligence* (New York: Macmillan, 1911), chap. 1.

16. W. Wundt, "Über Ausfrageexperimente und über die Methoden zur Psychologie des Denkens," *Psychologische Studien* 3 (1907):301–60.

17. See, e.g., J. Jastrow, "Community and Association of Ideas: A Statistical Study," *Psychological Review* 1 (1894):152–58.

18. See, e.g., M. W. Calkins, "Synaesthesia," *American Journal of Psychology* 7 (1895):90–107.

3

Metamorphoses in the Psychologist's Advantage

Karl E. Scheibe

Wesleyan University

The relationship between the psychologist and the material of psychological inquiry is not constant, but variable. In part, this variability is traceable to the dual origin of modern psychology, in physiology and philosophy. The material of physiology is tractable and relatively passive even when it is alive. It does not normally look back at the observer from the other end of the microscope. It has the enormously appealing property of being actual stuff. By contrast, the material of philosophy is material only in a loose sense. Theology, epistemology, ethics, logic, metaphysics—these are major philosophical topic areas. But this sort of material is fugitive, rather than fixed, not easily manipulated, and has disquieting properties of reflexivity. Epistemology is inquiry into what it is itself—namely, knowledge. The study of ethics is itself the product of ethical choice. Metaphysics consists of an inquiry into the nature of reality itself and cannot take place apart from a presumptive reality, including at least the observer as part of that which is observed. The dialectic method of philosophy supposes a kind of rough equality between subject and object, an interpenetration, a mutuality. Since modern psychology is a product of nineteenth-century materialist physiology and speculative philosophy, it is not surprising that the nature of psychological material is so varied, ranging from fixed neuronal specimens to the mirrored observations of the observer observing.

In this chapter, I will examine some of the forms taken by the relationship between the psychologist and psychological material. I shall refer to these as forms of the "psychologist's advantage," even though in some cases the magnitude of that advantage is quite small and transitory. In the minimal case this advantage is merely that of the person who happens to be talking in a

53

quiet, noncompetitive conversation among peers. But the psychologist always lays claim, at least implicitly, to some advantage—ranging from the slight and brief to the large and permanent—in relation to the material of inquiry. The character of this advantage is both problematic and significant. It is problematic in that such an advantage is not given in the nature of things, but must be achieved, and the mode of achievement depends on delicate and variable cultural understandings of what a psychologist is and what powers he or she should be expected to exercise. The presumption is normally that the psychologist's advantage has been legitimately earned and is properly exercised. Yet the psychologist's advantage can entail what Veblen termed a "trained incapacity" or what Dewey called an "occupational psychosis." These are not prima facie illegitimate claims to a privileged position, but rather more subtle and inclusive limitations imposed by the psychological position and perspective.

The significance of this issue has to do with both moral legitimacy and methodological practicality. In the best (and perhaps normal) case, the psychologist's advantage works positively for all concerned—the psychologist wants to know, the subject wants to be known; the psychologist wants to help, the client wishes to be helped—and the knowledge or talent of the psychologist is often such as to make knowing and helping not only possible but actual. On the other hand, the stance taken by the psychologist in relation to the subject can be both degrading and dehumanizing to that subject; in addition, it can happen that a stance is disabling methodologically. An example of the former case is the psychotherapist who uses his role for purposes of sexual exploitation.[1] Examples of methodological disability deriving from inappropriate forms of the psychologist's advantage are provided by the many studies of demand characteristics (subtle cues about expected behavior deriving from the total experimental context) and experimenter bias that have appeared in the last twenty-five years.[2] While a great deal of significance has commonly been attached to finding naive subjects, it has often been the researcher who has been naive. Thus a methodological disability has been produced by an inappropriate claim to the psychologist's advantage. More generally, the pretension by psychologists that subjects are only narrowly reactive to manipulated experimental conditions is related to the radical contemporaneity of experimental psychology, which amounts to a denial that human action is historically grounded. The ahistorical character of experimental psychology results from a claimed advantage of the psychologist over psychological material and results in a profound methodological disability.[3]

This examination of forms of the psychologist's advantage is presented with two qualifications or disclaimers. First, while to some degree the presentation will be historical, it should not be supposed that the history of psychology can be described as a distinct, linear progression of a set of forms. The weaker claim is made that the dominant forms of this advantage have changed systematically over time and will continue to change. The second qualification is akin to the first, for a full inventory of forms is too large a task for the compass of this chapter.

Before developing the historical argument, it is necessary to describe more fully the concept of the psychologist's advantage and the forms it can assume.

What is the Psychologist's Advantage?

First, it is the advantage that derives from authority and control: the rat in the Skinner box or maze is clearly in an inferior position to the experimenter—not only because of species differences, but also because it is the experimenter who controls the contingencies and structure of the environment. Similarly, the subject who shows up for an experiment on learning, perception, or social behavior is temporarily allowing the experimenter to assume a position of authority and control. I have frequently done the classroom demonstration of asking for a student to volunteer for an experiment, come to the front of the room, and sit in a chair. I wait for about thirty seconds and then inquire of the subject, who is always entirely passive and quietly attentive, "What are you doing?" The answer is invariably, "I am waiting for you to tell me what to do." I then ask the subject to do something like write his or her name on the blackboard, remove his or her glasses, or walk back and forth in front of the class. The point of the demonstration is simply to show the power that the experimenter has once the commonly understood rules of the experimenter-subject relationship are tacitly invoked. Kelman has observed that this advantage is often compounded by researchers choosing as subjects individuals who are in socially inferior positions of power—"children and old people, ethnic minorities and welfare recipients, mental patients and invalids, criminals and delinquents, drug addicts and alcoholics, college sophomores and military recruits."[4] In the interpretation of Milgram's studies of obedience, most attention is given to the apparent willingness of subjects to perform putatively harmful acts. But this obedience is but another instance of the ordinary docility of subjects, a docility that is the product of the advantage conferred on the psychologist.

The patient in psychotherapy is in a parallel position to the subject in an experiment, except that the patient does have the right to make some claim that the interests served by the proceedings be primarily his or her own. Even so, the classical form of psychoanalytic therapy is based on a clearly understood unilateral arrangement of authority and control. The time, place, and content of the analytic session are framed by the analyst. The patient is invited to exercise initiatives and to control content only within the limits set. The introduction of client-centered therapy by Carl Rogers was a clear attempt to restructure the lines of authority and control in therapy. (In his 1951 *Client-centered Therapy* Rogers included among the rules the stipulation that "the therapist treats the patient as an equal.")[5] But in even the most extreme form of nondirective therapy, the therapist retains control of the outer frames of the interaction, retaining the right, for example, to refuse to be directive in the face of the most urgent pleas from the client.

The second source of the psychologist's advantage derives from his or her greater knowledge. Observational research generates relational knowledge, which is accessible to the psychologist in a way that it is not accessible to the subject. It is characteristic of psychology texts to make some claim to special knowledge within the first few pages. In the text by David McClelland, we read: "The psychologist is simply someone who has special methods and special skills for examining the unexamined, for discovering what individuals and groups of individuals or cultures don't know about themselves."[6] And in that by Henry Gleitman: "What is psychology? It is a field of inquiry that is sometimes defined as the science of mind, sometimes as the science of behavior. It concerns itself with how and why organisms do what they do. Why wolves howl at the moon and sons rebel against their fathers; why birds sing and moths fly into the flames; why we remember how to ride a bicycle twenty years after the last try; why humans speak and make love and war. All of these are behaviors and psychology is the science that studies them all."[7]

The advantage from knowledge can be rather subtle, for not only does the psychologist know things that allow him to make predictions and give explanations. He or she is also *expected* to know a great deal—all about unexamined or unconscious thoughts, according to McClelland, or all about the acts of wolves, birds, and moths, as well as the full repertory of human actions, according to Gleitman. Empirical research informs the psychologist that subjects will say "3" a large proportion of the time when asked to pick a number between 1 and 4, and that individuals who have interest patterns similar to those of life insurance salesmen make good life insurance salesmen.[8] These are simply empirical generalizations. But in addition, the psychologist is supposed to know all sorts of things (and perhaps does) that have no obvious empirical basis. The advantage from what the psychologist is assumed to know can be very large. A good example is provided in the work of Milton Erickson, a psychiatrist by profession, to be sure, but a most powerful practitioner of the psychologist's advantage. Erickson was considered by his students and patients alike to be an absolute master at bringing about psychological change. One may open an Erickson text almost at random and encounter startling examples of his absolute mastery of the dynamics of thought and action in his patients. For example:

> *Well, you see she's come in and she doesn't know how to act in that strange and new situation. Therefore, she is going to strive desperately,*

because there is no formulated plan by which she can present herself. Since there is no formulated plan, she's going to be at a loss about how to conceal her problem the way she's been concealing it from herself for a long time. Since she has got no patterns of concealment when she comes into the office, she is going to betray a good deal of her problem right then and there if you look for it. After she gets acquainted with you, then she'll be able to start concealing more adequately."[9]

The psychologist knows much, is assumed to know much, and is able because of this knowledge, both real and attributed, to take an advantaged position vis-à-vis the subject or the patient.

The psychologist's third source of advantage is what I call his superior cleverness. Suppose that a psychologist sacrifices the advantage from both authority and control on the one hand and superior knowledge on the other. I argue that a possible advantage still remains; that deriving from what I have elsewhere referred to as "acumen" and here describe as "superior cleverness," a talent combining both special training and a natural ability to "see into others."[10] Even though two chess-players may be equal in their knowledge and their power or authority, an advantage accrues to the player with superior powers of penetration, since he is able to think a step ahead of his opponent and to take advantage of this ability to know his opponent's mind. In popular parlance, this sort of thing is often described as "out-psyching" the other; in more conventional psychological terminology, as empathy, or taking the role of the other. Another form of superior cleverness is displayed in Freud's *Psychopathology of Everyday Life*.[11] The subject fumbles to know, but the master knows with clarity. Freud seems to have an encompassing sense of the meaning of various slips and tics and mistakes. It is not just that he possesses conventional knowledge; he also seems to display an uncanny ability to penetrate appearances. The superior cleverness of the psychologist seems to be most clearly in evidence when he is in charge of relating stories of interpretive success. As in the case of the advantage from knowledge, it is possible to confer upon the psychologist an advantage of superior cleverness even though he might otherwise be unable to provide objective proof of his ability. Indeed, it is tempting to argue that the superior, penetrating cleverness of the psychologist functions most convincingly under the protective covering of an advantage from authority and control. An interpretation offered by a psychologist may be accepted not because it is correct, but because it is offered from the psychologist's advantaged position.

In sum, the psychologist's advantage can be supported in three ways: by superior authority and control, by greater knowledge, and by superior cleverness. It is appropriate to examine trends in the development of these kinds of advantage in the history of modern psychology.

The Genesis of Modern Psychology's Claims of Advantage

Kant considered empirical psychology to be an impossibility. This claim represents an a priori negation of the psychologist's advantage. For Kant asserted that the psychologist has no legitimate claims to superior authority or power over the subject matter, for the subject matter is mind itself and thus cannot be made subordinate to the observer, as it is in chemistry or physics. Nor, by extension, can the psychologist claim an advantage from accumulated knowledge or superior cleverness. For Kant, psychology was subordinate to philosophy; at best, psychological phenomena could provide material for the formulation of certain philosophical truths. In one sense, Kant's indictment of psychological subjectivism could be read as providing an opening for the emergence of an objective or behavioral psychology, and the long-term effect of Kant's abhorrence of psychologisms was perhaps just that. [12] But the more immediate consequence in the nineteenth century was to retard the breaking away of psychology from its philosophical base and to discourage experimental inquiry into the structure and function of mind. Psychology had no independent authority. Nor did psychology build up any empirical base at all throughout the first half of the nineteenth century; hence no advantage of this kind could be claimed. Certainly, one can think of no psychologist before the late nineteenth century with a great reputation for cleverness.

But incipient forms of the psychologist's advantage can be recognized by the middle of the nineteenth century. In Germany, philosophers who followed Kant succeeded in relaxing his strictures regarding empirical psychology. Leary has argued that Fries, Herbart, and Beneke succeeded in a "reconstruction of psychology," which had the effect of supporting the proposition that in principle psychology need no longer be subjugated to philosophy but could develop its own empirical base. [13] Brentano's *Empirical Psychology*, while not experimental, nevertheless argued that psychological acts could be the substance of a true science. Although these philosophers did not actually contribute to an empirical base by performing experiments, their compatriots with backgrounds in physiology and medicine, rather than philosophy, began to do just that. Fechner's book on psychophysics was published in 1860. Helmholtz demonstrated the measurability of the speed of neural impulses and determined that speed to be much slower than had previously been thought. The label "New Psychology" came to be used by mid-century to describe an enterprise with a fresh claim to authority, an enterprise that could in fact develop a base of empirical knowledge. The nervous system could be studied directly. Regular empirical results were obtained from Fechner's studies of psychophysics. With new instrumentation, it became possible to study reaction times and to address the personal equation problem that Bessel had formulated. French practitioners of psychiatry—Liebeault, Bernheim, and Charcot—were establishing a reputation for clever control, principally through application of hypnotic techniques. Freud was to shape and extend this tradition in his own ingenious way, becoming the first and foremost psychological detective. And, of course, in 1879, Wundt set up his laboratory in Leipzig, thereby establishing once and for all the legitimacy of the claim that psychology could be an experimental science, at least in a limited sense.

It is worth examining those limitations, particularly with respect to the psychologist's advantage. For although Wundt began to develop a number of experimental studies on problems in the areas of perception, attention, and memory, and although he developed introspective inquiry in a rigorous, careful way, the material he studied was only temporarily subject to the psychologist's advantage, and the individuals he studied were of about the same status as the experimenter. Nevitt Sanford describes the status of Wundt's observers thus: "In the experiments that got started in Wundt's laboratory the person whom today we are likely to call a 'subject' was called an 'observer.' These observers were real, live persons, key figures in the interaction, who could be counted upon to take responsibility for their actions, to tell the truth, to keep their promises."[14]

Wundt's was the so-called new psychology, to be sure, in that it was empirical, experimental, bold, and ambitious. But it was not inhumane and self-disabling in the way that subsequent developments in psychology made it appear. Wundt was neither a positivist nor a reductionist. In his experimental studies, he assumed only the provisional advantage of setting the conditions of the laboratory.[15] He seemed always to recognize that the roles of experimenter and observer (subject) were interchangeable. His observers were not naive, but highly trained. In a similar way, his contemporary Ebbinghaus undertook a most profitable study of the laws of learning by using himself as a subject.

Wundt's division of psychology into two branches—experimental psychology and *Völkerpsychologie*—is further testimony to his appreciation of the dangers of an exaggerated psychologist's advantage. For he recognized the inappropriateness of extending experimental methods to problems in the domain of social attitudes, politics, religion, language, and cultural forms and mores. These problems could be studied, to be sure, and studied empirically. But the observation was to be not "from above," but "on the level"; not with presumptions of universality, but with careful attention to the historical conditionality of human thought and action in the social and cultural domain. (Wundt's plans and principles for the development of *Völkerpsychologie* are set forth in his 1911 volume *Probleme der Völkerpsychologie*.)

The sense of caution and qualification exemplified by Wundt was simply overwhelmed by positivist enthusiasms. Consider this characterization of the new experimental psychology by the French psychologist Ribot, published in the very year of the founding of Wundt's laboratory:

> *The spirit of the natural sciences has invaded psychology. . . . One asks whether a collection of ingenious remarks, of analyses, of observations clothed in terms of elegant exposition . . . constitute a body of doctrine, a true science—whether it is not time to resort to a method more rigorous. Thus has arisen the separation, every day more apparent, between the old and the new psychology. . . . The old psychology is doomed. . . . The new psychology differs from the old in its spirit: it is not metaphysical; in its end: it studies only phenomena; in its procedure: it borrows as much as possible from the biological sciences.[16]*

Foreign students, including Titchener, Hall, Cattell, and Baldwin went to study with Wundt and brought back to America plans for founding psychological laboratories. By the end of the century, scores of laboratories had been established in colleges and universities throughout the United States. Accompanying the translation of the new psychology to these shores was a major metamorphosis in the psychologist's advantage. For in the hands of the young, vigorous, practically minded Americans, psychology was not just to be a means of exploring traditional philosophical and scholarly problems: it was to be a means of getting the millennium on stage.

A typical expression of this aspiration is that of Cattell, at a meeting of the International Congress of Arts and Sciences in 1904. Cattell allowed himself to imagine how and to what extent psychology could become a means of human betterment, seeing no reason "why the application of systematized knowledge to the control of human nature may not in the course of the present century accomplish results commensurate with the 19th century application of physical science to the natural world."[17] As handmaiden to human improvement, a claim is entered that psychology ought to be granted recognition and support. The widespread, rapid establishment in this period of laboratories and departments of psychology and the founding of journals and professional associations are testimony to a general ratification of this claim. The early years of the twentieth century in the United States saw the rapid institutionalization of psychology as a discipline. This was the period of the consolidation of the psychologist's advantage, especially the advantage from authority and control. This consolidation was achieved in part through the successful activities of psychology's organizational entrepreneurs, particularly G. Stanley Hall and James McKeen Cattell. But this could not have been achieved in an environment in which psychology was not wanted—and it was very much wanted at this time and in this place.

A New Metamorphosis

In 1910, William James died. At about the same time, James Mark Baldwin resigned his position at Johns Hopkins, never again to hold an academic position in the United States. Thus were eliminated from the scene of American psychology two major integrative forces; for both James and Baldwin wanted to view psychology as entire with philosophy. Although James early on established a demonstrational laboratory at Harvard and Baldwin established several laboratories after his sojourn with Wundt, neither practiced or advocated the experimental method as the sole, or even the major, avenue to psychological truth. Indeed, both were methodologically eclectic and theoretically wide-ranging. One reads James's *Principles of Psychology* and Baldwin's *Social and Ethical Interpretations* with a sense of wonder at the intellectual and scholarly range of their psychology. Not only does one find frequent references to major philosophical traditions integrated with recent empirical studies, one also finds an abundance of references to material from literature, the arts, and drama. The human experience provides artifacts on many levels and in many forms, all of which are material for those with the catholicity of spirit of James and Baldwin.

G. Stanley Hall's obituary of James waxes sentimental about his humane spirit but is dismissive of his lasting contributions to psychology: "A growing science leaves even its ablest representatives behind; and despite the originality of his thought, the erudition that he so lightly carried, his consummate skill in inner observation, and his literary charm, the work he has bequeathed to us will presently be superseded."[18]

Hall was correct in suggesting that a new era in psychology was at hand. In this critical period in the development of psychological thought, many traditions were to be superseded which would, with difficulty, have to be recovered in the last third of the century. By 1913, Watson had published his behaviorist manifesto. In Germany, Wundtian experimental psychology was to be rejected from yet another angle by the Gestalt psychologists, the first expression of this rejection being Wertheimer's 1912 paper on the phi phenomenon. To extend the inventory of major changes in psychological thought, the very same volume of the *American Journal of Psychology* that carried James's obituary notice also contained contributions by Freud and Jung, stemming from their visit to Clark University the previous year. Thus, within just four years, two leading representatives of the integrative and eclectic style of American psychology were removed from the scene. Gestalt psychology was born, and psychoanalysis came of age as a line of thought to be taken seriously. And of greatest importance for the mainstream of psychological theory and research in America, the principles of radical behaviorism were articulated.

This great turning point in the history of psychology brought with it major changes in the nature of the psychologist's advantage. In abolishing respect for mind and subjective experience, Watson also accomplished a subjugation of the psychologist's material—no longer mind, but behavior. Freud's scientifically garbed claims for interpretive power elevated the psychologists' claim to truth to a position entirely beyond the grasp of the patient or the layperson. Thus, in different ways both Watson and Freud established a dominating psychologist's advantage over the material of study or treatment. With its definitional base now established, psychology could go about accumulating experimentally (or clinically) based knowledge, at the same time ignoring all former claims to psychological understanding. The institutional position of psychology was firmly established by the beginning of World War I. One manifestation of this position was the establishment of the first massive, systematic program of psychological assessment in human history.[19] Further, Freud provided the advantage from cleverness, the prototypical image of the psychologist-savant. The Gestalt tradition is an exception to this general trend in terms of its regard for the subject as a collaborator rather than an object. This is a major reason for the persistent marginality of Gestalt psychology in the United States.

An interesting confluence of the predominant changes is represented in Yale University's Institute of Human Relations. From the strongest of institutional bases, an attempt was launched to combine the advantages of behaviorism with those of psychoanalysis. The institute was founded in 1929 and provided a base for the most influential psychologists of the post-1912 era. Morawski has elsewhere described the organization and function of the institute in its early years.[20] Suffice it to observe here that it represented a serious, fully pious utopian ideal: an attempt to apply scientific psychology in its most powerful form to the resolution of perennial human and social difficulties. It must be noted as well that its accomplishments never quite measured up to its aspirations.

Consolidating the Subjugation of Psychological Material

Kurt Danziger has in this volume and elsewhere described the origin and development of the role of the subject in the psychological experiment.[21] With the developing dominance of the language of objective science, a change occurred in the way experiments were done and described. Participants in experiments came to be referred to as "subjects" rather than "observers." Proper names were used less frequently, and academic psychologists came to be replaced by undergraduates and schoolchildren. All these changes betoken an elevation in the status of the psychological experimenter in relation to the material of inquiry, and thus an increase in the psychologist's advantage from authority and control.

Of course, behaviorists stopped referring to their work as being about human beings at all, but rather, described it as having to do with "organisms." Clark Hull at Yale and Edward Tolman at the University of California were the dominant psychologists of the second quarter of the twentieth century, and their famous disputes were mounted on experiments with rats. Hull's system represents the ultimate attempt at establishing the psychologist's advantage once and for all through strict adoption of the hypothetico-deductive method. That his system is now a curious museum piece from which only negative lessons can be drawn could hardly have been predicted at the time. Tolman's purposive behaviorism was at once less systematic than Hull's version and more humane. It has been said that rather than dehumanizing people, Tolman succeeded to a degree in humanizing the rat. Be that as it may, this is the period in which the psychologist's advantage was at its apogee; and this is evident not only in the dominance of the conceit that everything of psychological importance could in principle be demonstrated by the rat at the choice point in a maze.

This was a Dark Age for the human being in psychology, for the force of the scientific theology swept all before it. The following "confession of faith" by Kuo provides an unusually vivid illustration of the state of affairs:

> The so-called consciousness, if it exists at all, must be reducible to physical terms and capable of objective and quantitative treatment when we have better methods and techniques than the ones in existence at present. . . . Any controversy in psychology must be capable of promoting experimental researches so that the issue can be settled in the laboratory, or it must at least have some particular value for laboratory procedure. Otherwise there is no justification for the existence of any such controversies or problems in the science.[22]

If this sort of doctrine could be made to hold, then it would have an enormous effect in imparting an advantage to the psychologist. For it amounts to an enforced silencing of anyone who would dare to make any claims whatsoever about matters psychological if those claims could not be based on laboratory proofs. The implications of this claim are several and powerful. First, it amounts to a negation of any and all accumulated knowledge or wisdom about the human condition. Gone completely are the genial musings of a James or a Baldwin or the more abstruse explorations of a Wundt on problems of language and culture or the universalistic speculations of a Herbert Spencer or the half-informed, half-mad conjectures of William McDougall about the mainsprings of human life. What a relief! But also, what a loss! The second outcome of the doctrine of the laboratory as a *via regia* to truth was the institution of experimental studies of personality and social psychology, an extension of the laboratory to a domain that Wundt had considered inappropriate for experimental study. The subsequent crisis in social and personality psychology can be seen as a belated recognition that Wundt was right about this matter after all. The third implication is related to the second and has to do with disillusionment. While the academic, political, and social climate in the United States afforded psychology a nurturing institutional base from which to develop, the kind of arrogant braggadocio of which Kuo's statement is representative came to haunt the discipline; for psychology simply failed to come up with the goods, even with a vastly improved technology. The psychologist has lost much of the advantage once accorded him by a more credulous public. [23]

Gathering Clouds of Difficulty in the 1960s

It is not difficult to find indictments of experimental psychology in mid-century. Controversies among the various brands of learning theory had become wearisome. It was becoming quite noticeable that the results of experimental methods in traditional areas of inquiry such as learning and perception, as well as in social and personality psychology, were not accumulating as they should in a proper science. Experimental facts are extremely unstable in social and personality psychology, and attempts at replication an almost certain way to fail. In this domain, so-called facts derived from the laboratory were likely to prove false before the ink in which they were reported was dry. In 1963, Koch observed that the age of theory in psychology had come to an end and that a new, more self-critical period in the history of psychology had begun. [24]

Several experimental results published in the 1960s had the effect of challenging the very utility of the experimental model as traditionally employed in psychology. Orne's work on hypnosis showed that subjects who simulated hypnosis could effectively deceive experienced hypnotists into thinking that they really were hypnotized. [25] Later, Orne argued and demonstrated that unwittingly transmitted cues in the experimental situation could effectively inform the subject about how the experimenter expected him or her to behave. Thus, results of many experiments involving human subjects were shown to be potentially confounded by "demand characteristics." [26] Rosenthal demonstrated a reproducible contamination of experimental results by "experimenter bias." [27] In these studies, the results obtained were shown to depend regularly on an arbitrary manipulation of experimental hypotheses. From a different quarter, Rosenhan showed that psychiatric diagnoses of mental illness were highly questionable and unreliable, as he and a number of colleagues demonstrated the problem of trying to remain "sane in insane places." [28] Even more telling for the history of research in personality and social psychology were the studies of Milgram on obedience, in which subjects who were ostensibly serving as experimenters were induced to give pseudo-shocks to confederates who were ostensibly serving as subjects. [29] The effect here was indirect, for Milgram's intention was not to undermine the legitimacy of the experimental study of social psychology. But the consequence was to trigger an expression of concern over the ethics of psychological experimentation and the use of deception in research.[30]

A number of other developments in theory and research in the 1960s can be seen as attacks on the psychologist's advantage, or better, as qualifications of the psychologist's advantage, for the intention was not always to attack. Mischel's work initiated the "situation-trait" debate in personality research.[31] In a sense, his work was an indictment of the entire tradition of personality research, which rests on the notion that individual conduct is a manifestation of fixed personality characteristics. This sort of argument provided collateral support for massive arguments that were being launched against the entire tradition of psychological assessment. Personality assessment was called into question because of the demonstration of the power of "response sets"—social desirability, yea-saying—in determining results and because of the limited predictive utility of assessed characteristics in any event. Intelligence testing was called into question with allegations of cultural bias and demonstrations of a certain amount of chicanery surrounding foundational research in the field (the Cyril Burt controversy). The most widely used form of aptitude testing in the world, the Scholastic Aptitude Test, has been under continual attack for the past twenty years, on both technical and ethical grounds.[32]

Challenges to the psychologist's advantage have not been restricted to applied areas or to what might be considered to be the more vulnerable areas of personality, social, and clinical psychology. The most prominent areas of traditional experimental psychology have been given their lessons in humility as well. The cognitive revolution began in the 1960s, casting doubt on most of the conceptions that psychologists had nurtured about basic learning processes, as "mind" found a place of renewed respectability in the field. The title of an article by Jenkins is telling: "Remember That Old Theory of Memory? Well, Forget It."[33] In the area of perception, Gibson offered an even more sober set of judgments: "The conclusions that can be reached from a century of research on perception are insignificant. The knowledge gained from a century of research on sensation is incoherent. We have no adequate theory of perception. And what we have found in the search for sensations is a mixed batch of illusions, physiological curiosities and bodily feelings. The implications are discouraging. A fresh start has to be made on the problem of perception."[34]

It appears that after a hundred years of seeking the security of true scientific status through the adoption of a positivistic, mechanistic, and operationist set of assumptions, psychology is newly afflicted with self-doubt. Even those areas of psychology that are ordinarily thought of as being the most solidly scientific are riven with controversy over the most fundamental questions. Perhaps those eighteenth- and nineteenth-century philosophers who asserted that an independent, scientific psychology was impossible were right. There are those who think so.[35]

Psychology on the Level

My major argument about the historical trajectory of the psychologist's advantage can be summarized as follows. After emerging from the disciplinary aegis of philosophy in the late nineteenth century, psychology retained for a time the philosophical custom of addressing its subject matter without a permanently established advantage of authority, knowledge, or cleverness. But with the growing adoption by psychology of both the assumptive bases of positivism and the trappings of science (laboratories, quantification, instrumentation, and so on) it became possible for psychology to assume in the twentieth century, especially after 1912, a formidable disciplinary advantage in relation to its subject matter—organisms, behavior, traits. This advantage began to diminish in the 1960s, as the hegemony of major schools and grand theories of psychology died out and as the self-criticisms generated by psychology became increasingly widespread, forceful, articulate, and unavoidable. We may think of the distance between the psychologist and the subject as diminishing, as the psychologist loses loftiness and as the human beings who comprise the subject matter of the field are considered once again to be as truly human as those who inquire about them.

This general pattern can be seen in the history of research and of theory on a variety of standard problems in psychology. Elsewhere, I have considered the problem of self and identity in just these terms.[36] Beginning with James's chapters on "the stream of thought" and "the consciousness of self," a line of theory about the self was established in psychology that borrows heavily from an analysis of ordinary experience—what is sometimes called phenomenology. This line continued through the work of Baldwin and then Mead. The characterization of the self emerging from this line of work is full, rich, and human. But Mead's line, although fully psychological, became lost to psychology and absorbed by sociology as the passion for objectivism in psychology transformed work on the self into research on "the self-concept," typified by Ruth Wylie's exhaustive review of that topic in the late 1960s and 1970s.[37] But Wylie's work culminated in the same deadly judgment of misguided futility as that visited on so many areas of psychological research in this era. More recently, research and theory on the self have been reinvigorated, but now borrowing more heavily from the point of view established earlier by James, Baldwin, and Mead. One need only look at the recent work on so-called narrative psychology to see how this is happening.[38]

The period of psychology's love affair with scientism seems to be coming to an end. New approaches to the study of old problems are emerging, all based on a more modest, more temporary definition of the psychologist's advantage. One such approach is that of ethogeny, espoused most forcefully by Harré.[39] This approach eschews experimental methods for the study of social behavior but encourages the systematic accumulation and analysis of observations of customs and folkways. Harré's approach admits the historical conditionality of observations but, even so, is capable of producing striking generalizations about the forms and structures of personal and social conduct.[40] Similarly, Sarbin's advocacy of contextualism as a new root metaphor for psychology brings the observer and the subject of observation together on the same level.[41] Sarbin's contextual approach has in turn led to a new interest in the narrative as providing a major source of material for psychological inquiry. In the preface to a recent volume on narrative psychology, Sarbin enters a broad plea for change: "The[se] essays make clear that story making, storytelling and story comprehension are fundamental conceptions for a revived psychology. Each makes a case for the storied nature of human action. When taken together, these essays support my claim that narrative psychology is a viable alternative to the positivist paradigm."[42]

Now that this alternative is gaining currency, it is possible to see other developments in psychology as consistent with it. George Kelly's personal construct psychology is based on the notion that preestablished scientific categories preclude an understanding of the world from the subject or client's point of view.[43] Even the study of classical problems of cognitive psychology— learning, perception, and memory—has moved to a renewed appreciation of context as modifying the functioning of basic psychological processes.[44] Lately, the term "ecological psychology" has gained currency; this represents a new awareness of the importance of not negating the real world of psychological existence in favor of the more convenient laboratory study "from above." It is appropriate to remember that early on Brunswik advocated a concern with the "ecological validity" of laboratory findings. His proposal for "representative design" is a clear anticipation of the sort of methodology now being broadly proposed.[45]

A more modest psychologist's advantage would consist in the psychologist's recognition and respect for the human status of psychological material. The psychologist would be willing to address the subject or client "on the level," and such advantages as are assumed for purposes of direction would be clearly bounded in time. So the advantage from authority would not be ponderous or permanent; the advantage from knowledge could be shared, and the advantage from superior cleverness might go to either the psychologist or the psychologist's material, depending on the nature of the case.

Evidence for the value of a more modest psychologist's advantage can be derived from analogy with related areas of inquiry. Oliver Sacks is a clinical neurologist who has published a number of case histories of individuals who have suffered from one or another neurological problem. He says:

> There is no "subject" in a narrow case history; modern case histories allude to the subject in a cursory phrase ("a trisomic albino female of 21"), which could as well apply to a rat as a human being. To restore the human subject at the centre—we must deepen a case history to a narrative or tale; only then do we have a "who" as well as a "what," a real person, a patient, in relation to disease—in relation to the physical. The patient's essential being is very relevant to the higher reaches of neurology, and in psychology; for here the patient's personhood is essentially involved, and the study of disease and identity cannot be disjoined. . . . It is possible that there must, of necessity, be a gulf, a gulf of category, between the psychical and the physical; but studies and stories pertaining simultaneously and inseparably to both . . . may nevertheless serve to bring them nearer, to bring us to the very intersection of mechanism and life, to the relation of physiological processes to biography.[46]

This restoration of the subject to the center of inquiry is bringing a salutary change to psychological science. With this development, it becomes possible for psychology to escape the error of its radical contemporareity and thus to reclaim all human history and culture as material for its inquiry and analysis. Psychology can bring sense and order to human experience by retaining a commitment to observation and analysis, but without assuming a position of arbitrary advantage over ordinary human life that is at once methodologically disabling and morally degrading.

In recent years, a great deal of the effort of psychology's professional associations has been directed to the establishment and reinforcement of the psychologist's advantage through economic force and political persuasion in a lobbying effort to command support from our larger institutional structures. This is certainly one way to establish a warrant for psychology's claims. But in order to be legitimate, these efforts need to be supported by a solid, cumulative, and progressive discipline capable of producing a better understanding of the human condition. The form of the psychologist's advantage now emerging is both more modest and more promising as a means of revivifying research and theory within the field.

Notes

1. S. Butler, "Sexual Contact between Therapists and Patients" (Ph.D. diss. California School of Professional Psychology, Los Angeles, 1975); R. D. Glaser and J. S. Thorpe, "Unethical Intimacy," *American Psychologist* 41 (1986):43–51.

2. See, e.g., M. T. Orne, "On the Social Psychology of the Psychological Experiment," *American Psychologist* 17 (1962):776–83; idem and K. E. Scheibe, "The Contribution of Nondeprivation Factors in the Production of Sensory Deprivation Effects," *Journal of Abnormal and Social Psychology* 68 (1964):3–12; R. Rosenthal, *Experimenter Effects in Behavioral Research* (New York: Appleton-Century-Crofts, 1966).

3. See K. J. Gergen and J. G. Morawski, "An Alternative Metatheory for Social Psychology," in *Review of Personality and Social Psychology*, ed. L. Wheeler (Beverly Hills, Calif.: Sage, 1980), pp. 326–52; R. Harré, "Making Social Psychology Scientific," in *The Development of Social Psychology*, ed. R. Gilmour and S. Duck (New York: Academic Press, 1980), pp. 27–52; T. R. Sarbin, "The Narrative as a Root Metaphor for Psychology," in *Narrative Psychology*, ed. T. Sarbin (New York: Praeger, 1986), pp. 3–21.

4. H. C. Kelman, "The Rights of the Subject in Social Research," *American Psychologist* 27 (1972):989–1016.

5. C. R. Rogers, *Client-Centered Therapy* (Boston: Houghton Mifflin, 1951), p. 20.

6. D. C. McClelland, *Toward a Psychology of Being* (New York: Van Nostrand, 1964), p. iii.

7. H. Gleitman, *Psychology* (New York: Norton, 1981), p. 1.

8. K. E. Scheibe, *Mirrors, Masks, Lies, and Secrets; The Limits of Human Predictability* (New York: Praeger, 1979).

9. J. Haley, *Conversations with Milton H. Erickson, M.D.*, vol. 1 (New York: Triangle, 1985), p. 151.

10. K. E. Scheibe, "The Psychologist's Advantage and its Nullification," *American Psychologist* 33 (1978):869–81.

11. S. Freud, *The Psychopathology of Everyday Life* (New York: Norton, 1906; repr. 1965).

12. R. A. Littman, "Social and Intellectual Origins of Experimental Psychology," in *The First Century of Experimental Psychology*, ed. E. Hearst (Hillsdale, N.J.: Erlbaum, 1979), pp. 39–88.

13. D. Leary, "The Reconstruction of Psychology in Germany, 1780–1850" (Ph.D. diss., University of Chicago, 1977).

14. N. Sanford, "What we have Learned about Personality," in *A Century of Psychology as Science*, ed. S. Koch and D. Leary (New York: McGraw-Hill, 1945), p. 510.

15. W. Wundt, *Probleme der Volkerpsychologie* (Leipzig: Ernst Wiegandt, 1911).

16. Quoted in S. Koch, Foreword to "Wundt's Creature at Age Zero—and as Centenarian: Some Aspects of the Institutionalization of the 'New Psychology'," in *A Century of Psychology as Science*, p. 14.

17. J. M. Cattell, "The Conceptions and Methods of Psychology," *Popular Science Monthly* 66 (1904–05):186.

18. G. S. Hall, "William James," *American Journal of Psychology* 21 (1910):605.

19. See C. S. Yoakum and R. M. Yerkes, *Army Mental Tests* (New York: Holt, 1920).

20. J. Morawski, "Organizing Knowledge and Behavior at Yale's Institute of Human Relations," *Isis* 77 (1986):219–42.

21. K. Danziger, chap. 2 above; idem, "The Origins of the Psychological Experiment as a Social Institution," *American Psychologist* 40 (1985):133–40.

22. Z. Y. Kuo, "A Psychology without Heredity," *Psychological Review* 31 (1924):427.

23. S. Koch, "Epilogue," in *Psychology: A Study of a Science*, ed. S. Koch vol. 3 (New York: McGraw-Hill, 1959), pp. 729–88; G. Miller, "The Constitutive Problem of Psychology," in *A Century of Psychology as Science*, pp. 40–45; A. Giorgi, "Toward the Articulation of Psychology as a Coherent Discipline," and D. Robinson, "Psychology, Science and Explanation: Synonyms or Antonyms?", both in the same volume as the paper by Miller, pp. 46–59, 60–79, respectively.

24. S. Koch, *Psychology*.

25. M. T. Orne, "The Nature of Hypnosis: Artifact and Essence," *Journal of Abnormal and Social Psychology* 58 (1959):277–99.

26. M. T. Orne, "On the Social Psychology of the Psychological Experiment," pp. 776ff.

27. R. Rosenthal, *Experimenter Effects in Psychological Research* (New York: Appleton-Century-Crofts, 1966).

28. D. Rosenhan, "On Being Sane in Insane Places," *Science* 180 (1973):250–58.

29. S. Milgram, *Obedience to Authority* (New York: Harper and Row, 1974).

30. D. Baumrind, "Some Thoughts on Ethics of Research: After Reading Milgram's 'Behavioral Study of Obedience,' " *American Psychologist* 19 (1964):421–23; A. G. Miller, "The Social Psychology of the Research Situation," in *Social Psychology*, ed. B. Seidenberg and A. Snadowsky (New York: Free Press, 1976), pp. 23–48.

31. W. Mischel, *Personality and Assessment* (New York: Wiley, 1966).

32. J. Crouse, "Does the SAT Help Colleges Make Better Selection Decisions?", *Harvard Educational Review* 55 (1985):195–219.

33. J. J. Jenkins, "Remember That Old Theory of Memory? Well, Forget It," *American Psychologist* 29 (1974):785–95.

34. J. J. Gibson, "Conclusions from a Century of Research on Sense Perception," in *A Century of Psychology as Science*, pp. 229–30.

35. See K. J. Gergen, *Toward Transformation in Social Knowledge* (New York: Springer, 1982); J. Shotter, *Social Accountability and Selfhood* (Oxford: Blackwell, 1984); R. Harré, *Social Being* (Oxford: Blackwell, 1979).

36. K. E. Scheibe, "Historical Perspectives on the Presented Self," in *The Self in Social Life*, ed. B. Schlenker (New York: McGraw-Hill, 1985), pp. 33–64.

37. See ibid.

38. See ibid.

39. R. Harré, *Personal Being* (Oxford: Blackwell, 1983).

40. R. O. Kroger, "Explorations in Ethogeny: With Special Reference to the Rules of Address," *American Psychologist* 37 (1982):810–20.

41. T. R. Sarbin, "Contextualism: A World View for Modern Psychology," in *Nebraska Symposium on Motivation*, ed. A. W. Landfield (Lincoln: University of Nebraska Press, 1977), pp. 1–42.

42. T. R. Sarbin, Preface to *Narrative Psychology*, ed. T. Sarbin, p. vii.
43. G. A. Kelly, *The Psychology of Personal Constructs* (New York: Norton, 1955).
44. See U. Neisser, *Cognition and Reality* (San Francisco: Freeman, 1976); E. Tulving, "Episodic and Semantic Memory," in *Organization of Memory*, ed. E. Tulving and W. Donaldson (New York: Academic Press, 1972), pp. 382–403.
45. E. Brunswik, *Perception and the Representative Design of Psychological Experiments* (Berkeley: University of California Press, 1956).
46. O. Sacks, *The Man Who Mistook His Wife for a Hat* (New York: Summit, 1986), p. vii.

4

Impossible Experiments and Practical Constructions: The Social Bases of Psychologists' Work

Jill G. Morawski
Wesleyan University

What can occur in a psychological laboratory generally is taken to be unproblematic. We have a plethora of manuals outlining the proper form of design, measurement, and analysis in psychological experimentation. Detailed codes of ethics instruct us on the boundaries of human rights. The formal (written) transcription of the laboratory adventure is regulated by style manuals containing rules of discourse, which dictate even the acceptable number of words in an article's title. There are gaps in these instructions, of course, and areas where researchers will disagree—on interpretations of the data or on the morality of deception, say. Yet even the fuzzy areas are commonly understood, and for the most part the procedures for laboratory conduct are taken to be intellectually reasonable and correct.

Indeed, the instructions are taken to be reasonable in the sense of being both rational and open-minded, for they imply that the boundaries they impose have been established empirically. Even the ethical constraints are derived in part through empirical means. There are no other explicit bounds on what can be done, and if someone should suggest that the study of urinal behavior is inappropriate, then they are merely confounding research with emotionalism or personal taste. It is simply assumed, then, that experimentation is limited only by procedural rules that have logical and empirical foundations.

Any reflective researcher knows, and historians and sociologists of science have reported, that there is more to it than that. What actually occurs in the design and execution of an experiment includes complex negotiations about what is being observed and what counts as an observation. The written account of a laboratory event is itself the product of rhetorical deftness and artful editing. What kinds of experiments are conducted depends on the research community's customs, ethics, economics, policy interests, and even fads. What goes on in experimental laboratories is not limited solely by explicit methodological rules, but involves practical problem solving by commonsense reasoners.[1] It is also structured by existing social practices. Such limiting conditions can be detected, for instance, in deliberations about experiments on natural language that would require the protracted isolation of children. The social prohibitions against such experimentation are tacitly shared. Social rules likewise influence the study of the effects of hallucinatory drugs, psychosurgery, and prolonged sensory deprivation. While these are sensational cases, more mundane experimental programs are conditioned by similarly overarching customs and constraints.

Conventional histories of psychology recount none of these conditions of laboratory work. The purpose of the present inquiry is to illuminate some unexplicated dimensions of experimentation by examining what research psychologists would not or could not undertake to do, even if they so desired. The cases to be recounted occurred between 1910 and 1940, a transitory period in the discipline, extending from the decline of the prominent brass-instrument or structural psychology to the standardization of behavioral and logical positivist procedures. The cases illumine how procedural decisions about laboratory work were often informed by essentially social sanctions and how these decisions in turn determined what was to count as observation and an observed phenomenon.

Reconstructing the Cognitions of Experimenters

Before considering these cases, we should note that decisions about what could and could not be done depended, first, on a certain recognition of the identities of the participants (see previous chapters by Danziger and Scheibe). Decisions about *what* research could be done depended on *who* was going to do it and on *whom* it was going to be done. During the first three decades of the century, psychologists spent much time negotiating these roles.

Researchers worked to define the proper cognitive orientation of psychological scientists. As one textbook-writer put it, the aim of his book was to teach students "not psychology, but to psychologize." After elucidating the means for training the psychologist's mind, another textbook author claimed that "millions of human beings—unfortunate but all unconscious of what they are missing—go through life blind to the psychological world."[2] This claim intimates that if properly trained psychologists are identified by their special cognitive skills of observation and reasoning, then the ordinary person must be seen as a poor observer, one less capable or incapable of rational thinking and the proper scientific gaze. Contemporaneous with the clarification of these two interdependent but asymmetrical roles was the definition of the proper object of study. Psychological experiences came to be seen as either private or public, personal or shared, external or internal.[3] Personal, private experiences became synonymous with the subjective, which was not only the antithesis of objective psychology, but was itself to become a major object of scientific control and adjustment. In turn, the subjective attitude was associated with the untrained, the misbehaved, the layperson, and the unfortunate and was contrasted with the disposition of the scientifically trained mind, of the "objective observer." Thus the subjective and the objective were most convincingly dichotomized by classifying both practices and persons as either objective or subjective.[4]

Impossible Experiments

In the process of identifying objectivity with experimentation and specifically with the psychologically fit experimenter, psychology was reconstructing its subject. The distance between what had been called the public and the private was being stretched, and the dimensions of personal-impersonal and internal-external were being reconceptualized. The shift in these dimensions of experience had important consequences. Psychologists could gain access to the private, personal experiences of others and could demonstrate that ostensibly internal, or nonextended, experiences of others are actually extended and, consequently, accessible to direct observation. The experiment was public and impersonal, but it allowed entry into the private and the personal.

In order to see how experimentation offered the means not only to analyze, but also to correct the other's deception, it is important to recognize some of the reasons why such corrective techniques were valued. The realization of an authentic *science* of psychology, justly placed alongside other sciences in universities, was not the only goal and probably not the primary one either. Psychologists proclaimed plans to improve human life. This moral imperative was not new to twentieth-century psychology, but took form during the scientific revolution and was refined through enlightenment philosophies. However, the intent of practical change fared well in the American milieu and gained impetus in the Progressive era and later with the war effort.[5] After World War I, psychologists frequently expressed their reformist sentiments not through social advocacy, but through an attitude of scientific expertise. They capitalized on calls for scientific custodians of culture. The practical attitude of reform and improvement fitted well with the goal of corporate enterprises and expansionism. In this environment psychologists pressed to apply their ameliorative skills to human conduct in schools, hospitals, factories, and the home.[6]

With the construal of special identities and overarching societal commitments, psychologists faced two special constraints: their subjects' own interpretation of their experiences and social customs that restricted the extent to which the experiment could become public. These problems are illustrated in the following cases, in which psychological work, constrained by certain social practices, was reconstituted to foster a feasible and unhindered research program. In the first case, the problem of constraints was resolved by altering the psychological entities under investigation; in the second, by changing the subject. The third case describes other ways of reconstituting research, notably by using existing social relations.

Changing the Phenomena

Among the claims of the new psychology was a promise to establish a scientific understanding of sex differences. Numerous researchers claimed that twentieth-century research would lay the axe to "pseudo-scientific superstitions" about the real nature of the masculine and feminine realms. Between 1900 and 1920 these expectations seemed to be fulfilled, as hundreds of experimental studies explored sex differences in sensory abilities, intelligence, motor efficiency, color preferences, responses to fear, reading speed, stammering, and tastes, among other things. The overall results of the studies were equivocal, for while males excelled in some experiments, females excelled in others. By 1915 it was obvious that anyone looking to the assorted mental tests to ascertain the superiority of one sex over the other would find little to report.[7]

Aside from failing to provide political ammunition for the battle regarding the nature of the sexes, the experiments left some central questions unaddressed. Given that researchers did not repudiate sex differences altogether, there remained questions about why such differences occur and what may happen to them in the future, about causation as well as mutability or plasticity, and about the psychological basis of the commonly acknowledged differences between female and male characteristics. These were the questions that inspired the idea of an impossible experiment and eventually prompted the resourceful invention of new techniques—and new phenomena—for the study of sex differences.

The question of causation was translated in to one of nature versus nurture, which ultimately indicated the need for a special kind of experiment.[8] It required the creation of a controlled setting in which *all* environmental variables could be manipulated in order to assess the extent, if any, of biologically induced sex differences. Such an apparently impossible experiment is intriguing, not so much for its design as for the fantasy it inspired. The ethics and practicality of such a study were barely mentioned. What was of far greater importance was its desirability for numerous psychologists considered the experiment itself to be Arcadia, a social ideal. It soon became clear that an experiment on the social world of males and females implied freedom as well as control. After all, the perfect experimental condition necessitated elimination of all differential treatment of men and women and, hence, entailed what seemed like equality.

Perhaps the most bald assertion of the desirability of such experimental conditions was the claim that "The real tendencies of women can not be known until they are free to choose, any more than those of a tied up dog can be." The critic, A. Tanner, argued that the nature of sex differences "can not be demonstrated until men and women are not only nominally free but actually free to enter any profession."[9] Scientific methods, in controlling extraneous variables, would actually remove social oppression of women. As Helen Hull argued, it would result in knowledge with an "exorcising power."[10]

Over the next quarter of a century, several researchers publicly contemplated the taboo investigation, the perfect experiment. Beatrice Hinkle, a feminist psychiatrist, described such an experiment as a social revolution, for she held that the determinants of sex differences will be known only "when the tradition of women's inferiority has completely disappeared and the children of both sexes are given the same training and freedom with the same privileges and responsibilities."[11] The psychologist Helen Thompson Woolley began her dissertation on sex differences with a caveat about the limits of her inquiry: she confessed that finding male and female subjects who had similar social training and experiences "even in the most democratic community, is impossible." The closest approximation to these ideal "democratic" conditions was the coeducational college.[12] One psychologist, Iva Peters, went even further in imagining the experiment, in saying that, "given greater liberty and a more rational choice a new kind of sex selection might appear, in both man and woman. . . . Mental equality might come to be a factor of prime importance and aid in determining what combinations shall fuse to develop a new harmony." Despite such play of the imagination, Peters did realize that this plan "has its perils for the existing order."[13]

It is of significance that these forbidden experiments reflected a feminist challenge to American society. Feminist scholars, then as now, had a double vision by means of which they could simultaneously contemplate the world of those with power and the world of those without. Some feminists extended this dual perception not just to social science, but also to fiction, as is evident in Charlotte Perkins Gilman's 1915 feminist utopia *Herland*.[14] Other feminists chose more conventional ways of dealing with this duality. Hinkle, Tanner, Hull, Thompson, and Peters exemplify feminists who opted to describe their vision through a legitimate voice, specifically that of science.

The negotiated substitution of scientific method for political feminism was not one involving equals, however, and the phenomena of interest (sex differences) was shifted through the exchange. Many of these women began their professional training with strong feminist beliefs but eventually succeeded in reconciling them with the adoption of a modern scientific attitude. Science came to be seen as practically interchangeable with feminism, for it insisted on fairness and equality of treatment. Early in her career as a psychologist, Phyllis Blanchard wrote an autobiographical account of her realization that science would serve her better than the radical feminism she had cultivated previously. The process of adopting this apparently fruitful substitution is captured in her account:

> *I had originally intended to write, but the drive to understand human motives and conduct, which arose out of the necessity of solving my own problems, developed into a desire to understand all behavior, and I turned to the social sciences. Probably this was a happy decision. Had I been only a writer, I might have prolonged indefinitely my separation from reality. Through a more scientific approach, I began to see things as they actually were rather than as I wished them to be. I even came to understand that in spite of the intensity of my feeling about marriage I might be able to accept the outward form so long as the inner spirit of the relationship embodied freedom.*[15]

Such substitution of one body of ideas for another usually alters the problem under examination. As the historian Carroll Smith-Rosenberg found, the women of that period who took the option of substituting a conventional language for their own were to have their emancipatory ideals eclipsed by the prevasive androcentric nature of the language they adopted.[16] In the case of sex differences, the substitution of the language of science, particularly of a certain form of experimentation, brought about a seemingly minor, but eventually consequential, change in the subject.

The notion of the impossible experiment as a desirable, if perilous, reform was not unanimously shared by psychologists. Some researchers settled questions of the causality of sex differences in a more orthodox way by turning to biological explanations. Even after admitting that in "our present state of ignorance" any assessment of nature-nurture influences is "unwarranted," Stanford psychologists Winifred Johnson and Lewis Terman "merely" suggested that sex differences "may be largely the outcome" of physiological differences. In 1926, James Leuba argued that the "feminist" experiment actually *had* occurred, but that it had revealed no evidence of strong similarity between the sexes; this experiment produced only a few notable achievements by women in contemporary society.[17] Claims that differences are biologically induced also drew on the argument for the unity of the sciences, the claim that muscular and mental energy are not independent of each other, and that ultimately the various sciences should submit concordant findings about the sexes. Thus, if the physiologist discovered that women were not merely wombed men, then the social psychologist would also have to recognize this fact.[18] One researcher even suggested that we aid nature's evolutionary experiment by protecting and cherishing sex distinctions.[19]

The comments on biology also reveal tacit boundaries of scientific thought. Together with the need to parallel the activities of psychology with those of biology was a desire to demonstrate that psychology offered a unique understanding of these questions. Thus, the more fanciful approaches of perilous social reform and evolutionary experiments were eschewed. Instead, attention was given to other unexplored phenomena that provided psychology with its own territory: the psychological characteristics commonly known as "masculinity" and "femininity." G. Stanley Hall found that the undeniably boyish flappers represented a truer womanhood, for the flapper is unaware that "underneath her mannish ways" she embraces an evolved feminine mind.[20] With this change in research interests, the grounds of the question were shifted, and what was considered public and beyond tampering—social experiences as they related to an individual's gender identity—was made to be private and personal.

The phenomenon of sex differences was interiorized, and the internal psychology of femininity and masculinity, the private, personal experiences of thinking like a man or a woman, became accessible to the psychologist's gaze. This new phenomenon required a new mode of access, new methodological techniques, and the rationale for these innovations came from common sense along with claims for the unity of the sciences. The argument was straightforward: if other human sciences, notably anatomy, physiology, and pathology, reveal man as man and woman as woman, then "What reason to suspect psychology to enter a dissenting opinion?"[21]

This logic of redefining the phenomena laid the ground for a research program on femininity and masculinity that was to engage laboratory researchers productively for decades. Here was the creation of a new phenomenon that was accessible to experimental psychologists, although not to the experiencing subject. Here too was an alternative to the impossible experiment requiring utopian reform. The insurmountable problem of manipulating social conditions was circumvented, for the study of the internal, private dimensions of the male and female constitution required controlling only the immediate "psychological" environment, not the greater physical and social world. The revised concepts fitted well with the developing identities of psychologists. They also made the problem tractable; that is, researchers could work with them through practical tasks in the laboratory.

The mental test supplied the model for such command of the psychological interior, and Lewis Terman and Catherine Cox Miles used this model to construct the first test of masculinity and femininity, which they published in 1936 after ten years of research. It was called the Attitude-Interest Analysis test to mask its real purpose. The 910-item, multiple-choice test consisted of 7 subtests: word association, inkblot association, general information, emotional and ethical attitudes, interests, and opinions (many of these subtests were derived from sex-difference experiments of the previous twenty years). Items in the subtests were selected according to two criteria: that there was a high probability that males and females would answer them differently, and that they were efficient in terms of test administration. A subject would receive a masculine point if he or she responded negatively to questions like "Do you usually get to do things that please you most?", "Do you like to have people tell you their troubles?", and "Do you sometimes wish you had never been born?", and a feminine point by responding negatively to questions such as "Do you feel bored a large share of the time?", "Do people ever say you are a bad loser?", and "Were you ever fond of playing with snakes?" ' To accrue masculine points, subjects would need to reply that they disliked foreigners, dancing, being alone, and thin women; whereas to gain feminine points, they would need to indicate dislike of giving advice, bald men, sideshow freaks, and riding bicycles. Overall, scores of males and females differed by an average of 122 points. Out of 1,000 subjects, 10 of each sex had scores exceeding the mean of the other sex. These deviations were regarded as indicative of psychological abnormality, and Terman and Miles, along with other researchers, investigated the extent to which they were symptoms of (often latent) homosexuality, marital problems, and poor adult adjustment.[22]

Over the next twenty years, more than a dozen similar tests of femininity and masculinity were developed.[23] Like the Attitude-Interest Analysis Test, these tests included several properties that allowed the researcher almost complete authority in defining what counted as masculine and feminine, and hence in deciding what were meaningful sex differences and what were worrisome deviations. First, the very existence of an M-F test provided a definition that researchers could share among themselves and that they could renegotiate only through a highly complex, regulated ritual of test construction and validation. Thus psychologists also had a shared vocabulary by means of which they could develop theories about the origins of phenomena without conducting the ultimate social experiment. For instance, although Terman and Robert Yerkes worked in diverse areas of psychology, Terman on human traits and Yerkes on psychobiology and primates, with the definitive test they could discuss masculinity and femininity and eventually concur on the phenomena and their roots.[24]

Other properties of the tests gave researchers an even wider range of authority over definitions. By disguising the true nature of the tests, by requiring forced-choice answers, and by maintaining control over the scoring and interpretation (and often even over the results themselves) of the inventories, researchers further insured their definitions of the phenomena. Subjects had no say as to whether their actions had specific sexual meaning or whether they themselves were deviants with regard to sex role, sex identity, or sexuality. In fact, subjects were assumed to be prone to deceiving others and even themselves on these matters: "A man may be an athlete, may know all about automobiles and fly a plane—and yet be afraid of women. Everyone has known such people, for there are many, who use behavior labeled masculine and feminine by our society to hide their disorientation, often from themselves."[25] The M-F inventories would thus serve an important function as a diagnostic device for screening those who needed professional assistance in adjusting to a normal life and to social well-being.

Once rendered observable, measurable, and communicable, the concepts of masculinity and femininity are for many researchers a sufficient answer to questions of sex difference. If masculinity and femininity were so deeply rooted and if concepts relating to them fitted well (at least conceptually) with psychobiological and animal research, not to mention models of mental adjustment, then the ultimate experiment of complete sexual equality was unnecessary. If femininity and masculinity were once cultural symbols, then the test had transformed them into even more powerful ones. These new symbols not only had an observable reality into which few individuals were capable of penetrating; they were now malleable. The phenomena could be isolated and possibly even corrected by trained scientists.[26]

Changing the Subject

While some psychologists merely contemplated social experiments involving total control of the environment, others produced more concrete schemes. Some, like Edward L. Thorndike, called for real social experiments, claiming that even trial-and-error experimentation was better than a social life regulated by blind custom. At least four researchers offered elaborate accounts of perfect, but impossible, experiments that would simultaneously test their theories *and* improve human life. These accounts were disguised in the form of fictional utopias in which their inventors—G. Stanley Hall, William McDougall, Hugo Münsterberg, and John B. Watson—depicted worlds structured according to their own psychological theories and governed with the expert assistance of psychologists.[27] After all, in the utopian genre the outrageous was permissible.

Grand social schemes and imaginative fiction notwithstanding, psychologists had to find other means of investigating problems that, under proper experimental conditions, required maximum control of the social and physical environment. One solution, illustrated by the research on masculinity and femininity, was to redefine the problem or even the phenomenon in question. Another was to (literally) change the subject. Yerkes and Watson sought means to maximize environmental control through their substantial efforts to create a laboratory in which all social and physical conditions could be manipulated. Yerkes was to stock his research site with apes; Watson was to fill his with human infants. At one point they even contemplated a research station housing both children and chimps.[28] A joint research institute would enable them to explore the most crucial psychological questions concerning modern life, from the nature of sexuality, cognition, and addiction to social hierarchies of power.

Watson's abrupt departure from academic life meant the end of such collaborative plans, although he continued to entertain fantasies of an ideal laboratory. Yerkes, however, was more successful. This primate laboratory was a concrete realization of his (and others') broadened conception of the subject of psychology. By 1911 he had produced a textbook with just such an expanded definition; while citing "objects of consciousness" as a major subject, he also included "conscious objects" such as "the child, the gorilla, the horse, the dog, the squirrel."[29] After years of careful organizing and negotiating, he established an experimental anthropoid station where environmental conditions could be controlled and where crucial experiments that could not be performed on human subjects could answer questions about social life.[30] Through use of the "comparative" method, findings on nonhumans could be generalized to human conduct. Through these studies, the truth of female submissiveness, male domination, social hierarchies, fixed personality differences, chemical addictions, and maternal affection could be uncovered. The comparative method offered a means of exploring evolutionary issues; but it seems that the method was even more valuable as an entrance into inaccessible aspects of human affairs.

In one "wholly naturalistic study of captive subjects," for instance, the researchers observed mother-infant interactions and were able to report on behaviors that could not be observed readily in humans. They produced detailed accounts of aggressive maternal defense, sexual interactions between mothers and their infants, and forms of corporal punishment.[31] This mother-infant research, although reported in the language of human social interaction, was not extrapolated directly to human behavior. Other studies generalized in this fashion, however. In his reports of experiments on conjugal relations among chimpanzees, Yerkes claimed that much human behavior is unconsciously, subconsciously, or otherwise consciously concealed, and that the "uninhibited" chimpanzee could illumine these hidden aspects of life. Yet in some experiments this special chimpanzee characteristic was irrelevant: only with nonhuman subjects could researchers study the psychological effects of psychosurgery, varied forms of ovariectomy, drugs, and hormones.[32]

This early work on primates, with its easy slippage between the experiential worlds of humans and nonhumans, was generally well received and was soon integrated into textbooks. However, Yerkes' study of conjugal relations met with a rebuttal, a critique written in the voice of a female chimpanzee. The account appears in Ruth Herschberger's *Adam's Rib*, in the chapter in which Josie, an adult female chimp who has been used for psychological experimentation, criticizes the theory, methodology, and ethics of an experiment. The experimenters had reported that when an adult male and an adult female were caged together for the duration of the chimpanzee estrus cycle and received bits of food from a chute ten times a day, the male ate most of the food.[33] Josie questioned the researchers' conclusion that the male, therefore, was "naturally dominant," displaying "masculine ascendancy," while the female was the "naturally subordinate" of the pair, engaging in "favor-currying" and "prostitution." She pointed out that the final score of the contest was not as much of a landslide as implied:

> Well, I'll tell you what the score was. I was top man at the food chute for fourteen days out of the thirty-two. Jack was top man for eighteen. This means I won 44 percent of the time, and Jack won 56 percent. He's champion, I'll grant you that; but still it's almost fifty-fifty. If Jack hadn't been dragged in as the biggest male in the whole colony . . . well, it sounds like sour grapes.[34]

Josie also chastised the experimenters for failing to report the discounting of the days of estrus and the availability of food other than that dispensed via the chute. She questioned the use of only male experimenters and, more important, the use of an interpretive language that anthropomorphically read chimpanzees' sexual desire in terms of females being "sexually receptive," exhibiting "sexual allure" and "prostitution," compared with males showing "masculine ascendancy" and "dominance," making "commands" and "demands." When Herschberger, prior to writing *Adam's Rib*, personally confronted the primary experimenter, Yerkes, with these methodological and interpretive problems, her concerns were dismissed.[35] It was then that she engaged the voice of a chimp to try to make her comments heard.

In Yerkes' and other animal laboratories, the grounds of research were again shifted slightly. The shift was twofold, changing the subject of research, from humans to nonhumans, and what counted as "private," inaccessible experiences to the "public" life of nonhumans. There is some irony in the fact that many researchers, like Yerkes, turned to nonhuman subjects to study social-psychological conditions that were significant aspects of their everyday lives. In research with primates, family interactions, sexual relations, and power hierarchies were popular research topics. In Yerkes' records of his personal life, these social relations—especially those of power, leadership, and heterosexual relations—appear to have been salient, if often awkward, aspects. Research with primates tended to mirror the social relations of the experimenters' own corporate (competitive and hierarchical), patriarchal culture.[36] Thus, the tense, highly restricted relations between men and women that researchers like Yerkes and Watson reported in autobiographical and informal accounts reappear with only superficial alterations in the studies of primate male and female interactions. Just as women were not typically welcomed as members of the Yale faculty, to which Yerkes and his co-workers belonged, so female chimps were found to demonstrate those very characteristics which, in humans, would make them unsuitable for prominent, demanding professional positions. And just as these researchers struggled in a complicated hierarchy of faculty, university administrators, foundation officials, and government bureaucrats, so they were captivated by the social hierarchies among (only male) primates.

This apparent mirroring of corporate, patriarchal culture in interpretations of primate activities is only part of what these studies accomplished. The research also served as a forum in which what counts as "nature"—biological, innate, determined, fixed, phenomena—was negotiated; consequently the research supplied one foundation for defining what counts as "human nature" or personhood.

Psychological research with nonhumans supposedly provides an aperture for looking into private, personal experiences. Yet in practice, the research has often served simply to mirror what experimenters already thought constituted the private and personal, as we have just seen. At times it has also been the place where experimenters redefine or delete those aspects of social life that they desire or refuse to acknowledge. The actions of nonhumans placed in constructed environments have been convenient for defining human desires. For example, violence toward outgroups and homosocial desire can be redefined as concomitants of "natural" power hierarchies. If such observation is made without critical reflection, the consequences are often substantial. The unreflective use of corporate, patriarchal models of social arrangements places strict limits on imaginative thought and on what can be learned from research. Just as these models constrain one's self-conceptions, so too they can impinge on the lives of others, notably by imposing norms for conduct (work hierarchies, interpersonal relationships and so on) and by creating scientific justifications for injurious social practices. The use of nonhuman subjects extends the possibilities for prescribing social conduct, since it enables researchers to make ready claims about the nature of "nature" and, hence, to establish their findings as real, fixed, and universal.

Tacit prohibitions of experiments that impinge on individual privacy or alter the public domain have occasionally led to reformulation of the phenomena under scrutiny or to the use of nonhuman subjects. But there have also been other ways to deal with the problems. Researchers could always penetrate the personal, private realm by examining their own experiences. Experiments on drugs, especially opium and mescal, were sometimes conducted in this manner. Such experiments intruded only on the privacy of the researchers, who circumvented public prohibitions by taking the drugs either in the laboratory or at home.[37] However, probably because this strategy would closely resemble, if not count as, either introspection or philosophical speculation, it was rarely adopted.

Another way for researchers to capitalize on their personal, private domains was to use their social privileges with others closely related to them, notably family members. Researchers had considerable license to manipulate the physical and social environment of their intimates. Watson was not the only psychologist to submit his children to experiments requiring control over the environment.[38] W. N. Kellogg raised an infant chimpanzee with his son, and for over a year child and chimp shared a physical and social environment in which they dressed, ate, and played together.[39] B. F. Skinner's "heircon-ditioner," a total environment for young infants, was tested on his daughter.[40]

Yet another means of circumventing social prohibitions and gaining access to private, personal experiences involved the use of institutionalized individuals or those now called "captive populations." With the consent of management, for instance, researchers could perform experiments on workers in factories. Schools and colleges were other places in which individuals were limited in their choice of actions and in which researchers could manipulate significant aspects of the public domain.

Further, researchers could abandon experiments altogether. Questionnaire and interview techniques offered two alternatives that relaxed experimental demands for a controlled environment and manipulated variables. With the finest training in experimental methods and an interest in nervous disorders, G. V. Hamilton developed an "objective psychopathology." Hamilton turned to the interview technique, which combines the "never quite trustworthy methods of field and clinical observation" with "scientifically formulated methods." This combination entailed converting the subject's reports of direct experience into an "objective tracing of stimulus-response sequences." Thus, through interviews, he was able to explore sexual behavior, "unsatisfied major cravings," and later, the psychodynamics of marriage.[41] Such alternative methods were never to gain the same legitimacy as experimentation, however.

Controlling public space or extracting information from the personal realm of others was possible only under certain circumstances. Access was available only because of social relationships of disparate power or authority, such as those in schools, hospitals, and the family. Such institutionalized relationships contain interpersonal asymmetries that either place intrinsic limitations on the individual's options to act or grant privileges to certain parties to govern the actions of other individuals by enforcing sanctions, usually through reward, threat, or punishment.

New Social Relations

The emerging roles of the experimenter and the subject, in both their psychological and social dimensions, and the transformation of subject matter were initiated by researchers. Thus there is little documentation of subjects' reactions to experimentation. The only available sources of subjects' responses aside from experimental reports are the articulate comments of social critics. Mental testing provides a good case: there are no records of refusal to accept or submit to mental testing apart from a few skeptical psychologists and professional critics like Walter Lippmann and Stephen Leacock.[42] The same is true of responses to experimentation. There is an amusing poem by Amy Lowell, for example, which tells of her indignation over a psychologist's request that she be a subject in a creativity study.[43] Franklin D. Roosevelt gave a similarly forthright reply when it was announced that four experimental chimpanzees had been named after him (Frank, Lynn, Rose, and Velt). Through a press aide, Roosevelt expressed disdain over the use (and misuse) of nonhumans in experiments designed to understand humans.[44]

There is a special sense in which the subject was rendered silent. The laboratory became a place where only experimenters spoke, just as experimenters became the only representatives in records of research, both published and unpublished. The opportunity for subjects to speak was diminished further with the adoption of purely behavioral techniques. Using operational behavioral criteria, subjects' completion of a task in a particular manner, regardless of knowledge, opinions, or beliefs to the contrary, became the sole indicator of whether subjects were creative individuals, latent homosexuals, adequate readers, introverts, or whatever. The implementation of fixed-response tests and the use of deceptive techniques reduced even further the opportunities for subjects to speak.[45]

The fact that such silence was eventually taken, not as a matter of *rights*, but of *abilities*, was due to the successful reconstruction of psychological experiences by recasting the identities of experimenters and subjects and reformulating the phenomenon under study. These role revisions aligned egocentricity with subjectivity and the subject and impartiality with objectivity and the experimenter. With these alignments, two noteworthy conventions were established. First, experimenters gained an advantage whereby they had access to experiences of the subject that had once been deemed private, personal, and even unextended, while subjects were held to have even more limited access to these experiences than was believed formerly. Second, experimenters developed an ethic of detachment that denied their own most private, personal experiences while simultaneously legitimating their ultimately private experience of laboratory observation. Just as the subjects' private experiences became accessible to the experimenter, so the experimenters' private, personal experiences were deemed trustworthy, were suppressed, or were considered subjective observations.

The relocation of psychological phenomena, the reduction or denial of the subject's opportunity to speak, and the experimenter's privileged position (in space and in conversation) remained relatively unquestioned (except for rare commentaries on experimental bias) until the 1960s. Given the presumed logic of these practices, it seemed reasonable to conduct experiments that exposed soldier-subjects to test blast sites in order to assess psychological reactions to atomic bombs, to induce a camp of schoolboy subjects to be aggressive toward one another, and to submit a similar group of young subjects to authoritarian leadership.[46] Plans in the research notebooks of Clark Hull reveal the exorbitancies that could result from such restructuring of privacy. Skeptical of a clinical (Freudian) psychologist's claim that a certain class of mental patients had a high frequency of constipation, Hull meticulously designed an experiment that would objectively test this observation. Experimenters would assess the feces of patients with various mental disorders; of course, the daily assessment would proceed with standardized measures (wax models of feces) of constipation. A similarly skeptical, but not entirely unbelieving, attitude Freud's theory of infantile sexuality inspired Hull to design experiments measuring the erections of infant males, particularly while they were breastfeeding.[47]

The new psychology of the subjects and the experimenters, therefore, created new conventions of the private and the personal, thereby altering social relations. Although psychology was not the only profession to silence its subjects, it did so more notably than others. Viewing the social relations of experimentation as simply relations of power augmented by the authority granted to professional scientists, however, is inadequate. Social power—the means to accomplish certain outcomes through imposing sanctions on others—is not unidimensional. Rather, it involves a dialectic of control in which those subject to the sanctions must actively comply (or more precisely, must maintain an identity which affords the possibility of compliance or conformity). Participants in experiments enter into them with certain understandings of what they can, should, and ought to do. In addition, institutional structures restrict social actions, imposing limitations that facilitate certain actions just as they constrain others. These constraining and facilitating conditions are not fixed but depend on the specific historical context in which the interaction transpires.[48] In other words, the high-school classroom of 1916 imposed different (as well as some similar) constraints on the relations between students and authority figures than the classroom of 1988 does.

Laboratory social relations are determined in part by inherent structural constraints and historical conditions; but they also depend in important ways on shared understandings—that is, on the tacit social knowledge of all participants. Experimenters must work to attain such understandings. Special social efforts on the part of the experimenter are recognized even in nonhuman research. Psychologists studying planeria have claimed that their research suffered because they did not know their subjects as well as researchers using rats knew theirs.[49] In human research, it was possible to "know" your subjects better by controlling who they are (using children or "unsophisticated adults" enables researchers to presume certain things about the subject's awareness), controlling the stimulus (such as the use of pain), and/or veiling the objectives of the study.[50]

What does this mean for our understanding of what is or is not possible in experimental events? Above all, it reconfirms that there are social boundaries, and that just as these boundaries restrict what actions can take place, so they also facilitate certain actions. What can be done in psychology experiments always has fuzzy boundaries which can change over time and across settings. For instance, by changing the phenomenon under examination from readily observable sex differences to differences unperceived by the ordinary observer and by changing the subject from humans to nonhumans, the limitations on what could be studied experimentally were shifted. The social relations of the experimental setting were then renegotiated. This renegotiation, for the most part, has progressively silenced the subject, while expanding the social influence of the professional researcher.

The experimental method, adopted primarily from neighboring sciences, offered psychology a protocol for work, while aiding its acceptance as a science. The procedures gave psychologists latitude to redefine what were to count as psychological phenomena and as subjects. Yet the procedures also involved constraints: as a social institution, experimentation had to coexist with other conventions concerning public life and individual conduct. Although such conventions forbade the conduct of certain experiments, various social prohibitions were skirted by renegotiating the identities of all participants, as well as the phenomena under investigation. The power of the reformulated identities is exemplified in the increased range of experiments that are considered socially appropriate. When accorded the identity of detached, impersonal, rational spectators, psychologists gained sanction to explore the private, personal dimensions of others. They could talk about a person's sexual orientation and gender identity, and their accounts would be taken as both acceptable and accurate. In instances where psychologists could not gain ready access to experiences, in conjugal relations and male power hierarchies, for example, the use of nonhumans provided entry into these sensitive areas. Thus, in early twentieth-century psychology, dreams of perfect experiments (such as the equal treatment of boys and girls) gave way to the realization of technical strategies for reconceptualizing the participants and phenomena under study.

The special identity accorded the experimenter had consequences for the social relations of the experiment. Subjects' accounts of experiences became less an explicit part of the drama, and their silence became apparent not just in the experimental situation, but outside it as well. Social arrangements in experiments were such that the subjects' responses were either restricted or reinterpreted in the language of experimentation. It is not surprising, then, that the range of manipulations that could be performed on subjects increased.

The new conventions meant that some previously impossible experiments could be performed. But this development also meant that experimenters became subject to a complex set of procedural rules laboriously laid out in manuals, codes, and editorial guides. These rules stipulate what they can do, say, and write; in other words, researchers themselves are now subject to a new set of controls on their thoughts, actions, and utterances. Consequently, the results of experimentation have limited capacity for enlightenment and creative insight. Such imposed constraints and restricted models of human nature do not lend themselves to producing imaginative knowledge. Paradoxically, the new experimental method, a distinctly twentieth-century form of institutionalized behavior, has affected the observers as well as the objects of observation. Through multiple transformations of experiences and identities, experimentation has altered the intellectual products, as well as the processes, of inquiry.

Notes

1. See Bruno Latour and Steve Woolgar, *Laboratory Life, The Social Construction of Scientific Fads* (Beverly Hills, Calif.: Sage, 1979); Donald A. MacKenzie, *Statistics in Britain, 1865–1930: The Social Construction of Scientific Knowledge* (Edinburgh: Edinburgh University Press, 1981); K. D. Knorr, R. Krohn, and R. Whitely, eds., *The Social Process of Scientific Investigation, Sociology of the Sciences Yearbook*, vol. 4 (Dordrecht: Reidel, 1980); Steve Woolgar, "Laboratory Studies: A Comment on the State of the Art," *Social Studies of Science* 12 (1982):481–498; G. D. L. Travis, "Replicating Replication? Aspects of the Social Construction of Learning in Planarian Worms," *Social Studies of Science* 11 (1981):11–32; Ludwik Fleck, *Genesis and Development of a Scientific Fact* (Chicago: University of Chicago Press, 1979); D. Cartwright, "Determinants of Sci-

entific Progress: The Case of Research on the Risky Shift," *American Psychologist* 28 (1973):222–31.

2. Robert M. Yerkes, *Introduction to Psychology* (New York: Henry Holt, 1911), p. 13; Carl E. Seashore, *Introduction to Psychology* (New York: Macmillan, 1923), p. viii.

3. For an early discussion of these dichotomous qualities, see Mary Whiton Calkins, *First Book in Psychology* (New York: Macmillan, 1910), pp. 3–6.

4. Textbook-writers typically used a psychological language of egocentricity versus objectivity, complicity versus disinterestedness, ignorance versus knowledge, confused versus directed. On subjects' self-deceptions, John Dashiell writes: "Perhaps the subject states that he sees an orange-red; he may really be red-green color blind. . . . He may sincerely insist that he is the prey to no embarrassment, resentment, or other agitation, while at the same time telltale evidence may be appearing on the experimenter's dials." With an advanced attitude of experimentation, the researcher acts "in a detached, objective manner, putting aside his own desires and wishes in such matters" (*Fundamentals of Objective Psychology* [New York: Houghton Mifflin, 1928], pp. 12, 15). See also Max F. Meyer, *Psychology of the Other-One* (Columbia: Missouri Book Company, 1921).

5. David E. Leary, "The Intentions and Heritage of Descartes and Locke: Toward a Recognition of the Moral Basis of Modern Psychology," *Journal of General Psychology* 102 (1980):283–310; Dorothy Ross, "American Social Science and the Idea of Progress," in *The Authority of Experts*, Thomas L. Haskell, ed. (Bloomington: Indiana University Press, 1984), pp. 157–79.

6. See J. M. O'Donnell, *Origins of Behaviorism: American Psychology, 1870–1920* (New York: New York University Press, 1985); Loren Baritz, *Servants of Power* (Middletown, Conn.: Wesleyan University Press, 1966); Michael Sokal, "The Origins of the Psychological Corporation," *Journal of the History of the Behavioral Sciences* 17 (1981):54–67; idem, "James McKeen Cattell and American Psychology in the 1920's," in *Explorations in the History of American Psychology*, J. Brozek, ed. (Lewisburg, Pa.: Bucknell University Press, 1984); Ben Harris, " 'Give me a Dozen Healthy Infants': John B. Watson's Popular Advice on Childrearing, Women, and the Family," in *In the Shadow of the Past: Psychology Portrays the Sexes*, M. Lewin ed. (New York: Columbia University Press, 1984), pp. 126–54.

7. See Helen Thompson Woolley, "The Psychology of Sex," *Psychological Bulletin* 11 (1914):353–79; L. Hollingworth, "Sex Differences in Mental Traits," *Psychological Bulletin* 13 (1916):377–84; idem, "Comparison of the Sexes on Mental Traits," *Psychological Bulletin* 15 (1918):428; and C. Allen, "Recent Studies in Sex Differences," *Psychological Bulletin* 27 (1930):394–407.

8. The emergence of the nature-nurture debates over sex differences and the role of female intellectuals in these debates are explored by Rosalind L. Rosenberg, *Beyond Separate Spheres: Intellectual Origins of Modern Feminism* (New Haven: Yale University Press, 1982).

9. A. Tanner, "The Community of Ideas of Men and Women," *Psychological Review*, 3 (1896):549–50.

10. Helen R. Hull, "The Long Handicap," *Psychoanalytic Review*, 4 (1917):442.

Hull and other feminists argued that scientific studies linking women's deficiencies with their biological makeup were themselves oppressive forces that negatively affected women's psychological conditions and achievements. See also Faith Fairfield, "Glandular Activity and Feminine Character," *Atlantic Monthly* 37 (1926):801–04.

11. Beatrice Hinkle, "On the Arbitrary Use of the Terms 'Masculine' and 'Feminine'," *Psychoanalytic Review* 7 (1920):19.

12. Helen B. Thompson (Woolley), *The Mental Traits of Sex* (Chicago: University of Chicago Press, 1903), pp. 2–3. In the conclusion of her study, Woolley suggested that if the sexes really had inherent differences, then it would not be necessary to indulge in so much effort to make girls and boys adhere to lines of conduct appropriate to their sex. Leta Hollingworth suggested that we rear both boys and girls with the goal of parenthood and then assess their relative achievements; like Woolley, she exposed the differential conditions of the grand experiment of social life and even believed that the "New Woman" was "conscientiously experimenting with her own life." These comments were made in 1931–32 and are reprinted in L. Hollingworth, *Public Addresses* (Lancaster, Pa.: The Science Press, 1940), pp. 16 and 60.

13. Iva Lowther Peters, "A Questionnaire Study of Some of the Effects of Social Restrictions on the American Girl," *Pedagogical Seminary* 23 (1916):561, 568.

14. On this dual perception and its uses in feminist science fiction, see Pamela J. Annas, "New Worlds, New Words: Androgyny in Feminist Science Fiction," *Science Fiction Studies* 5 (1978):143–55. Charlotte Perkins Gilman, *Herland* (New York: Pantheon, 1979). An analysis of Gilman's scientific work is given by Ann Palmeri, "Charlotte Perkins Gilman: Forerunner of a Feminist Social Science," in *Discovering Reality*, ed. Sandra Harding and Merrill B. Hintikka (Dordrecht: Reidel, 1983), pp. 97–119.

15. Phyllis Blanchard, "The Long Journey," repr. in *These Modern Women: Autobiographical Essays from the Twenties*, ed. Elaine Showalter (Old Westbury, N.Y.: Feminist Press, 1978), pp. 108–09.

16. For an insightful analysis of how the feminist work by the "new women" of the period was blurred and subverted, see Carroll Smith-Rosenberg, "The New Woman as Androgyne: Social Disorder and Gender Crisis, 1870–1936," in *Disorderly Conduct: Visions of Gender in Victorian America* (New York: Knopf, 1985), pp. 245–96.

17. W. B. Johnson and Lewis B. Terman, "Some Highlights in the Literature of Psychological Sex Differences Published since 1920," *Journal of Psychology* 9 (1940):327–36; J. H. Leuba, "The Weaker Sex," *Atlantic Monthly* 137 (1926):454–60. For similar arguments supporting biological sex differences and criticisms of studies demonstrating otherwise, see J. G. Morawski, "The Measurement of Masculinity and Femininity: Engendering Categorical Realities," *Journal of Personality* 53 (1985):196–223; and Woolley, "Psychology of Sex."

18. Johnson and Terman, "Some Highlights," p. 331.

19. A. Wreschner, cited by Woolley, "Psychology of Sex," p. 374.

20. G. Stanley Hall, "Flapper Americana Novissima," *Atlantic Monthly* 129 (1922):771–80.

21. Joseph Jastrow, "The Feminine Mind," in *The Psychology of Conviction* (Boston: Houghton Mifflin, 1918), p. 285.

22. Lewis B. Terman and Catherine Cox Miles, *Sex and Personality* (New York: McGraw-Hill, 1936).

23. For an account of the development and proliferation of these tests, along with the criticism to which they were eventually subjected, see J. G. Morawski, "Measurement of Masculinity and Femininity"; idem, "The Troubled Quest for Masculinity, Femininity, and Androgyny," in *Review of Personality and Social Psychology*, vol. 7, ed. Phillip Shaver (Beverly Hills, Calif.: Sage, 1987), pp. 44–69; Miriam Lewin, "Rather Worse than Folly? Psychology Measures Femininity and Masculinity: I: From Terman and Miles to the Guilfords," and "Psychology Measures Femininity and Masculinity: II: From '13 Gay Men' to the Instrumental-Expressive Distinction," both in *In the Shadow of the Past: Psychology Portrays the Sexes*, pp. 155–78, 197–204, respectively.

24. See correspondence between Robert Yerkes and Lewis Terman from 1920 until the 1940s, Robert M. Yerkes Papers, Sterling Library, Yale University, and Lewis M. Terman Papers, Stanford Archives, Stanford University.

25. K. Franck and E. Rosen, "A Projective Test of Masculinity-Femininity," *Journal of Consulting Psychology* 13 (1949):247.

26. On the transformation of events and objects through laboratory work, see Bruno Latour, "Give me a Laboratory and I will Raise the World," in *Science Observed: Perspectives on the Social Study of Science*, ed. Karin Knorr-Cetina and Michael Mulkay (Beverly Hills, Calif.: Sage, 1983), pp. 144–70.

27. Edward L. Thorndike, "Sex in Education," *The Bookman* 23 (1906):214. On psychologists' utopian plans, see J. G. Morawski, "Assessing Psychology's Heritage through our Neglected Utopias," *American Psychologist* 37 (1981):1081–95.

28. Letters from Robert M. Yerkes to John B. Watson, 14 May 1913 and 8 June 1913; Watson to Yerkes, 29 Nov. 1916 and 29 Mar. 1919; Yerkes Papers. See also Robert M. Yerkes, "Progress and Peace," *Scientific Monthly* 2 (1915):195–201; idem, "The Road of Psychology," *The Open Road* 4 (1922):56–63.

29. Yerkes, *Introduction to Psychology*, pp. 8–9.

30. Robert M. Yerkes, "The Yale Laboratories of Primate Biology," *Scientific Monthly* 56 (1943):287–90; idem, *Chimpanzees: A Laboratory Colony* (New Haven: Yale University Press, 1943); idem, "Creating a Chimpanzee Community," *Yale Journal of Biology and Medicine* 36 (1963):205–23.

31. Robert M. Yerkes and Michael I. Tomilin, "Mother-Infant Relations in Chimpanzee," *Comparative Psychology* 20 (1935):321–48, quote on p. 321.

32. Robert M. Yerkes, "Conjugal Contracts Among Chimpanzees," *Journal of Abnormal and Social Psychology* 36 (1941):175–99. On the range of experiments conducted on the primates, see idem, Publications from the Yale Laboratories of Primate Biology, Inc., 1925–1939 (New Haven, 1940), p. 14, Yerkes Papers.

33. Ruth Herschberger, *Adam's Rib* (New York: Pellegrini and Cudahy, 1948), pp. 7–8. The chapter is entitled "Josie Takes the Stand." The experiments are reported in Robert M. Yerkes, "Social Behavior of Chimpanzees: Dominance between Mates, in Relation to Sexual Status," *Journal of Comparative Psychology* 30 (1940):147–86; idem, *Chimpanzees, A Laboratory Colony*, chap. 5.

34. Herschberger, *Adam's Rib*, pp. 7–8.

35. Ruth Herschberger to Robert M. Yerkes, 2 Mar. 1944; Yerkes to Herschberger, 30 Mar. 1944, Yerkes Papers.

36. For an examination of connections between primatology and cultural values, see Donna Haraway, "Animal Sociology and a Natural Economy of the Body Politic, Part I: A Political Physiology of Dominance," *Signs* 4 (1978):21–36; idem, "Animal Sociology and a Natural Economy of the Body Politic, Part II: The Past is the Contested Zone: Human Nature and Theories of Production and Reproduction in Primate Behavior Studies," *Signs* 4 (1978):37–60; idem, "The Biological Enterprise: Sex, Mind and Profit from Human Engineering to Sociobiology," *Radical History Review* 20 (1979):206–37; Janet Sayers, *Politics: Feminist and Anti-Feminist Perspectives* (New York: Tavistock, 1982).

37. See, e.g., Henrick Kluver, "Mescal Visions and Eidetic Vision," *American Journal of Psychology* 37 (1926):502–15.

38. Rosalie R. Watson, "I am the Mother of a Behaviorist's Sons," *Parents' Magazine*, Dec. 1930, pp. 16–18, 67; John Watson, *Psychological Care of Infant and Child* (New York: W. W. Norton, 1928).

39. W. N. Kellogg and L. A. Kellogg, *The Ape and the Child: A Study of the Environmental Influence upon Early Behavior* (New York: McGraw Hill, 1933).

40. B. F. Skinner, "Baby in a Box," *Ladies Home Journal* 62 (Oct. 1945):30–31, 135–36, 138; idem, *The Shaping of a Behaviorist* (New York: Knopf, 1979).

41. G. V. Hamilton, *An Introduction to Objective Psychopathology* (St. Louis: C. V. Moby, 1925); idem, *A Research in Marriage* (New York: Medical Research Press, 1929).

42. Walter Lippmann, "Tests of Hereditary Intelligence," *New Republic* 32 (1922):328–30; idem, "A Future for the Tests," *New Republic* 33 (1922):9–10. See also idem, "The Mental Age of Americans," *New Republic* 32 (1922):213–15; idem, "Reliability of Intelligence Tests," *New Republic* 32 (1922):275–77. Stephen Leacock, "A Manual for the New Mentality," *Harper's* 48 (1924):472–80; Grace Adams, "The Rise and Fall of Psychology," *Atlantic Monthly* 153 (1934):82–92.

43. Amy Lowell, "To a Gentleman who Wanted to See the First Drafts of My Poems in the Interests of Psychological Research into the Workings of the Creative Mind" (originally "To the Imprudent Psychologist"), in *The Complete Poetical Works of Amy Lowell* (Boston: Houghton Mifflin, n.d.), pp. 535–36.

44. Robert Yerkes to Franklin D. Roosevelt, 27 Feb. 1934; Stephen Early (assistant secretary to the president) to Yerkes, 21 Mar. 1934, Yerkes Papers.

45. There is one notable exception to subjects' silence, one situation in which their voices have been recorded, or, more accurately, in which experimenters have used their voices. Occasionally subjects' reactions to experimental conditions have been used to debunk or discredit experiments. Thus, what subjects report may be of interest to researchers who hold opposing views or who have obtained conflicting results in their own studies. Here the subject is accorded authority, or at least granted enough competence, to demonstrate the opponent's argument.

46. E. L. Walker and J. W. Atkinson, "The Expression of Fear-related Motivation

in Thematic Apperception as a Function of Proximity to an Atomic Explosion," in *Motives in Fantasy, Action, and Society*, ed. J. W. Atkinson (New York: Van Nostrand, 1958), pp. 143–59; M. Sherif, O. J. Harvey, B. J. White, W. R. Hood, and C. W. Sherif, *Intergroup Cooperation and Competition: The Robbers' Cave Experiment* (Norman, Okla.: University Book Exchange, 1961); K. Lewin, R. Lippitt, and R. White, "Patterns of Aggressive Behavior in Experimentally Created 'Social Climates,' " *Journal of Social Psychology* 10 (1939):271–99.

47. Clark Hull, "Idea Books," Clark Hull Papers, Sterling Library, Yale University.
48. For an analysis of constraints, see Anthony Giddens, *The Constitution of Society* (Berkeley: University of California Press, 1984).
49. G. D. L. Travis, "Replicating replication?"
50. For a fuller account of the psychologist's advantage, see chap. 3 above. See also Karl Scheibe, *Mirrors, Masks, Lies, and Secrets: The Limits of Human Predictability* (New York: Praeger, 1979). For an early claim that psychologists need to learn the social nature of the subject, see Saul Rosenzweig, "The Experimental Situation as a Psychological Problem," *Psychological Review* 40 (1933):337–54.

5

Shared Knowledge:
The Experimentalists,
1904–1929

Laurel Furumoto

Wellesley College

"For many years I wanted an experimental club—no officers, the men moving about and handling (apparatus), the visited lab to do the work, no women, smoking allowed, plenty of frank criticism and discussions, the whole atmosphere experimental, the youngsters taken in on an equality with the men who have arrived."[1] Thus, in 1904, shortly after his thirty-seventh birthday, Cornell's E. B. Titchener described his vision of a society for the advancement of experimental psychology in a letter to a colleague at Harvard, Hugo Münsterberg.

In this chapter, I will examine the early history of this small, elite scientific society and the life and career of the psychologist who inaugurated it. The story has relevance to the history of experimentation in that it illustrates very clearly how one psychologist's cognitive authority came to be exerted in a particular social arrangement which had significant consequences for the subfield of experimental psychology.[2] Titchener's personality exhibited a peculiar admixture of erudition, charm, and dogged insistence, which often enabled him to lead and control those in his immediate environment very effectively. While in the eyes of many of his contemporaries the force of these personal qualities may have elevated him to a level somewhat larger than life, the obedience he commanded from his students and associates would not have been possible in the absence of mutually held values. An instructive example of this is provided by the exclusion of women from Titchener's society. Although Titchener originated the policy, it seems implausible that it could have been maintained without the tacit approval of the other members. The impact of this exclusion was to deprive women in the field of the opportunity of establishing collegial ties and of being part of an informal communication

94

network, essentials for scientific research.[3] Experimental psychology, in turn, was deprived of women's participation, contributions, and point of view, as Titchener's discriminatory policy effectively relegated them to the periphery of the field.

Titchener's club, begun in 1904, came to be called "the Experimentalists," and for more than twenty years, until his death in 1927, he dictated how it was run. Attendance was by invitation only to the heads of psychology laboratories, primarily in elite eastern universities. In addition to men who had arrived, a select group of youngsters—promising advanced graduate students and junior faculty—were invited from the chosen laboratories.

Titchener insisted that the meetings be kept informal; he frowned on the reading of papers, encouraging instead reports of work in progress, discussion, and hands-on demonstration of apparatus. The only subject matter welcomed for inclusion was that which Titchener considered legitimate psychology. This excluded from consideration mental testing and comparative and applied psychology, among other things. Titchener vigilantly enforced two other practices: no prohibition against smoking and no women at meetings. Finally, Titchener did not want what went on in the meetings to be disseminated publicly. He was opposed to publishing proceedings, and when in the early years of the group some published notes did appear, he expressed his displeasure to those responsible.

Information on Titchener's background, personality, and the way in which he came to conceptualize psychology is provided in the following section, with the intent of shedding some light on his reasons for sponsoring the Experimentalists and his insistence that the group observe a certain protocol. It is useful to keep in mind the observation of one historian of psychology that the originator of the Experimentalists was a breed apart from his American colleagues: "Titchener was not typical of those who founded American experimental psychology in the 1890's. He maintained the image of a 19th-century aristocratic Oxford scholar when others were rapidly moving toward the image of modern twentieth century man."[4]

E. B. Titchener

Origins, Education, and Cornell

E. B. Titchener was born in 1867 in Chichester, a town seventy miles south of London, close to the English coast. He was a descendant of an old, respected family, counting among his paternal ancestors a great grandfather who was a mayor of Chichester and a grandfather who was an influential barrister.[5] However, when Titchener was in adolescence, both his father and his paternal grandfather died, and soon after the family found itself financially bereft. Nevertheless, Titchener was able to further his education by earning a scholarship to a public preparatory school. He subsequently spent five years at Oxford, where he took his A.B. degree. The first four years he devoted to studying classics and philosophy, making his way by means of scholarships and summer jobs; the fifth he spent in the laboratory of the physiologist Burdon Sanderson, who was apparently responsible for suggesting to Titchener that he study psychology with Wundt.[6]

Titchener followed the suggestion to study with the German scion of experimental psychology, spending two years in Leipzig, where he earned his doctorate in 1892. Frank Angell, an American graduate student with whom Titchener struck up a cordial friendship during his first year of study in Germany, was to play an important role in bringing Titchener to the United States. In the fall of 1891 Angell went to Cornell to set up a psychological laboratory, but after only one year resigned from his position to accept a job at Stanford, which was just opening its doors. His admiration for Titchener's abilities prompted Angell to recommend Titchener as his replacement at Cornell.[7] Titchener apparently had an opportunity to return to Oxford, in addition to the offer of a position from Cornell. Moreover, there were serious drawbacks to Cornell. Aside from necessitating leaving England to live in the American wilderness, which Ithaca surely was in the 1890s, Titchener had doubts about Cornell's stature as an academic institution. Howard C. Warren, who was studying in Leipzig at the time that Titchener was completing his doctorate, remembered "the day when Titchener received the call to Cornell; we were in Wundt's lecture hall . . . waiting for the lecturer, and T. asked me whether Cornell really ranked as a first class university."[8]

It seems that it was the lure of the laboratory which tipped the scales in favor of Cornell. Many years later Titchener confided to a younger colleague, "When I had the choice between creating my subject at Oxford, with no chance of a laboratory, and coming here, I came here."[9] E. G. Boring, who took his Ph.D. with Titchener in 1914, also considered the laboratory to have been the decisive factor influencing Titchener's decision: "In those days a laboratory was a laboratory, Titchener . . . often said; and . . . [Titchener] only twenty-five years old, hurried to Ithaca, New York, with its laboratory, as an assistant professor of psychology. He never left Cornell; and within psychology Cornell and Titchener (became) almost interchangeable words."[10]

A vivid impression of the legendary psychologist toward the end of his career is conveyed in the recollections of Titchener's nephew, written for the *Cornell Alumni News* in the late 1960s. The author, who was the son of Titchener's sister, had become well acquainted with his uncle in his years as an undergraduate at Cornell during the early 1920s. First and foremost in his reminiscences was "the code by which Uncle Bradford guided his life—the code of the British gentleman. . . . That code, carried out to the point of brusqueness, dictated at one extreme, absolute intellectual integrity, and at the other, rigid rules of etiquette."[11] Another central feature of Titchener's image his nephew recalled was that of the British intellectual, who had gained the reputation of being the best-informed individual in any gathering. And, in his nephew's opinion, "he worked very hard to maintain that status. The result was that his students and colleagues regarded him with a mixture of fear and reverence."[12]

Psychology as Experimentation

To understand Titchener's stance on a variety of issues surrounding the question of what could legitimately be thought of as psychology requires an appreciation of how he conceptualized the emerging discipline. In this regard it is important to note that Titchener embraced a positivist philosophy in which psychology was conceived as wholly a natural science. He discovered positivism while a student in Leipzig and became one of a group of younger psychologists, which included Külpe and Ebbinghaus, that adopted this perspective. In doing so, Titchener placed himself squarely in opposition to Wundt, whose adherence to German idealist philosophy led him to espouse a model of psychology "which had at most one foot in the camp of the natural sciences."[13]

Titchener's commitment to positivist philosophy is revealed by his adoption of experimentation as the criterion for judging what was and what was not psychology. Very early in his career, he came to construe the role of experimentation in psychology in a way vastly different from Wundt. For Titchener, "the experimental method made a scientific psychology possible. For him questions that could not be explored using the method were not properly part of psychology."[14] In Titchener's own words, *"Experimental psychology* is just psychology; the science which describes 'mental' processes, and enumerates their conditions."[15] One of his earliest Ph.D. students, Walter Pillsbury, in an assessment of Titchener's psychology, characterized his former adviser's attitude toward experimentation as follows:

> When he came to America the extension of the experimental method became his dominant interest. He was full of enthusiasm for the laboratory and all that went with it. From the first year at Cornell he began to gather apparatus and plan new pieces for the investigations of his students. . . . He believed in the possession of apparatus and its use. He practically laid down the law for the laboratory that there is no psychology without introspection and little useful introspection without experimental aids.[16]

For Titchener, then, advancing experimentation was equivalent to advancing psychology, and there is evidence that during his early years at Cornell he was intently pursuing this aim. It is most clearly manifested in his manuals of experimental psychology, which set forth for the student and the instructor alike the background, subject matter, and methods of the psychological enterprise as interpreted by their author. It is also apparent in Titchener's idea of a club that would bring together established experimentalists and novices so that the latter would be appropriately inducted into the field, as defined by Titchener. In the following section, I will consider these endeavors of Titchener's to institutionalize psychology as experimentation.

Promoting Experimental Psychology

In his lengthy obituary of Titchener, E. G. Boring included a detailed account of the life and career of his doctoral adviser and long-time mentor. Commenting on the decade of the nineties at Cornell, Boring acclaimed it one of "remarkable accomplishment" for Titchener. In addition to building up the laboratory, directing the work of several graduate students, and giving lectures to undergraduates, he also found time for an impressive amount of scientific work and writing. He produced sixty-two articles and two books by the end of 1900 and was heavily involved in translating works by Wundt and Külpe.[17]

The manuals. The next decade was marked by a decline in Titchener's rate of publication, which Boring attributed to his involvement in a major undertaking, preparing the four volumes of his *Experimental Psychology*. These laboratory manuals, two addressed to the student and two to the instructor, represented an enormous investment of time and energy. Titchener himself worked out in the laboratory all the experiments contained in the manuals, devising procedures requiring only simple apparatus that would be available even to psychology laboratories with limited means. He revised instructions, added cautions, and modified procedures until students performing the experiments were able to obtain unequivocal results. As Boring notes, this achievement necessitated "a tremendous amount of careful, laborious work in the laboratory."[18]

The manuals were much more than a collection of painstakingly devised laboratory exercises; they also included an exhaustive up-to-date compilation of the psychological literature, which has been referred to as encyclopedic. Quoting again from Pillsbury's 1928 article on Titchener's psychology: "At the time the volumes were published they gave a summary of the results on topics treated that had probably not been equalled in any language. It is still a very useful work of reference. . . . If one desires today to look into any of the topics discussed, the literature up to the date of publication can be found accurately stated and evaluated there."[19] The companion student and instructor manuals having to do with qualitative methods were published in 1901.[20] The other two manuals, which deal with quantitative methods, occupied

Titchener for several years more, appearing in 1905.[21] Boring tersely, yet candidly, summed up the motivation behind this herculean labor thus: "What Titchener wanted to do was to establish psychology as a science."[22] In fact, the manuals can be seen as Titchener's bid to spread the word throughout the English-speaking academic world that psychology was an experimental science. As the manuals were approaching completion, Titchener launched another project, different in nature but with the same goal of promoting psychology as an experimental science.

The Club. In a printed form letter dated 15 January 1904, Titchener appealed to a select group of psychologists for their assistance in organizing "an American society for the advancement of Experimental Psychology."[23] While asserting that the field of experimental psychology in America now stood second, if to any country, only to Germany, Titchener nevertheless believed that there existed "a serious need of organization and consolidation of forces."[24] In his view, "Not only would the directors of laboratories benefit by interchange of ideas and discussion of programmes; but the younger men also—and this is a point upon which I desire to lay especial weight—would realize, by association, the community of their interests, the common dangers to which their profession is exposed, and their responsibilities to the science."[25]

Titchener disavowed any desire "to interfere with the existing American Psychological Association."[26] While crediting the twelve-year-old association (hereafter APA) with having "done admirable work for American psychology at large," he said he believed it to be "evident that the opportunities which it offers for scientific and social intercourse have not met the special requirements of Experimental Psychology."[27] Foreshadowing the restrictions that the society was to adopt regarding who it would accept as members and what was acceptable as subject matter, Titchener recommended that the club's membership "be confined to men who are working in the field of experimental psychology" and "that its discussions be confined to subjects investigated by the experimental method."[28] He expressed the hope that his readers would approve of his scheme and assured them: "The intention underlying these proposals is, very simply, that the experimentalists shall come together for a couple of days every year, to talk, think, and act nothing but Experimental Psychology."[29]

The Experimentalists

Titchener, along with certain other experimental psychologists, notably Lightner Witmer at the University of Pennsylvania, had long been dissatisfied with the APA. In fact, six years prior to Titchener's proposal, Witmer had launched an abortive attempt to found a new society limited exclusively to experimentalists. G. Stanley Hall, who had only a few years earlier hosted the founding meeting of the APA at Clark University, had written to Titchener about Witmer's plan: "A line from Witmer says that he wants to join you, me and others in forming a new Psychological organization which shall put the lab on a proper basis and exclude half breeds and extremists. Do you want to consider it?"[30] Although tentative plans were laid for an organizational meeting at Clark over the Christmas holidays, Witmer did not succeed in establishing a society of experimentalists. In his account of Witmer's failed attempt, historian of psychology C. James Goodwin comments that, ironically, it was Titchener himself who proved to be the chief stumbling block. It seems that Titchener dissuaded both Hall and Witmer from going ahead with the plan for a new society because he wished to avoid public repudiation of the APA, which the establishment of a rival society would signify. Titchener at the time suggested an alternative plan to another colleague, which, as Goodwin observes, "was virtually identical to what eventually emerged in 1904. . . . He had 'advised informal friendly gatherings of experimentalists by personal invitation, at the leading laboratories, year by year, the inviter presiding'."[31]

So it is clear that, as early as 1898, Titchener and some other psychologists were distinctly unhappy with the APA and were thinking about the possibility of forming another professional interest group. What were the grounds for their disaffection? Titchener's quarrel with the APA is often traced to its failure to respond to his request that it oust a member whom Titchener believed to be guilty of plagiarism. This led to Titchener's resignation from the APA in protest in the mid-1890s. However, Goodwin points to a more fundamental difficulty with the APA, one that Titchener shared with other experimentalists:

> It was dominated by interests other than those of experimental psychology, which Titchener took to mean the study of the basic units of human conscious experience, analyzed through the use of experimental and introspective procedures. The most notable of these other interests was philosophy. . . . Other topics outside the boundaries of Titchener's definition of 'experimental' were, for example, mental testing, child study, abnormal psychology, and animal psychology. All of these were of interest to American psychologists.[32]

Despite the long-standing displeasure of many experimental psychologists with the APA, approximately half of the fifteen responses to Titchener's form letter in 1904 expressed reservations about creating a rival society. Hugo Münsterberg was among those who questioned the need for a new psychological association. He suggested instead that Titchener rejoin the APA, confessing "I am unable to see what two psychological associations can do in this country side by side."[33] Münsterberg foresaw a major problem in trying to hold two psychological meetings each year in different locations. Reminding

Titchener that in the United States the distances that had to be traveled to meetings were so great "that no one cares to make such long trips too often," he also worried that there were too few psychologists in the country to support two meetings.[34] Münsterberg observed that there had already been "this year a regrettable conflict between the Psychological Association, which met at St. Louis, and the Philosophical Association which met at Princeton."[35] There were grounds for the concern of Münsterberg and several others that a new association might imperil the APA. The APA's twelfth annual meeting, to which he referred, had been held in a high school and had been very poorly attended, featuring just twelve papers, as compared with twenty-six the year before.

Titchener, undeterred by the objection that his proposed society would pose a threat to the already none too robust APA, issued another form letter approximately three weeks after the first. He began by claiming that "the large proportion of favourable answers" he had received "shows that the need of such an organization is keenly felt" and indicated that there was "pretty general agreement" about the features that the new society should have, listing them as follows:

(1) no fees; no officers; organization as simple as possible;

(2) membership small; meetings entirely informal;

(3) for the present at least, membership confined to men;

(4) for the present at least, no affiliation to any existing society;

(5) meetings to be held at the larger university laboratories;

(6) place and date of meetings to be so chosen as to avoid conflict with the meetings of other scientific societies;

(7) special effort to be directed towards the encouragement of grad-uate students and the younger independent workers in Experi-mental Psychology;

(8) papers, demonstrations, symposia, etc., to be strictly confined to subjects investigated by the experimental method.[36]

Granting that all these points would be "entirely open to discussion among those who accept[ed] membership in the society," Titchener asked his correspondents to indicate whether they would be willing to become active members and whether they could attend a meeting at Ithaca during the Easter vacation.[37]

That first meeting was rather sparsely attended compared with those in later years, and most of those attending (seven out of twelve), were affiliated with the host institution. It attracted representatives from the laboratories of only four other institutions—Yale, Pennsylvania, Clark, and Michigan.[38] However, the Cornell gathering was significant in that it established guidelines for future meetings, as the Experimentalists continued to meet each spring until 1928 with the exception of one year during World War I (1918). Although the group had no officers, each year there was a host, the head of one of the participating laboratories. The host sent out invitations to the heads of the other laboratories, who, in turn, invited and brought along with them some of their staff and advanced graduate students. The meetings were run informally, emphasized discussion of work in progress, and, as Titchener had envisioned, provided an unparalleled opportunity for young men just entering the profession to become acquainted with those who were already well established.[39]

Not only was the society an important communication network and source of contacts within the profession, it also, on more than one occasion, engaged in decision making that affected the profession as a whole. Two notable cases were the recommendation to the APA that it abandon the plan to host the International Congress of Psychology, which emanated from the 1910 meeting of the Experimentalists at Johns Hopkins[40] and the plans for the role of psychology in the war effort, which were formulated at the Harvard meeting in 1917.[41]

A prominent feature of the group was what Boring has labeled "Titchener's insistent regnancy. . . . Always Titchener dominated the group."[42] For example, hosts consulted Titchener about whom to invite, and, according to Boring, Titchener "was virtually the arbiter of invitations. Not only were there certain persons in certain years who were understood to be ostracized from Titchener's presence; there were also those whose status as experimentalists lay in doubt."[43] Thus it was with trepidation that Columbia's Robert S. Woodworth was invited to the 1922 meeting hosted by Raymond Dodge at Wesleyan. Boring reports that Woodworth "was in Titchener's bad graces" because, finding he could not attend the meeting at Cornell in 1920, he had posted Titchener's invitation to him on the bulletin board at Columbia "with the added query 'Who wants to go?' In Titchener's view one did not do that with invitations."[44]

As for the fate of those who strayed from the straight and narrow path of what Titchener viewed as psychology, the experience of Gordon Allport is instructive. In his autobiographical sketch, Allport tells of his single encounter with Titchener, which occurred in the early 1920s when he was a graduate student at Harvard doing his dissertation under the direction of Herbert S. Langfeld:

> I had been invited to attend the select gathering of his group of experimentalists, which met at Clark University . . . just as I was finishing my thesis. After two days of discussing problems in sensory psychology Titchener allotted three minutes to each visiting graduate to describe his own investigations. I reported on traits of personality and

> *was punished by the rebuke of total silence from the group, punctuated by a glare of disapproval from Titchener. Later Titchener demanded of Langfeld, "Why did you let him work on that problem?"*[45]

Boring, who was host for the Clark meeting, also vividly recalled the incident and Titchener's total dismissal of Allport and his work: "There was a long discussion of David Katz's modes of appearance of colors, and after that Langfeld was asked for a report and he put up Gordon Allport to tell about his analysis of personality. Allport's communication was followed by a long silence, and then Titchener said 'As we were saying, the modes of appearance of colors are . . . .'"[46]

Exclusion of Women

In addition to assuming an uncompromising stance in regard to matters of decorum and what counted as legitimate psychology, Titchener rigidly enforced a ban on women at meetings of the Experimentalists. At the time the group began, there were about two hundred scientists in North America who identified themselves as psychologists, a little over 10 percent of whom were women.[47] Of course not all the women would have qualified as experimentalists, but there were several, including some of Titchener's own students, who did. In fact, if one consults the list of fifty-six psychologists who took their doctorates with Titchener, which was appended to the obituary by Boring, one finds that slightly over one-third were women.[48] And of the group of eleven students who took their degrees with Titchener prior to the advent of the Experimentalists in 1904, six were women.

The abundance of women among Titchener's doctoral students could be attributed to institutional factors. In the 1890s, at a time when many universities were unwilling to admit women as Ph.D. candidates, Cornell not only admitted them, but, what was even more unusual, regarded them as eligible for fellowships.[49] However, it appears that Titchener was not merely tolerating an institutional policy that brought many women graduate students to Cornell. There is evidence in the prefaces of his two instructor's manuals of experimental psychology that he found many of his women students credible as potential experimentalists. In the preface to the first manual he acknowledged it as "a product of the laboratory," embodying "the work of a long roll of students."[50] Of the few students whose names he selected for mention, half (three out of six) were women. Similarly, in the preface to the second manual, he gave particular thanks to nineteen of his students, ten of whom were women.

At least two of his early woman students are known to have developed into full-fledged experimental psychologists: Margaret Floy Washburn (Ph.D. 1894) and Eleanor Acheson McCulloch Gamble (Ph.D. 1898). Washburn, who became a professor at Vassar College, was unquestionably the more eminent of the two, her research achievements winning her the distinction of being the second woman ever elected to the National Academy of Sciences, in 1931.[51] Gamble also became a respected experimental psychologist who held a professorship at Wellesley College and continued her research, teaching, and writing despite an increasingly severe visual handicap which rendered her almost blind by the time of her sudden death at the age of sixty-five. Writing to a younger male colleague in 1907, Titchener, who was not lavish in his compliments, referred to Gamble as "an old pupil of mine, and a very good psychologist."[52] Yet, the existence of accomplished women experimentalists among his own former students and elsewhere notwithstanding, Titchener felt impelled to prohibit women from his experimental club. This gesture exemplified a gender-biased attitude painfully familiar to educated women in that era who were seeking access to the academic and scientific professions in general and to psychology in particular.[53]

The first form letter distributed by Titchener in mid-January 1904 was somewhat ambiguous regarding the status of women in the Experimentalists, stating: "that . . . membership be confined to men who are working in the field of experimental psychology."[54] The word *men* could have been interpreted generically in the context of the letter. In the next form letter, sent out in early February, Titchener outlined the features of his new society, and the third point in the list left no room for doubt: "For the present at least, membership confined to men."[55] As can be seen from the quote at the beginning of this chapter, Titchener's letter to Münsterberg in late January was also explicit about excluding women from his proposed club. Titchener's incoming correspondence during January and February 1904 contains only three letters which refer to the plan to exclude women from the group: two psychologists mildly questioned the policy, and one strongly endorsed it. But the bulk of the correspondence was silent on the issue.

E. C. Sanford at Clark felt caught in a dilemma, because he knew that there were women experimental psychologists who should be invited to the meetings, yet feared that their presence would be an inhibiting influence on the men.

> *The question with regard to women in the association is a poser. Several of them on scientific grounds have full right to be there and might feel hurt (in a general impersonal way) if women are not asked. On the other hand they would undoubtedly interfere with the smoking and to a certain extent with the general freedom of a purely masculine assembly. Would it be possible to give them also the chance to say whether they would like to come—assuring them by a personal note that transactions would not come off except in a partially smoke-charged atmosphere?[56]*

While in basic agreement with Titchener's proposal for the new society, a psychologist at the University of Toronto, August Kirschmann, did express some sympathy for the plight of the women: "I find it a little hard on ladies who take an interest in Experimental Psychology if we exclude them altogether."[57] Lightner Witmer also regretted that the ban on women meant "excluding a number of very capable experimentalists" yet felt compelled to support it, explaining his position as follows:

> *I am quite positive in my objection to inviting women. . . . I am sure*
> *from my experience, that you cannot run an informal meeting of men*
> *and women. . . . We want a small vigorous association where we can*
> *speak our minds with perfect freedom. . . . The larger and more het-*
> *erogeneous the organization the more likely is vigorous discussion to*
> *be misinterpreted and to be taken as an offence by individuals who*
> *may happen to be attacked. I think that the presence of women in*
> *the organization adds greatly to this danger, owing to the personal*
> *attitude which they usually take even in scientific discussions. I favor*
> *a small association, no invited guests, and no women members.*[58]

There was thus virtually no opposition from his correspondents to Titchener's policy of excluding women from the Experimentalists' meetings, even though it was freely admitted by Titchener and others—including Sanford, Kirschmann, and Witmer—that there were several women who in terms of scientific credentials warranted inclusion. Furthermore, as mentioned earlier, Titchener himself had numerous women doctorate students, beginning with his first graduate student at Cornell, Margaret Floy Washburn.

Titchener never explained why women were unacceptable as members of his society. That he wanted above all to have free, informal interchange between older and younger men in the area of experimental psychology, with the goal of socializing the next generation into the profession, seems clear. Sanford and Witmer both suggest that the presence of women would interfere with this process, and it is a fair assumption that Titchener thought so too.

The exclusionary policy remained in effect throughout Titchener's lifetime with, it seems, little, if any, protest from the other men in the group. Only two recorded incidents from the early years of the society could be interpreted as challenges to his position, and even these are open to other interpretations. The first involved James Rowland Angell of the University of Chicago. Angell, invited to the inaugural meeting of the Experimentalists, did not attend. He did contribute a paper, however, and perhaps it is significant that it was written by a woman graduate student, Matilde Castro.[59] The other incident took place at the meeting held at the University of Pennsylvania in 1907. Titchener later described the event in a letter to Münsterberg, telling him that James Leuba, a professor at Bryn Mawr College, had sent some of his women students to the meeting. Titchener indicated to Münsterberg that the "girls" were "promptly turned out," and he dismissed the whole incident as a "sheer misunderstanding."[60]

The only unambiguous protest to Titchener's exclusionary policy came from Christine Ladd-Franklin, a woman who was unquestionably qualified to be a member of the group in terms of scientific credentials. Twenty years Titchener's senior, Ladd-Franklin had completed her doctoral studies in mathematics and logic at Johns Hopkins in 1882.[61] Soon after, she had developed an interest in the topic of vision and had published a paper on binocular vision in 1887, in the first volume of the *American Journal of Psychology*.[62] In 1891–92 she had had the opportunity to study in Europe, carrying out experimental work on vision in the laboratory of G. E. Müller in Göttingen. She had also traveled to Berlin, where she had worked in Helmholtz's laboratory and attended the lectures of Arthur König. By the conclusion of her year of study, Ladd-Franklin had worked out her own theory of color vision, an evolutionarily based model, which she had presented to the International Congress of Psychology in London.

Her marriage to Fabian Franklin, a member of the mathematics faculty at Johns Hopkins, just after she had completed her doctoral work there, had foreclosed the possibility of an academic career. In that era married women were not viewed by institutional authorities as suitable candidates for those academic positions that were open to women.[63] Only through persistent effort was Ladd-Franklin able to secure appointments to teach some courses in her areas of specialization at Johns Hopkins and at Columbia, albeit intermittently and on a part-time basis. But in spite of her marginal institutional base, she managed to remain active in scientific pursuits throughout her lifetime, promoting her theory of color vision, conducting research on vision, attending and giving papers at meetings, and publishing. She was labeled "a remarkable woman" by one of her younger colleagues at Columbia, R. S. Woodworth.[64] He was impressed not only by "her keen logical mind" and "power of criticism," but also by her vitality, the zeal with which she promoted her views, and "her cheerful aggressiveness."[65]

Ladd-Franklin began corresponding with Titchener in 1892, as soon as he arrived in the United States to take up his post at Cornell. Both were endowed with dominating personalities, which would be pitted against each other twenty years later in a contest over the policy of exclusion of women from the Experimentalists. In 1912 Ladd-Franklin, perhaps the most outspoken of the women psychologists of that era in her feminist views, reacted incredulously when Titchener first barred her from a meeting of the Experimentalists that she wanted to attend.[66] She had written to ask if she might present a paper at his April meeting. "I am particularly anxious to bring my views up, once in a while, for hand-to-hand discussion before experts, and just now I have especially a paper which I should like very much to read before your meeting of experimental psychologists. I hope you will not say nay!"[67]

Titchener's reply has not been preserved, but the surviving evidence suggests that he wrote informing Ladd-Franklin that women were not welcome to attend the Experimentalists' meetings. Her next letter to Titchener conveys her indignant reaction to this discriminatory practice: "I am shocked to know that you are still—at this year—excluding women from your meeting of experimental psychologists. It is such a very old-fashioned standpoint!"[68] She also pointed out how irrational it was for Titchener to invite to that year's meeting at Clark University "the students of G. Stanley Hall, who are not in the least experimentalists and exclude the women who are doing particularly good work in the experimental laboratory of Professor Baird."[69] She was also unwilling to accept the notion that it was legitimate to exclude women from the meetings because they would interfere with the men's smoking: "Have your smokers separated if you like (tho I for one always smoke when I am in fashionable society), but a scientific meeting (however personal) is a public affair, and it is not open to you to leave out a class of fellow workers without extreme discourtesy."[70]

Although Ladd-Franklin failed to persuade Titchener to let her attend the Experimentalists' gathering at Clark, she did not admit defeat on the matter. Two years later the Experimentalists decided to meet at Columbia, where Ladd-Franklin was teaching courses in logic and color vision. Shortly before the meeting, she wrote to Titchener, thanking him for having referred to her as belonging to the group of psychologists that "had some logic in them."[71] In view of this compliment, she considered it all the more contradictory that Titchener should persist in excluding her from his Experimentalists' meetings: "Is this then a good time, my dear Professor Titchener, for you to hold to the mediaeval attitude of not admitting me to your coming psychological conference in New York—at my very door? So unconscientious, so immoral,—worse than that—so unscientific!"[72] It seems that Ladd-Franklin was permitted to attend one session at the Columbia meeting. At the others, according to Boring's account, "tradition was kept supreme."[73] In spite of the fact that Ladd-Franklin persisted in protesting Titchener's policy until at least 1916, when she attempted to enlist John B. Watson in her cause, tradition indeed remained supreme.[74]

Nor did the group rush to open its doors to women immediately after Titchener died in 1927. In 1928, the committee of five charged with the task of developing a plan for reorganizing the society hesitated to break with the traditional ban on women members. Although two women—Margaret Floy Washburn and June Etta Downey—were discussed favorably, the committee "decided not to prejudice this issue" and declined to elect any women that year.[75] The next year the organizing committee was enlarged, and in

1929 it met at Princeton, where several important decisions were made regarding the future of the society. In keeping with tradition, the society was
to be restricted to experimental psychologists meeting "for the purpose of informal discussion."[76] However, in a break with the past, the group also decided
"that there should be no restriction of membership with regard to sex."[77]

The Experimentalists reconstituted themselves as the Society of Experimental Psychologists at the Princeton meeting. The charter group consisted
of twenty-six members, among them Washburn and Downey. Downey, a
professor and chair of the Department of Psychology and Philosophy at the
University of Wyoming, was never to attend a meeting; in her mid-fifties
when elected, she died suddenly just three years later.[78] Washburn, a professor
at Vassar College, was in her late fifties when admitted to the society. Although
she had the opportunity to host the society for its 1931 meeting, her participation in the group was cut short when, in 1937, she suffered an incapacitating
cerebral stroke from which she never recovered.[79]

By the late thirties, then, neither of the women elected to the society in
1929 remained in the group, and no other women had been elected to membership. This dearth of women in the society was not a temporary phenomenon. A group photo taken in 1947, twenty years after Titchener's death,
when the society met at Princeton, shows thirty-nine psychologists, all men.

In fact, it was not until 1958 that another woman, Eleanor J. Gibson, was
admitted to the society. And as recently as the early 1970s, the membership
list of the organization showed only one more woman, Dorothea Jameson
Hurvich, added to the rolls in 1970. In both cases, their spouses had belonged
to the group for over a decade before they were elected to membership,[80]
which suggests that sponsorship and access to the communication network of
the group provided by a spouse were key ingredients in their election to membership.

In summary, the elite society organized by E. B. Titchener in 1904 to promote
psychology as an experimental science provided an important communication
network and opportunities for contact among a select group of established
and neophyte psychologists. Collegial relationships were fostered, and knowledge was shared at the annual meetings. The gatherings also, on more than
one occasion, served as a forum for decision making that would affect the
larger profession. For over two decades, Titchener dominated this group, in-
sisting, among other things, that the subject matter of the meetings be confined
strictly to what he defined as experimental psychology. Also by Titchener's
fiat, and with the acquiescence of the other members, certain groups of psychologists, such as women and those not considered experimentalists, were
excluded from the meetings. The evidence suggests that this prolonged policy
of social ostracism took a heavy toll on women's participation and advancement

in experimental psychology. Deprived because of their gender of the collegial ties and informal communication so vital to the successful pursuit of experimental work, they faced virtually insurmountable obstacles to advancing their careers as scientists.

The cost to experimental psychology of losing women as practitioners is more difficult to assess. I would like to suggest, however, that by excluding women, the subfield may have deprived itself of a perspective recently articulated by a group of women scholars who regard it as a distinctively, but not exclusively, feminine approach to knowledge. What Belenky, Clinchy, Goldberger, and Tarule describe as "women's ways of knowing" stand in sharp contrast to the masculine approach to scientific knowledge (epitomized by Titchener), with its emphasis on objectivity, detachment, control, and domination.[81] The epistemological orientation associated with this masculine approach, which Belenky and her colleagues call "separate knowing," is tough-minded, being based on impersonal procedures for establishing truth. The more typically feminine epistemological orientation that Belenky and her co-workers call "connected knowing," is an approach that places a premium on learning through empathy and involves intimacy and equality between the self and the object of study. If Titchener's group had allowed participation by women, with their special ways of knowing, who is to say how profoundly different the subfield of experimental psychology might have become? But to imagine that is another story.

Notes

1. Letter from E. B. Titchener to Hugo Münsterberg, 1 Feb. 1904, Münsterberg Papers, Boston Public Library.
2. For an inquiry into how the epistemological authority of scientific specialists is brought to bear in social arrangements inside and outside science, see Kathryn Pyne Addelson, "The Man of Professional Wisdom," in *Discovering Reality: Feminist Perspectives on Epistemology, Metaphysics, Methodology, and Philosophy of Science,* ed. Sandra Harding and Merrill B. Hintikka (Dordrecht: Reidel, 1983), pp. 165–86.
3. For an insightful discussion of how women scientists are hindered in their research role by restricted access to the informal communication system in science and to informal contacts among colleagues, see Barbara F. Reskin, "Sex Differentiation and the Social Organization of Science," *Social Inquiry* 48 (1978):6–37.
4. Arthur L. Blumenthal, "Shaping a Tradition: Experimentalism Begins," in *Points of View in the Modern History of Psychology,* ed. Claude E. Buxton (Orlando, Fla.: Academic Press, 1985), p. 71.
5. Rand B. Evans, "Edward Bradford Titchener: A Sketch" (brochure printed by the American Psychological Association to accompany a photographic exhibit on E. B. Titchener, 1 Nov. 1972–1 Apr. 1973, and an exhibit of memorabilia,

Apr. 1973–1 Oct. 1973, located in the headquarters of the APA, Washington, D.C.), p. 1.
6. Ibid., p. 2.
7. Frank Angell, "Titchener at Leipzig, *Journal of General Psychology* 1 (1928):198.
8. Howard C. Warren, in A *History of Psychology in Autobiography*, vol. 1, ed. Carl Murchison (Worcester, Mass.: Clark University Press, 1930), p. 451.
9. Titchener to Hunter, 24 Jan. 1907, Titchener Papers, Department of Manuscripts and University Archives, Cornell University Libraries.
10. Edwin G. Boring, "Edward Bradford Titchener 1867–1927," *American Journal of Psychology* 38 (1927):493.
11. Raymond F. Howes, "Recollections of E. B. Titchener," *Cornell Alumni News*, Apr. 1969, p. 20.
12. Ibid., pp. 21–22.
13. Kurt Danziger, "The Positivist Repudiation of Wundt," *Journal of the History of the Behavioral Sciences* 15 (1979):205. For other recent scholarship that discusses the differences between Wundtian and Titchenerian psychology, see Arthur L. Blumenthal, "Wilhelm Wundt: Psychology as the Propaedeutic Science," in *Points of View in the Modern History of Psychology*, ed. Claude E. Buxton (Orlando, Fla.: Academic Press, 1985), pp. 19–50; Thomas H. Leahey, "The Mistaken Mirror: On Wundt's and Titchener's Psychologies," *Journal of the History of the Behavioral Sciences* 17 (1981):273–82; and Ryan D. Tweney and Stephen A. Yachanin, "Titchener's Wundt," in *Wundt Studies: A Centennial Collection*, ed. Wolfgang G. Bringmann and Ryan D. Tweney (Toronto: C. J. Hogrefe, 1980), pp. 380–95.
14. Tweney and Yachanin, "Titchener's Wundt," p. 388.
15. E. B. Titchener, "Some Current Problems in Experimental Psychology," *Natural Science* 4 (1894):446.
16. W. B. Pillsbury, "The Psychology of Edward Bradford Titchener," *Philosophical Review* 37 (1928):97.
17. Boring, "Titchener," p. 494.
18. Ibid., p. 497.
19. Pillsbury, "Psychology of Titchener," pp. 99–100.
20. E. B. Titchener, *Experimental Psychology: A Manual of Laboratory Practice*, vol. 1, *Qualitative Experiments*, part 1, *Students' Manual*; part 2, *Instructor's Manual* (London: Macmillan, 1901).
21. E. B. Titchener, *Experimental Psychology: A Manual of Laboratory Practice*, vol. 2, *Quantitative Experiments*, part 1, *Students' Manual*; part 2, *Instructor's Manual* (London: Macmillan, 1905).
22. Boring, "Titchener," p. 497.
23. "E. B. Titchener and the Beginnings of the Society of Experimental Psychologists," *Newsletter of the Division of the History of Psychology: American Psychological Association* 13, no. 2 (1981):17.
24. Ibid.
25. Ibid.
26. Ibid.

27. Ibid.
28. Ibid.
29. Ibid.
30. Quoted by C. James Goodwin, "On the Origins of Titchener's Experimentalists," *Journal of the History of the Behavioral Sciences*, 21 (1985):386.
31. Ibid.
32. Ibid., p. 384.
33. Münsterberg to Titchener, 30 Jan. 1904, Titchener Papers.
34. Ibid.
35. Ibid.
36. "Titchener and the Society of Experimental Psychologists," p. 18.
37. Ibid.
38. C. H. Judd, "Meeting of Experimental Psychologists at Cornell University," *Journal of Philosophy, Psychology and Scientific Methods* 1 (1904):238–40.
39. Edwin G. Boring, "The Society of Experimental Psychologists: 1904–1938," *American Journal of Psychology* 51 (1938):410–21.
40. See Pillsbury to Titchener, 26 Apr. 1910, Titchener Papers.
41. See Robert M. Yerkes, ed., *Psychological Examining in the United States Army*, Memoirs of the National Academy of Sciences, vol. 15 (Washington: Government Printing Office, 1921), p. 7.
42. Boring, "Society of Experimental Psychologists," p. 410.
43. Ibid.
44. Ibid., p. 415.
45. Gordon W. Allport, in *A History of Psychology in Autobiography*, vol. 5, ed. Edwin G. Boring and Gardner Lindzey (New York: Appleton-Century-Crofts, 1967), p. 9.
46. Edwin G. Boring, "Titchener's Experimentalists," *Journal of the History of the Behavioral Sciences* 3 (1967):323.
47. For an account of these early women psychologists, see Laurel Furumoto and Elizabeth Scarborough, "Placing Women in the History of Psychology: The First American Women Psychologists," *American Psychologist* 41 (1986):35–42.
48. Boring, "Titchener," p. 506.
49. For discussions of the struggles of women to gain access to graduate education in the late nineteenth century, see Margaret W. Rossiter, *Women Scientists in America: Struggles and Strategies to 1940* (Baltimore: Johns Hopkins University Press, 1982), and Elizabeth Scarborough and Laurel Furumoto, *Untold Lives: The First Generation of American Women Psychologists* (New York: Columbia University Press, 1987).
50. Titchener, *Experimental Psychology*, vol. 1, part 2, p. vii.
51. See Scarborough and Furumoto, *Untold Lives*, pp. 91–107, for an account of Washburn's life and career.
52. Titchener to Hunter, 24 Jan. 1907, Titchener Papers.
53. For detailed accounts of the obstacles confronting women aspiring to careers in the sciences and more particularly the social sciences and psychology in the late nineteenth and early twentieth centuries, see Rossiter, *Women Scientists*, (for

women scientists, in general), Rosalind Rosenberg, *Beyond Separate Spheres: Intellectual Roots of Modern Feminism* (New Haven: Yale University Press, 1982) (for women in the social sciences), and Scarborough and Furumoto, *Untold Lives* (for women psychologists).

54. "Titchener and the Society of Experimental Psychologists," p. 17.
55. Ibid., p. 18.
56. Edmund C. Sanford to Titchener, 19 Jan. 1904, Titchener Papers.
57. August Kirschmann to Titchener, 5 Mar. 1904, Titchener Papers.
58. Lightner Witmer to Titchener, 25 Jan. 1904, Titchener Papers.
59. C. H. Judd, "Meeting of Experimental Psychologists," p. 240.
60. Titchener r to Münsterberg, 29 Feb. 1908, Münsterberg Papers.
61. Johns Hopkins refused to grant her the degree she had earned because she was a woman. On the occasion of its fiftieth anniversary in 1926, it belatedly awarded Ladd-Franklin the Ph.D. For a fuller account of Ladd-Franklin's life and experience at Johns Hopkins, see Elizabeth Scarborough and Laurel Furumoto, *Untold Lives*, pp. 119–24.
62. Christine Ladd-Franklin, "A Method for the Experimental Determination of the Horopter," *American Journal of Psychology* 1 (1887):99–111.
63. See Scarborough and Furumoto, *Untold Lives*, pp. 71–90, for a more detailed discussion of the marriage-versus-career dilemma faced by highly educated women in the late nineteenth and early twentieth centuries.
64. R. S. Woodworth, "Christine Ladd-Franklin," *Science* 71 (1930):307.
65. Ibid.
66. See Scarborough and Furumoto, *Untold Lives*, pp. 109–12, for an account of Ladd-Franklin's feminist stance.
67. Christine Ladd-Franklin to Titchener, undated, Christine Ladd-Franklin and Fabian Franklin Papers, Butler Library, Columbia University.
68. Ladd-Franklin to Titchener, undated, Christine Ladd-Franklin and Fabian Franklin Papers.
69. Ibid.
70. Ibid.
71. Ladd-Franklin to Titchener, 21 Mar. 1914, Christine Ladd-Franklin and Fabian Franklin Papers.
72. Ibid.
73. Boring, "Society of Experimental Psychologists," p. 414.
74. See John B. Watson to Ladd-Franklin, 14 Apr. 1916 and 18 Apr. 1916, Christine Ladd-Franklin and Fabian Franklin Papers.
75. Boring, "Society of Experimental Psychologists," p. 417.
76. Ibid., p. 418.
77. Ibid.
78. For a fuller account of Downey's life and career, see Christina Van Horn and Laurel Furumoto, "June Etta Downey: The Psychologist, the Poet, and the Person" (Unpublished manuscript).
79. See Scarborough and Furumoto, *Untold Lives*, pp. 91–107.
80. "Report of the Society of Experimental Psychologists, Inc., 1971–72," David

Krech Papers, Archives of the History of American Psychology, University of Akron, Ohio.

81. Mary Field Belenky, Blythe McVicker Clinchy, Nancy Goldberger, and Jill Mattuck Tarule, *Women's Ways of Knowing: The Development of Self, Voice, and Mind* (New York: Basic Books, 1986). For an analysis of the gendered nature of science, see Evelyn Fox Keller, *Reflections on Gender and Science* (New Haven: Yale University Press, 1985), and the insightful review of Keller's book by Jill G. Morawski, "Toward Science without Gender," *Contemporary Psychology* 31 (1986):95–96.

6

The Hawthorne
Experiments and
the Politics of
Experimentation

Richard Gillespie
University of
Melbourne

From its inception, modern psychology has marked its progress by the degree to which it could apply the experimental method. Psychologists mark the birth of the discipline by the dates on which psychological laboratories were established: by Wilhelm Wundt at Leipzig in 1879 and by G. Stanley Hall at Johns Hopkins in 1883. E. G. Boring's influential history of experimental psychology began with a chapter on the evolution of scientific method and measured psychology's progress by the extent to which it had purged philosophy and absorbed in its place the ethos and methods of the natural sciences. The founders of American psychology and the generations that followed assumed that experimentation and measurement would guarantee the development of a body of objective knowledge, permit the establishment of an applied science, and give psychology an intellectual and professional status equal to that of the natural sciences.[1]

The common assumption among social and behavioral scientists, as among natural scientists, is that their social power derives from their command of a body of objective knowledge, which in turn is derived from scientific experimentation. Yet historical and sociological studies suggest that the relationship between knowledge and power is more complex. Scientific knowledge has come to seem an increasingly contingent phenomenon, a construction that reflects ideological commitments, cultural and national styles, and local technical conditions. Scientific method should be seen not as providing a universal technique for the generation of objective knowledge, but rather, as a flexible resource, a highly variable collection of epistemological assumptions and experimental techniques that are themselves shaped by scientists' social values and their commitment to particular scientific beliefs. This is not to say that scientific knowledge can be reduced to the political beliefs of the experimenters, but that social factors are an intrinsic part of scientific knowledge. At the same time, scientists' claims that they are discovering objective facts and laws are perceived to be the professional ideology of a group whose status rests on society's acceptance of their expertise. Thus there is a dialectical relationship between knowledge and power: scientists' social power derives from their control of a body of supposedly objective knowledge; yet that very knowledge is accepted as objective only if scientists already have sufficient power within their discipline and in the broader society.[2]

Scientific experimentation constitutes a screen that conceals the interpenetration of scientific knowledge with its social and political context. Without even being aware of the process, scientists bring to their research a set of political values and technical goals that shape both their theories and their experimental observations. Far from creating a scientific knowledge free of social and political values, the experimental process serves to conceal and reify those values. This is of particular importance in the social and behavioral sciences, for here it is social relations themselves that are refracted through the process of scientific experimentation and presented to us as objective, value-free scientific knowledge.[3]

In this chapter I will demonstrate the political character of scientific experimentation through an analysis of the history of the Hawthorne experiments. They make a particularly appropriate subject because, first, they were among the earliest and remain among the most renowned large-scale experiments in the social and behavioral sciences—indeed, they have acquired the status of a creation myth in social psychology and in the subdisciplines of industrial and organizational psychology, management theory, industrial sociology, industrial psychiatry, and the anthropology of work. Second, they seem to exemplify the importance of experimentation; they are acclaimed, in psychology and sociology textbooks and elsewhere, because they capture the excitement and surprise of experimental findings overturning the cherished assumptions of experimenters, of stunning and totally unexpected discoveries emerging from the careful application of the scientific method.

But the extension of the laboratory into the factory and the resulting experimentation constituted an essentially political process, for the science and politics of work are inseparable. Industrial managers and researchers believed that scientific experimentation on the organization of work and industrial relations would provide a body of objective knowledge that could be applied impartially in the work place, thereby reducing conflict between labor and capital. However, as we shall see, the experimenters accepted in large measure the work-place relations of industrial capitalism and repeatedly rejected the viewpoint of workers. In so doing, they unconsciously reified management ideology so that it became scientific knowledge. The scientific findings of the Hawthorne experiments thus reflected the political values of the experimenters and the employers and provided techniques and a scientific ideology for an intensification of production and supervision.

The most effective way of demonstrating the political character of the Hawthorne experiments is to compare the standard account, as presented in the official reports of the experiments, with a historical interpretation based on the original experimental records and the papers and correspondence of the researchers. Where the official publications describe a process of scientific discovery arising from careful experimentation, a close examination of the archival records reveals that practical concerns and ideological commitments permeated the very process of experimentation and interpretation of experimental results.[4]

The Standard Account

The official accounts of the Hawthorne experiments, echoed in histories and textbooks, are beguilingly straightforward and unproblematic. We are informed that between 1924 and 1933 managers at the Hawthorne works of Western Electric Company, in collaboration with Elton Mayo and his colleagues at the Harvard Business School, conducted a series of experiments on worker productivity, job satisfaction, and work-place organization. They began by attempting to measure the effects of varying levels of lighting on the production of several groups of workers, assuming that increased lighting would result in higher production. However, it proved impossible to isolate the effects of changes in lighting from many other variables; indeed, when lighting levels were reduced, the workers' production actually remained the same or increased, contrary to both common sense and the expectations of the researchers. This extraordinary result drove the researchers to conduct further experiments, all of which attempted in some way to identify those other variables and to assess their importance for production.[5]

In the relay assembly test room study, the most famous of the experiments, the researchers aimed at isolating, through experimental control, the other factors affecting production and worker satisfaction. Six women were placed in a test room, where their production, working conditions, health, and social interactions were carefully monitored. Production increased as the researchers introduced improvements in working conditions, such as rest periods and a shorter working day; at the same time, the workers expressed satisfaction with the improvements and attributed the rise in production to these experimental changes. But when, in the crucial twelfth test period, the researchers removed the special conditions, production continued to increase! One of the researchers later described this moment as "the great *éclaircissement*, the new illumination, that came from the research."[6] It seemed that the workers' attitude to their work was as important, perhaps more important, than the changes in working conditions. Separated from their fellow workers and given special attention by researchers and supervisors, the workers had responded so enthusiastically that the total experimental environment had overwhelmed the individual changes in conditions. This subsequently became known as the "Hawthorne effect."

The researchers then developed a new series of experiments, all designed to explore this new insight. A massive program of interviewing the factory workers revealed, we are told, that complaints about working conditions and supervision could not be taken at face value but must be understood in the context of the workers' personalities; workers brought to the factory a host of attitudes and sentiments that shaped their reactions to the work environment. A second study, involving close observation of a group of bank-wiring workers in an experimental setting much closer to a normal working environment than had obtained in the relay assembly test, revealed the existence of an informal social group among the workers. The most dramatic effect of this informal group was that it restricted output and to a degree protected the workers from the directives of engineers and supervisors. In sum, the researchers claimed that the experiments provided scientific evidence that managers must look beyond the technical organization of the factory; productivity and the behavior of workers were influenced as much by personal attitudes and informal social organization as by formal lines of organization and authority.

The most striking feature of the standard account of the Hawthorne experiments is its emphasis on the drama of scientific discovery, of comfortable assumptions being overturned by the force of unexpected and irrefutable scientific evidence. The authors of *Management and the Worker*, the most detailed of the official accounts, stress that in addition to reporting the experimental results, theoretical conclusions, and practical applications of the experiments, they are presenting a history of the process of discovery. Here, the reader is assured, is an objective history of the experiments, a narrative made all the more authentic because it reports the "trials and tribulations of a research investigator" and bears "the stamp of human imperfection."[7] The description of the experimental process is presented as an assurance of the objectivity of the knowledge produced. Yet this standard account is thoroughly misleading, for it conceals the complex process by which scientific knowledge was constructed out of the web of confusing data and conflicting interpretations. In the following sections I will contrast the standard account of *discovery* with an alternative interpretation based on archival sources, which emphasizes the *construction* of scientific knowledge.

Lighting Tests

The lighting tests at Hawthorne were part of a larger research program designed to demonstrate the importance of higher levels of electric lighting for industrial efficiency. Conducted under the auspices of the government's National Research Council (NRC), the research was funded by electrical manufacturers and utilities, who expected that a committee of engineers and psychologists would provide scientific data which could be used to establish industrial lighting codes. Between 1924 and 1927 Western Electric engineers and electrical engineers from Massachusetts Institute of Technology (MIT) conducted a series of three tests on the relationship between levels of lighting and levels of production, with mixed results. The researchers found it next to impossible to control the many other factors that seemed to affect production and thus could not isolate the influence of levels of illumination.[8]

The third set of tests provided the clearest evidence of the difficulty of isolating variables. Two groups of coil-winders were matched so that their skill and average production were equal. In one section of a divided test room the control group worked under a steady illumination of 11 foot-candles throughout the test, while in the other section the test group was subjected to progressively lower levels of lighting. Production in both control and test groups increased slightly, the test group maintaining its output in the face of decreasing illumination, complaining only when the lighting had been reduced to 1.4 foot-candles. Fritz Roethlisberger, who was to become one of the central figures in the Hawthorne experiments, but who was not involved in the early research, later commented that after the lighting tests "a few of the tougher minded experimenters already were beginning to suspect their basic ideas and assumptions with regard to human motivation." Most later commentators have echoed this view of the lighting tests, seeing them as exemplifying the triumph of the human factors studied by psychologists and sociologists over the mechanistic, economic assumptions of engineers and managers.[9]

A closer examination of the surviving records of the lighting tests shows that the engineers conducting the research were aware of the importance of psychological factors from the very beginning however. In a report to the NRC prior to the commencement of the Hawthorne tests, for example, the chairman of the lighting committee, MIT electrical engineer Dugald C. Jackson, had raised the following questions to be resolved in the experimental design: "How can the human equation be eliminated or properly recorded, such as the antagonistic attitude of workers, effect of the physical condition, effect of their habits outside working hours, etc?"[10] The significance of the lighting tests was not, as the standard account has it, that the results forced the researchers to recognize the importance of psychological and social factors. Rather, the tests demonstrated the great difficulty of *controlling* variables such as psychological interest among workers, variations in supervision between groups, and competition between control and test groups. Far from the researchers being surprised by the fact that the coil-winders had maintained production in the face of inadequate lighting, they had actually predicted it; indeed such a prediction had been a necessary part of the experimental protocol, since the test was designed to set a lower limit on lighting levels. The experimenters fully expected that the skill of the workers, combined with the incentive to maintain production in order to sustain their earnings, would combine to keep production steady until the lighting became impossibly low, for "with each succeeding decrease in illumination the tendency will be to work harder and harder."[11]

How then did the lighting tests influence the progress of the Hawthorne experiments? Clearly it was not because test results revealed to previously ignorant managers the importance of supervision, wage schemes, worker solidarity, or the human factor. Management had long been manipulating such factors on a daily basis—in the case of worker solidarity either by trying to break collective restriction of output or by attempting to turn it to account through the introduction of group payment schemes. But the tests did suggest to the Hawthorne managers that their traditional skills in the organization and supervision of work could be subjected to scientific experimentation.[12]

The introduction of experimental methods to the study of the organization of work had started prior to the Hawthorne experiments, of course. Frederick Winslow Taylor had published his *Principles of Scientific Management* in 1911, in which he reported his experiments with time and motion studies and the rationalization of work. Taylor claimed that through the careful regulation of when and how work was performed, he had quadrupled the daily production of a pig-iron handler. At the same time, several liberal European industrialists had experimented with shorter hours of work and the introduction of rest periods and had demonstrated that workers were capable of producing as much in eight hours as in twelve. These investigations culminated in a concerted program of research on "industrial fatigue" during and after World War I, conducted for the most part under government auspices, in which physiologists and psychologists studied the physical and mental aspects of industrial fatigue and sought to alter industrial operations and work-place conditions so as to reduce fatigue and increase production. At the same time, applied psychologists had demonstrated during the war that their skills could be of great benefit in the selection and classification of personnel. As a result, the new field of industrial psychology flourished in the early 1920s. The decision by Hawthorne managers to continue experimentation after the cessation of the NRC's lighting tests reflected an interest in such industrial investigations. Moreover, as manufacturing subsidiary of American Telephone and Telegraph (AT&T) and co-owner of Bell Telephone Laboratories, the huge industrial research organization, Western Electric was imbued with the value of scientific and industrial research.[13]

Relay Assembly Test Room

Before the lighting tests were finished, the Hawthorne managers had decided to continue experimenting, using the test room constructed for the third test and the experience of several Hawthorne engineers. The managers listed the following problems that they hoped would be answered by the new tests:

1. *Why does output drop in the afternoon?*
2. *Do operators actually get tired out?*
3. *Desirability of establishing rest periods.*
4. *Changes in equipment.*
5. *What is the attitude of the operators?*
6. *Effects of a shorter working day on output.*[14]

These were standard questions regarding the relationship between fatigue and production, drawn from the extensive literature on the subject, and were not, as the standard account of the experiments would have us believe, an attempt to break through the "puzzling" results of the lighting tests.

The Hawthorne managers were not particularly interested in the analysis of fatigue, however, or in furthering scientific knowledge. Their concern was the organization of production in their own factory and determination of the most efficient conditions for specific industrial processes. AT&T's decision to introduce machine-switching, automatic telephone exchanges had meant that Western Electric was required to manufacture 200 new pieces of equipment involving some 36,000 manufacturing operations. By 1922 separate time standards and piece rates departments had been established within the technical branch, whose task was to determine the cheapest and fastest manufacturing methods. It was the superintendent of the technical branch, George Pennock, who had made the decision to establish the relay assembly test room. The reason for choosing relay assembly for the study seems to have been that it involved the kind of highly repetitive, labor-intensive work most commonly associated with fatigue, and because the assembly of relays for the telephone system absorbed large numbers of semiskilled workers at the plant. By the late 1920s Hawthorne was producing over seven million relays a year, and while most of the parts could be produced by highly specialized machines, the thirty-five or more parts for each relay had to be assembled by hand, adjusted, and inspected—all labor-intensive operations in which the speed of the individual assembler determined productivity.[15]

The researchers' interest in a close analysis of individual productivity was reflected in the design of the test room. Five relay-assemblers sat side by side at a bench; to their right a sixth worker, the layout operator, prepared trays of relay parts for the five to assemble. The finished relay was dropped down a chute in the bench in front of each worker, where it triggered a recording mechanism to punch a hole in a paper tape moving at constant speed. The strips of paper thus recorded the individual production time for each relay and the total production for each worker. Across the test room sat two experimenters, a piece-rate engineer and a clerk, who supervised the workers and prepared two documents. A log sheet recorded work times, personal time out for each operator, time taken for preparing relays that failed inspection, time spent waiting for parts, and other fluctuations in production. Every fifteen minutes the output tape was counted, and the totals were entered. A "daily history record" was kept as a diary of the test; in it, the experimenters recorded changes in test procedures, observations of workers' behavior, and workers' remarks. This latter record is an invaluable source for the historian trying to understand the social and political dynamics of the relay test. Nor did the investigation stop at the test room; the experimenters questioned the six workers about their home life, families, and social activities, inspected their employment records, and arranged for monthly physical examinations at the factory hospital.[16]

The organization of the test periods reflected the engineers' interest in rest periods and hours of work. After establishing a base production rate for the five assemblers by checking their production in the regular department, the researchers moved the workers into the test room for a period of acclimatization in May 1927. In the third period they were shifted onto a special group rate of payment, in which, instead of sharing the bonus of the regular department, they kept for themselves any bonuses accruing from increased production in the test room. This change was introduced to ensure the cooperation of the workers. The subsequent eight test periods, from August 1927 to September 1928, experimented with a variety of rest periods and shorter hours of work. Average hourly output for the group increased in every period in the test room except one, from 49.4 relays per hour at the beginning to a maximum of 64.1 relays in the ninth test period.

It did not take long for the workers to realize that their special position endowed them with hitherto undreamed-of power. They had become a privileged elite among relay-assemblers, even among the entire Hawthorne work force; they participated in meetings about the progress of the test in the office of one of the plant managers, during which their opinions were earnestly solicited; and they were provided with free morning tea and enjoyed rest periods and shorter hours of work. But they nevertheless saw room for improvement in their working conditions and began to demand further changes, at first hesitantly and then more stridently. The women had resented the hospital visits from their inception, and the researchers were able to induce them to cooperate only by allowing them to turn the visits into parties, at which cake and tea were served and a radio played. Repeated attempts by the researchers to stop the parties failed, and they remained a symbol of the women's ability to effect changes in their working lives in exchange for their participation in the experiment. In addition, the workers' complaints about lighting, mistakes in wage payments, and overzealous inspection of their completed relays were dealt with promptly by the researchers and were resolved to the workers' satisfaction—in marked contrast to the regular department, where they were constantly "bawled out" by their supervisors.[17]

But supervision in the test room, even if generally conducted in a more friendly and less confrontational fashion, was more intense and more focused. The close observation of the workers and the detailed records of individual production constantly reminded the workers that the researchers hoped and expected that production would increase. And on at least one occasion the researchers threatened that the free morning tea would be discontinued if production and cooperation did not improve. A major confrontation ensued over the extent to which the workers could talk in the test room. Talking was permitted as long as it did not interfere with production, but this was an impossible line to hold. Conversations about movies, clothes, and boyfriends naturally gained momentum, until work slowed and the women laughed and talked freely. The researchers saw such behavior as a threat to the experiment, but repeated attempts to put a stop to the disruptions failed. One of the women was particularly resistant to admonitions, exclaiming on one occasion: "For the love of Mike! They tell you to work how you feel, and when you do it, it isn't good enough. . . . I work like I feel and I don't feel like working any different." When the researchers overheard her encouraging her friend to work more slowly, they decided to remove the two women from the test.[18]

The replacement of the two women had a dramatic effect on production in the test room. Output in periods 2–7, covering 37 weeks, had risen 12.3 percent over the starting level for the group; now, in the 7 weeks of period 8, it jumped a further 12 percent. Several factors appear to have contributed to this increase. First, the two new women brought into the test room were faster workers than those they replaced; one held the record as the fastest relay-assembler in the regular department. Second, the removal of the two original women constituted an explicit threat to the remaining workers that they would be removed from the privileged conditions of the test room if they did not perform adequately. Third, the fastest relay-assembler soon became the leader of the group, encouraging and chastising her fellow workers into increasing their production. Nevertheless, the atmosphere in the test room soon returned to normal, and the workers once again laughed and talked freely, and the researchers had to negotiate benefits to ensure their continued cooperation.

Workers and supervisors emphasized different factors when accounting for the increase in production over the first twelve test periods. The workers, in written questionnaires and in discussions with the managers, emphasized those factors they liked about the test room and hoped would be retained, especially the rest periods, the morning tea, the increased freedom, the small bonus scheme, and the fewer types of relay than in the regular department (a change introduced to make calculation of output easier). The researchers focused on the value of rest periods in reducing monotony and fatigue in repetitive assembly work, thereby increasing production. The test room was intended as a place to test innovations in production organization to see if it would be worthwhile introducing them on a larger scale throughout the factory. Thus, after the apparent success of rest periods in the test room, they were introduced in the regular relay department in February 1928, where they were received enthusiastically. On the other hand, the researchers downplayed or dismissed changes such as the reduction in number of relay types and the shift to special group payment, because these were changes that they were not in a position to introduce in the regular departments of the factory. Thus, although they noted that changes in supervisory style in the test room might also have contributed to production, they never emphasized this in their early reports, for it was not clear how such changes could be introduced outside the test room.[19]

Contrary to the standard account of the experiments, however, the researchers did not ignore the impact of social and psychological factors on production. The standard narrative is that the researchers did not realize the importance of social and psychological factors until the twelfth test period, in which the removal of rest periods and the restoration of regular hours did not result in the anticipated fall in production to the original level. Yet in the first progress report, prepared during the seventh period, the researchers had noted that "in addition to the material and physical differences, there are the mental and psychological, which would obviously surround a group of people for such a test," and that these psychological effects had undoubtedly helped overcome monotony and had increased output. These observations, it should be noted, date from before Elton Mayo and his colleagues became involved in the Hawthorne experiments.[20]

Elton Mayo first visited Hawthorne in April 1928, at the invitation of the company researchers. He brought a new approach to the relay assembly test by focusing on the psychological and physiological states of the workers, thereby shifting the emphasis away from the manipulation of single variables. Yet Mayo's intervention did not result in a consensus among all participants as to what the experiments meant; rather, his own preconceptions and commitments were simply added to those of the workers and the company researchers. In previous research in Philadelphia and New England, he had explored the possibility of using blood-pressure measures as an index of fatigue, hoping to find an "objective standard" for a worker's productive capacity. But the results at Hawthorne were as inconclusive as those in the other factories; the blood-pressure measures showed less fatigue among workers taking rest periods, but did not correlate well with individual or collective fluctuations in output.[21]

Mayo reinterpreted the removal of the two women from the relay test so that it became evidence for his view that the psychological and physiological states of workers were closely interrelated and could affect production. Mayo described the incident as one where "a former worker in the test room . . . was permitted to withdraw because she complained of fatigue, became paranoid and 'turned Bolshevik'." On examining her medical record, Mayo discovered that her blood analysis showed a low hemoglobin level and red blood cell count; this, he believed, was evidence of the intimate connections between "pessimistic or paranoid preoccupations, fatigue and organic disability." In this way, Mayo transformed any challenge by workers to managerial control into evidence of psychological disturbance; the woman's assertions that she would work as she liked became evidence of fatigue and bolshevism, while her objections to having her conversation secretly recorded were labeled paranoid.[22]

In addition, Mayo sought to discount the relay-assemblers' interpretations of the data by demonstrating that the women's statements were emotional responses, rather than objective assessments. In both conversation and questionnaires the women had mentioned the improved work flow, the absence of driving supervision, and the small-group wage incentive. But, Mayo insisted, the working conditions at Hawthorne were excellent overall, and the women's comments on how the test room was better should not be taken as an objective critique of the regular department: "This is simply a type of statement almost inevitably made when a not very articulate group of workers tries to express an indefinable feeling of relief from constraint." For Mayo the relay test was evidence that the researchers had created a more humane industrial environment, one that strengthened the " 'temperamental' inner equilibrium" of the workers.[23]

The official accounts of the relay assembly tests report that the researchers— by which they mean both the company researchers and the imported academics—quickly recognized the truth of Mayo's view that the increased production in the relay test lay in the changed mental attitude of the workers. However, this was by no means the case. After reviewing the experimental data and interviewing the workers, two of the company researchers concluded that "explanations of test group behavior may not lie in as obscure causes as is generally supposed"; in particular they stressed the importance of increased earnings, observing that the women showed a keen interest in their daily percentages and had a much clearer understanding of the piece-work system than other workers. Even in 1932, the two researchers who had supervised

the relay test remained doubtful as to what the relay test had proved, as the
following conversation over a draft report reveals:

> Chipman: "I thought it was good. Of course I could give a different
> set of explanations of those things myself, but I agree
> with you."
>
> Hibarger: "Well, we know that we could take either side of any
> question and prove or disprove it whatever we want."
>
> Chipman: "Yes, they say that figures don't lie, but we have shown
> that we can take a set of figures and prove anything we
> want to."[24]

The published accounts of the relay assembly test are thus highly constructed
accounts, reflecting the intellectual and ideological commitments of the authors, and cannot be viewed as objective reports of unproblematic experimentation. Meaning was imposed upon a set of complex, unruly data that
was open to many interpretations, depending on the viewpoint of the observers.
The seemingly authoritative standard account provided in *Management and
the Worker* and in Mayo's writings, in which all doubts and disagreements
are omitted in favor of a description of shared scientific discovery, is misleading.
This is not to say that it is dishonest; it is evident that in each case the authors
believed that they were writing an account that was accurate in both detail
and spirit. It is worth noting, however, that the major official accounts were
written several years after the events and by authors who had not been involved
in the design and supervision of the relay assembly test, a situation that made
it easier for them to undertake a rational reconstruction from a huge quantity
of experimental records.

Experimentation in the relay assembly test room was an inescapably political
activity. As we have seen, the participants' interpretations of the experimental
data varied according to their class; managers, workers, and academics constructed accounts that would strengthen their power with respect to the other
groups. The relay assembly test was also political in that it necessarily reflected
the political relationships of these groups outside the test room; there was
never any doubt that managers and academics had the power to impose their
interpretations and ignore the workers' arguments. In the official accounts
the experimental results in the relay test were taken as incontrovertible proof
that increased production came from enlightened supervision and a friendly
working atmosphere, rather than from improvement in specific working conditions, such as hours of work or rest periods. At the same time workers were
seen as emotional children whose views on working conditions should not be
taken too seriously. The test room transformed the daily industrial conflict
between managers and workers into a set of experimental variables. Yet, scientific experimentation, far from providing an objective view of industrial

relations, enabled management to portray its class interests as objective and scientific. This process can be clearly seen in the interviewing program undertaken at Hawthorne.

Interviewing

As with the transition from the lighting tests to the relay assembly test, the authors of the official accounts were eager to present the establishment of the interviewing program as a natural methodological development from the relay assembly test. In *Management and the Worker* Roethlisberger and Dickson imply that the interviewing program resulted from the discovery in the twelfth-period of the relay tests that the social situation of the worker was more important than any of the variables being manipulated in the test room. There are two distinct problems with this suggestion: first, the interviewing program began in early September of 1928, at the beginning of the twelfth period, so could hardly have been developed in response to its supposedly startling discoveries; and second, the original experimental records reveal that more practical reasons lay behind the interviewing program. We shall also see that the researchers differed over the goals of the interview program and hence over the way to interpret the interviews.[25]

The interviewing program was introduced by the company researchers as a means of identifying existing problems in employee-supervisor relations and of providing materials for an expanded supervisory training program. It was expected that interviews with the workers would provide a picture of their morale, their likes and dislikes, and their attitudes to their bosses. Workers' comments could then be used in three ways. Consistently unfavorable comments about working conditions could be used as a basis for corrective action, where deemed appropriate. Compilations of representative comments, favorable and unfavorable, would provide "a picture of the thoughts and feelings of the workers." And comments on supervision would be discussed in conference groups of supervisors and used as the basis of a supervisory manual. Interviewing was an extension of the research program involving the relay test; but, rather than being the response to an intellectual breakthrough, it was envisaged by the company researchers as a means of developing practical management policies by studying the entire work force. This shift in emphasis from manufacturing methods to management techniques reflected a change in the company personnel conducting the research. With Mayo's assistance, personnel managers had effectively taken over the research by late 1928, and at the start of 1929 an industrial research division was created within the industrial relations branch to direct all personnel research and supervisory training at Hawthorne.[26]

Mayo and his protégé Fritz Roethlisberger, on the other hand, saw the interviews as providing a window onto the seething personal life of the individual worker, whose complaints were most likely to be determined by irrational drives and unconscious associations. Since his experiences working as a psychiatrist during World War I, Mayo had sought to apply psychiatric techniques to industrial unrest and to the attitudes and beliefs of workers. In his industrial research in Philadelphia from 1923 to 1926 he had encountered great difficulties in persuading employers that such techniques would have a practical outcome in terms of industrial efficiency and in persuading workers to submit to intensive interviews.[27] Mayo was therefore most enthusiastic about the interviewing program at Hawthorne and sought to persuade the company researchers of the value of his psychiatric approach. Mayo and Roethlisberger spent considerable time at Hawthorne, teaching clinical interviewing techniques based in part on Piaget's work with children. In particular, they stressed that the interviewer should treat everything the workers said as symptoms, not facts, and argued that the process of interviewing was itself therapeutic, for the worker would experience an emotional release and come to a clearer understanding of his or her subjectivity. Attracted to a perspective that so neatly undermined workers' complaints, the company researchers absorbed Mayo's approach quickly, and interviewers were subsequently trained to detect the "personal adjustment" of the workers.[28]

The very nature of the interviewing program lent itself to strengthening management control over the work process. Worker complaints were collected individually, leaving researchers to compile the data and construct what they believed were workers' attitudes. The structure of the experimentation encouraged the researchers to perceive workers as individuals with no collective experience or attitudes. This perspective was most apparent in the accounts of the Hawthorne experiments by Mayo and Roethlisberger, who argued that the majority of workers' complaints were expressions of sentiment or rationalizations of sentiment and consequently not a reliable guide to work-place conditions. Complaints about low piece rates were more likely to be due to the worker being less efficient than a fellow worker than a reflection of low rates in the company. The latent content of complaints was more important than its manifest content: "The same underlying complaining attitude might be present, even though the employee might on one occasion be complaining about smoke and fumes and on another occasion about his supervisor." Revealingly, the authors denied that this continuity might be justified, that the worker might indeed see an economic and political pattern behind poor working conditions and the behavior of the foreman.[29]

Bank Wiring Test Room

In the final major study of the Hawthorne experiments, the bank wiring test, the focus shifted to a study of the social structures and social relationships in the test room and their influence on production. Later commentators, following the lead of the official accounts, have presented this change as the logical outcome of the researchers becoming aware of the shortcomings of the previous tests. Thus *Management and the Worker* reports that the researchers had become dissatisfied with the interviewing program, because, although it captured the workers' personal situations, it missed the social relations within the factory. Accordingly, the bank wiring room was established as a place to observe these social relations without disturbing the work environment. [30]

However, several other, more prosaic factors seem to have had a greater influence on the design of the bank wiring test than did the logical development of scientific research. First, the interviewing program was discontinued because it seemed an unnecessary expense during the depression, not because the researchers were dissatisfied with the material obtained from it or with its positive impact on workers and supervisors. Second, the shift from a psychological to a more sociological approach was due primarily to the introduction of a new researcher into the experiments. A colleague of Mayo's at Harvard, social anthropologist W. Lloyd Warner, had a significant input into early conceptualizations of the bank wiring test. Whereas Mayo and Roethlisberger argued that interviews revealed only the psychological adjustment of the individual worker, Warner suggested to the company researchers that workers' personal beliefs could tell them something about the social structure of work, and that workers' collective attitudes and behavior had to be treated as a legitimate aspect of the factory. [31]

Third, the research design of the bank wiring test was shaped to a large extent by the conditions placed on the researchers by the foreman of the bank wiring department. The initial proposal was that Mayo's psychological approach be grafted onto the methods developed in the relay assembly test room, with emphasis primarily on the individual worker's relationship to work and the causes of individual maladjustment. But the foreman objected to any research design that would involve significant change from practices in the regular department. He insisted that supervisors be permitted to exercise their normal power, that workers be kept on the department's group rate, and that the test room not be protected from the disruptions of changing work schedules that normally attended production. He did so because he disliked the researchers' argument, used frequently in supervisory training sessions, that production in the relay assembly test room had increased because of the absence of traditional supervisors. Like many other supervisors at Hawthorne, the foreman felt that the altered payment system and the many small, but significant, changes in the organization of production in the relay test room were the major factors. The researchers acceded to his demands, and the bank wiring test room faithfully reproduced conditions in the regular department, the only additions being an observer, who had no supervisory powers, and an interviewing program. [32]

The observer's great discovery in the bank wiring test was that the workers restricted their output. Although the bogey—the amount management expected workers to produce—was 8,000 connections per day, the workers ignored this standard, substituting their own norm of what they considered a fair day's work, between 6,000 and 6,600 connections. Yet the researchers in the bank wiring test did not unexpectedly "discover," as a result of new experimental approaches, that the workers were restricting their output. They were well aware that a piece-rate engineer had previously noted the phenomenon in the bank wiring department, and restriction of output was a well-known, topical problem in personnel management circles.[33]

Nor can the bank wiring test be credited with the experimental discovery of the meaning of restriction of output. Interpretations of the bank-wirers' behavior differed over time and reflected the political perspectives of the researchers. The initial report of the bank wiring test was prepared by William J. Dickson, a young company manager with an undergraduate degree in economics. Dickson's report was remarkably sympathetic to the workers' behavior, arguing that restriction of output was a result of existing industrial organization. He suggested that the workers controlled their production because they knew that if their output consistently reached or exceeded the bogey, management would rerate the job; any attempt to increase their wages through increased production would have only a short-term benefit and would run counter to their interests in the longer term, for they would then find themselves producing more just to protect existing wage levels. Restriction of output, Dickson suggested, was thus a reflection of group solidarity, an indication that workers shared common purposes, ideas, and sentiments. Even the workers' immediate supervisors shared in this solidarity, because their earnings also depended on the group's production, and thus they also had an interest in protecting rates. The solution to restriction lay in guaranteeing that rates would not be reduced and in avoiding coercive forms of supervision.[34]

Subsequent interpretations of the bank wiring test refused to acknowledge the possibility that restriction was a logical, conscious, collective response by workers to the existing piece-rate system. Dickson's reports disturbed the upper management at Hawthorne, which was unwilling to accept that its elaborate management structure could be so ineffective. His reports were also severely criticized by Mayo, who was unimpressed by Dickson and Warner's view that the workers were behaving in a rational, economic manner, rather than irrationally and emotionally. Dickson bowed to pressure from both Mayo and upper management and quickly prepared a supplementary report, in which restriction was no longer portrayed as a collective response by workers to managerial authority and the pay system, but was described as an unconscious reaction by workers to a system that did not provide them with an incentive to work harder. By the time *Management and the Worker* was published several years later, this interpretation had crystalized. Roethlisberger and Dickson dismissed the argument that the bank-wirers restricted their output because they were motivated by economic interest and feared a rate reduction if they achieved the bogey. And they dismissed the possibility that the workers were capable of collective action, concluding that "the ideology expressed by the employees was not based upon a logical appraisal of their situation." The workers' economic arguments were seen as rationalizations of behavior actually driven by sentiments, notably their unconscious desires to be part of a group.[35]

The Politics of Experimentation

Reflecting on the writing of *Management and the Worker* forty years later, Fritz Roethlisberger admitted that "the consumer of knowledge can never know what a dicky thing knowledge is until he has tried to produce it."[36] Fortunately, the existence of a rich collection of archival materials enables the historian to construct a plausible account of the development of the Hawthorne experiments. This can then be compared with the standard account found in the official publications. On this basis, I argue that, whereas the standard account emphasizes a process of scientific discovery, achieved through the application of the scientific method, experimentation was an inherently political activity, in several respects.

First, the scientific findings of the experiments reflect the political values of the experimenters; workers, managers, and academics interpreted the experimental data in ways that reinforced their class interests within the factory. Information on workers' interpretations of the experiments is patchy, but we have seen that the women in the relay assembly test room held that the experimental results revealed the value of improved working conditions, looser supervision, and payment in small groups; while workers throughout the factory were willing to pour out complaints in the interviewing program in the hope that upper management would improve factory conditions. The managers involved in the research preferred interpretations that underscored the need for middle managers such as themselves to increase direct control of production. They stressed the importance of proper supervision of workers, seeing the supposed improvement in supervisory style in the relay test as a major cause of increased production, while citing the restriction of output in the bank wiring test as evidence of inattention by supervisors to the social organization of work. The managers went on to argue that the social relations of work must be brought under the control of specialized personnel managers, and the most important practical outcome of the experiments at Hawthorne was the introduction of supervisory training programs that taught supervisors how to deal with human relations in their work groups.[37] For Mayo the experiments revealed the nonlogical, emotional nature of workers' behavior; industrial peace would be achieved only when an enlightened management adopted the insights into human relations developed by psychiatrists, psychologists, and anthropologists. And he went on to argue that the Hawthorne experiments supported his political observations; the organized resistance by bank-wirers to the hierarchical organization of the work place revealed the social disintegration evident throughout modern society; conversely, the increased production and contentment of the workers in the relay assembly test, resulting from enlightened and humane supervision, demonstrated how human understanding by leaders could create a harmonious society.[38]

Second, the construction of the standard account of the Hawthorne experiments was itself a political process, determined by the respective political power of the participants. Not surprisingly, the workers played no part in this process, for while they had the power to influence the conduct of the experiments, their interpretations were ignored by managers and academics—indeed, part of the function of the "discovery" that workers were nonlogical was that it made it legitimate for the researchers to dismiss the workers' views. Meanwhile, differences in interpretation between and among managers and academics were submerged in the major official publications, all of which were written at Harvard by Mayo and his protégés. When drafts of *Management and the Worker* were circulated among company researchers and upper management, Mayo was able to use his considerable influence within Western Electric to resist pressure for alterations. The book described the many researchers simply as "the investigators" or "the experimenters," terms that were supposed to apply to the researchers actually participating in any test; but in practice, they seemed to refer to Roethlisberger and Dickson and what their opinions would have been had they been involved in every test.[39]

Third, the Hawthorne experiments provided the scientific foundations for two important changes in the politics of production: the gradual emergence of personnel management as a specialized function and the sudden transformation of industrial relations in the New Deal and World War II. Whereas in the 1890s and 1900s control of the technical organization of production passed increasingly from the shop floor to production engineers, a process that came to be known as "scientific management" or "Taylorism," so in the 1910s and 1920s the larger manufacturing companies began to remove personnel functions from shop-floor supervisors and to create specialist personnel departments. Foremen increasingly lost their power to hire, fire, or promote their workers, and personnel managers in many large manufacturing companies operated a system of paternalistic welfare policies designed to weaken and discourage unionization and win the loyalty of the work force. By the early 1920s the vice-president in charge of personnel for AT&T and Western Electric was arguing that management must take into account the "human element" in industry. Thus personnel managers were already concerned with the social organization of production before the Hawthorne experiments. Although the research at Hawthorne was initiated by production engineers within the technical branch, after the early stages of the relay test the research was taken over by personnel managers within the industrial relations branch. These managers saw the research as a means of establishing the importance of their responsibilities in a manufacturing company dominated by engineers. And they sought experimental evidence for increasing their control over supervisors, who clearly had the most direct, immediate influence on the social relations of production; thus the most important management technique to come out of the Hawthorne experiments was supervisory training. The experiments at Hawthorne allowed personnel managers to claim that they had special expertise in understanding the organization of production and enabled them to extend the boundaries of their power within the factory.[40]

Although personnel management provided the incentive for the Hawthorne experiments and an audience for the results, it was the turmoil in industrial relations that ensured their prominence. The calm of the 1920s and early 1930s had been shattered by the militancy of new industrial unions of mass-production workers and industrial relations had been reshaped by New Deal legislation that protected workers' rights to organize and bargain collectively with their employers. Personnel management flourished in this environment, and a function that had previously been the responsibility of middle managers was transformed overnight into the province of executives; henceforth, no managerial decisions could be made without considering their impact on labor relations. Executives were suddenly receptive to arguments by Mayo and his colleagues that managers had contributed to the current turmoil in industry by ignoring the importance of human relations in their companies. Personnel managers echoed Roethlisberger's claim that the findings of the Hawthorne experiments, with their emphasis on human needs and the social organization of production, offered "the road back to sanity" in industrial relations.[41]

The Hawthorne experiments and the human relations approach derived from them appealed greatly to industrial managers, because they codified a managerial perspective that recognized the necessity of gaining the support and active participation of workers, while retaining all the key elements of managerial control. Henceforth the supervisor was to be the leader of a team, who, by using his leadership skills well, could gain the cooperation of his workers; he should be able to utilize the informal groups on the shop floor and to identify and gain the cooperation of their (informal) leaders. By consulting workers over proposed changes and listening to their complaints, the supervisor could reduce their resistance to the technical organization of work and could bind the workers to him through ties of personal loyalty. This perspective was reinforced by government legislation, most notably the Taft-Hartley Act of 1947, which restricted union activities to collective bargaining over wages, hours, and conditions, and to a lesser extent, promotion and discipline. Human relations thus constituted a powerful managerial ideology, which was incorporated in industrial relations and promoted endlessly in supervisory training programs, business education courses, and management journals. In all these writings the Hawthorne experiments figured prominently as the supposedly objective findings on which all these new theories and practices were based.[42]

Finally, if we stand back from the fine details of the Hawthorne experiments, we can see that the decision to undertake social scientific research in the work place was itself a political process. When the experiments began, social and behavioral scientists were just starting to move out of the university into society; claims for the social utility of their knowledge had been made since the last decade of the nineteenth century, but only after World War I did experts try in any coherent fashion to develop techniques of social control based on academic research, modeling themselves explicitly on the successes achieved by scientific medicine in the previous three decades. In 1921 the Personnel Research Federation (PRF) was established under the aegis of the NRC as a means of encouraging and coordinating scientific research on industrial relations. In the same year several of the nation's leading psychologists, including James McKeen Cattell, John B. Watson, Lewis M. Terman, Walter D. Scott, Walter V. Bingham, and Robert M. Yerkes, formed the Psychological Corporation, to provide psychological consultants to industry. In his presidential address at the first meeting of the PRF, Yerkes argued that "there is every reason to believe that human engineering will shortly take its place among the important forms of practical endeavor." It was essential, however, that it be conducted in a disinterested manner, for personnel research could succeed only if all members of society accepted its objective judgment. The introduction of experimental methods was the central strategy of social and behavioral scientists seeking to study and control the organization of work and industrial relations. They firmly believed that experimentation would guarantee the objectivity of their findings and recommendations, and that it would ensure their professional standing on an intellectual and moral plane above that of capitalists and workers, whose views were limited by self-interest. Experimentation became the keystone of the professional ideology of social and behavioral scientists, and the Hawthorne experiments became an exemplar.[43]

By contrast with the standard account of unexpected discovery, I have argued that the Hawthorne experiments should be seen as part of a complex system of manufacture, in which it is impossible to separate fact from value, experimental data from interpretation, scientific knowledge from ideology. The scientific knowledge produced by the experiments was an inextricable amalgam of experimental data, researchers' values, practical expectations, and the hierarchical assumptions of capitalist industrial organization. Far from experimentation increasing the objectivity of the social and behavioral sciences, it may well serve simply to conceal further the inherently political nature of the enterprise. Yet social and behavioral scientists continue to embrace a positivist conception of knowledge. Recent critiques of the Hawthorne experiments still seek, through statistical reworkings or analysis of published accounts, to identify the "correct" interpretation of the data or to show that the experiments were "bad" science.[44] Perhaps that is because the social and professional status of social and behavioral scientists would be undermined if they analyzed their knowledge as a social product.

Notes

1. For classic statements reflecting these views, see J. McKeen Cattell, "Address of the President," *Psychological Review* 3 (1896):134–48: Edwin G. Boring, *History of Experimental Psychology* (New York: Century, 1929); Kurt Lewin, "Experiments in Social Space," in idem, *Resolving Social Conflicts* (New York: Harper, 1948), chap. 5; Gordon W. Allport, "The Historical Background of Modern Social Psychology," in *Handbook of Social Psychology*, ed. Gardner Lindzey (Cambridge, Mass.: Addison-Wesley, 1954), vol. 1, pp. 3–56.

2. For recent surveys of the historical sociology of scientific knowledge, see Henrika Kuklick, "The Sociology of Knowledge: Retrospect and Prospect," *Annual Review of Sociology* 9 (1983):287–310; and Steven Shapin, "History of Science and Its Sociological Reconstructions," *History of Science* 20 (1982): 157–211. On the contingent nature of scientific knowledge and scientific method, see, e.g., Bruno Latour and Steve Woolgar, *Laboratory Life: The Social Construction of Scientific Facts* (London: Sage, 1979); and John Schuster and Richard Yeo, eds., *The Politics and Rhetoric of Scientific Method: Historical Case Studies* (Dordrecht: Reidel, 1986).

3. Psychologists critical of the positivist character of their discipline have tended to argue that the social and behavioral sciences should not emulate the natural sciences, thereby basing their argument on the mistaken assumption that the natural sciences are capable of achieving objectivity. See, e.g., Kenneth J. Gergen, "Social Psychology as History," *Journal of Personality and Social Psychology* 26 (1973):309–20.

4. The original experimental records are held in the Hawthorne Studies Collection, Baker Library, Graduate School of Business Administration, Harvard University; hereafter HSCM, with reference to the microfiche set. Other manuscript collections cited in this chapter are the papers of Elton Mayo (EM) and Fritz Jules Roethlisberger (FJR), also held in the Baker Library; the Dugald Caleb Jackson papers (DCJ), held in the Institute Archives and Special Collections, Hayden Library, Massachusetts Institute of Technology; the Thomas Alva Edison papers (TAE), held at the Edison National Historic Site, West Orange, N.J.; and the Laura Spelman Rockefeller Memorial Records (LSRM) and Rockefeller Foundation Records (RF), held at the Rockefeller Archive Center, Pocantico Hills, Tarrytown, N.Y. For a detailed history of the Hawthorne experiments and fuller citations of the archival records referred to in this chapter, see Richard Gillespie,

"Manufacturing Knowledge: A History of the Hawthorne Experiments" (Ph.D. diss., University of Pennsylvania, 1985).

5. The major official accounts, written by participants in the experiments, are Elton Mayo, *The Human Problems of an Industrial Civilization* (New York: Macmillan, 1933); T. N. Whitehead, *The Industrial Worker*, 2 vols. (Cambridge, Mass.: Harvard University Press, 1938); F. J. Roethlisberger and W. J. Dickson, *Management and the Worker* (Cambridge, Mass.: Harvard University Press, 1939); and Elton Mayo, *The Social Problems of an Industrial Civilization* (Boston: Division of Research, Graduate School of Business Administration, Harvard University, 1945). For the standard account of the Hawthorne experiments as found in textbooks and popular works, see William S. Sahakian, *History and Systems of Social Psychology*, 2d ed. (Washington, D.C.: Hemisphere, 1982), pp. 183–93; Jonathan L. Freedmen, David O. Sears, and J. Merrill Carsmith, *Social Psychology*, 3d ed. (Englewood Cliffs, N.J.: Prentice-Hall, 1978), pp. 413–15; Charles Perrow, *Complex Organizations*, 2d ed. (New York: Random House, 1979), pp. 92–98; C. S. George, Jr., *The History of Management Thought* (Englewood Cliffs, N.J.: Prentice-Hall, 1968), pp. 128–30; Thomas J. Peters and Robert H. Waterman, Jr., *In Search of Excellence* (New York: Warner Books, 1984), pp. 5–6, 92–94.

6. F. J. Roethlisberger, *Management and Morale* (Cambridge, Mass.: Harvard University Press, 1941), p. 15.

7. Roethlisberger and Dickson, *Management and the Worker*, p. 4.

8. E. F. Nichols, "Report of Committee on Research," *Transactions of the Illuminating Engineering Society* 19 (Feb. 1924):125–30; Dugald C. Jackson, "Lighting in Industry," *Journal of the Franklin Institute* 205 (1928):285–303.

9. Dugald C. Jackson, Appendix H of "Factory Illumination-Production Tests at Hawthorne Works of the Western Electric Co.," DCJ/5/330; Roethlisberger, *Management and Morale*, p. 11.

10. Minutes of the Division of Engineering and Industrial Research, National Research Council, 21 Nov. 1924, NRC/Engineering and Industrial Research/Committee on Industrial Lighting, 1924–25.

11. Jackson, "Progress Report of the Illumination Test," in letter from J. W. Barker to T. A. Edison, 11 Sept. 1926, TAE/NRC/1924, quote on p. 3; idem, Appendix H, pp. 12–14.

12. On scientific management techniques in Western Electric and at the Hawthorne works, see R. Gillespie, "Manufacturing Knowledge," pp. 22–31; H. F. Albright, "Fifty Years' Progress in Manufacturing," *Western Electric News* 8 (1919):22–29; and J. W. Bancker, "Records and Reports of Work," *Annals of the American Academy of Political and Social Science* 65 (1916):252–72.

13. Frederick Winslow Taylor, *The Principles of Scientific Management* (New York: Harper, 1911). On the American research on industrial fatigue and the widespread interest in research on industrial efficiency, see R. Gillespie, "Industrial Fatigue and the Discipline of Physiology," in *Physiology in the American Context, 1850–1940*, ed. G. L. Geison (Bethesda, Md.: American Physiological Society, 1987), pp. 237–62.

14. "Relay Assembly Test Room [henceforth RATR] Progress Report," no. 1, 3 Dec. 1927, sec. 1, HSCM/3, B1–F11.

15. W. F. Hosford, "Preparation for Manufacture of Machine Switching Equipment," in Western Electric Co., *Engineering-Manufacturing Conference, Chicago, 27–31 October 1919*; S. P. Shackleton and H. W. Purcell, "Relays in the Bell System," *Bell System Technical Journal* 3 (1924):1–42.

16. "RATR Progress Report," no. 1, secs. 2–3.

17. The account of the social dynamics of the test in this and the following paragraphs is based on the "RATR Daily History Record," HSCM/11–15.

18. "RATR Daily History Record," 12 Jan. 1928.

19. "RATR Progress Report," no. 1, secs. 8–9.

20. Ibid., secs. 2, 5.

21. E. Mayo to T. K. Stevenson, 7 May 1928, HSCM/159, D8–13; "RATR Progress Report," no. 3, 30 June 1928, sec. 5, HSCM/5–6, D1. On Mayo's previous research, see Gillespie, "Manufacturing Knowledge," esp. chap. 2.

22. Mayo to Stevenson, 7 May 1928; Mayo to B. Ruml, 30 Apr. 1928, LSRM/53/572.

23. Mayo, *Human Problems*, pp. 53–94, quotes on pp. 78–79, 72.

24. RATR, "Outline for Progress Report" [Sept. 1931], pp. 20–23, HSCM/9, B11–13; I. Rousseau to H. A. Wright, 15 Oct. 1931, HSCM/63, A1–9; D. D. Davisson, "An Observer's Impressions of the Relay Assembly Test Room," 7 July 1932, HSCM/58, A1–9; RATR, "Record of Observations," 26 Feb. 1932, HSCM/59–62.

25. Roethlisberger and Dickson, *Management and the Worker*, pp. 182–86.

26. "Summary Note of Employee Interviewing Program, Inspection Branch, September 1928 to February 1929," HSCM/109, A3–9.

27. For details of Mayo's intellectual development and research prior to Hawthorne, see Gillespie, "Manufacturing Knowledge," chap. 2, and Richard C. S. Trahair, *The Humanist Temper: The Life and Work of Elton Mayo* (New Brunswick, N.J.: Transaction Books, 1984).

28. E. Mayo, "The Interview," in "A Plan for Improving Employee Relations on the Basis of Data Obtained from Employees, Project 2: Interviewing Techniques," HSCM/148–49, B1; "An Account of the Work of the Industrial Research Division, April 1931," sec. 2, "Development and Use of the Employee Interview as a Research Tool," HSCM/152–53; Roethlisberger, "Method of Interviewing," 1930, HSCM/105, E3–G2.

29. Roethlisberger and Dickson, *Management and the Worker*, pp. 255–69.

30. Ibid., pp. 373–91.

31. W. L. Warner to W. J. Dickson, 27 Feb. 1931, HSCM/159, F7–8.

32. M. L. Putnam to H. S. Wolff, 11 May 1931, HSCM/73, C2–4; "Procedure on Establishing Bank Wiring Test Room," HSCM/73, A1–8; H. A. Wright to Wolff, 25 Sept. 1931, HSCM/73, C5–6.

33. The piece-rate engineer's study of bank wiring is reported in "An Engineering Study of Human Fatigue," HSCM/73, C8–11. For a contemporary study of restriction of output, see Stanley B. Mathewson, *Restriction of Output Among Unorganized Workers* (New York: Viking Press, 1931).

34. Dickson to Wright, 28 Oct. 1931, HSCM/74, C1–11; A. C. Moore and W. J. Dickson, "Report on Bank Wiring Test Group for the Period Nov. 9, 1931, to Mar. 18, 1932," 21 Mar. 1932, HSCM/74, A1–B1.

35. Warner to Dickson, 27 Feb. 1931, HSCM/159, F7–8; "Supplement to Report on Bank Wiring Test Group," 7 Apr. 1932, HSCM/74, A1–B1; Roethlisberger and Dickson, *Management and the Worker*, pp. 531–35, 575–77, quote on p. 535.

36. F. J. Roethlisberger, *The Elusive Phenomena* (Boston: Division of Research, Graduate School of Business Administration, Harvard University, 1977), p. 53.

37. This was most eloquently argued by the Hawthorne researchers in the final chapter of Roethlisberger and Dickson, *Management and the Worker*, pp. 590–604.

38. Mayo, *Human Problems*, pp. 138–80; idem, *Social Problems*, passim.

39. For an account of the writing of *Management and the Worker*, see Gillespie, "Manufacturing Knowledge," pp. 405–27.

40. For a general study of these transformations in American industry, see Daniel Nelson, *Managers and Workers: Origins of the New Factory System in the United States, 1880–1920* (Madison: University of Wisconsin Press, 1975). The AT&T vice-president was E. K. Hall; see his "Management's Responsibility for and Opportunities in the Personnel Job," American Management Association, Convention Address Series, no. 1 (1922).

41. David Brody, *Workers in Industrial America* (New York: Oxford University Press, 1980), chaps. 3–5; Howell John Harris, *The Right to Manage: Industrial Relations Policies of American Business in the 1940s* (Madison: University of Wisconsin Press, 1982); Bryce M. Stewart and Walter J. Couper, *Reconversion in Industrial Relations* (New York: Industrial Relations Counselors, 1946); Roethlisberger, *Management and Morale*, p. 9.

42. See Gillespie, "Manufacturing Knowledge," pp. 436–83. On the new type of foreman, see American Management Association, *The Development of Foremen in Management* (New York: American Management Association, 1945); Burleigh B. Gardner and William F. Whyte, "The Man in the Middle: Position and Problems of the Foreman," *Applied Anthropology* 4 (1945):1–28.

43. Robert M. Yerkes, "What is Personnel Research?", *Journal of Personnel Research* 1 (1922):56–63; Michael M. Sokal, "The Origins of the Psychological Corporation," *Journal of the History of the Behavioral Sciences* 13 (1977):54–67. For a comprehensive overview of industrial psychology in the United States, see Loren Baritz, *The Servants of Power: A History of the Use of Social Science in American Industry* (Middletown, Conn.: Wesleyan University Press, 1960).

44. See esp. Richard Herbert Franke and James D. Kaul, "The Hawthorne Experiments: First Statistical Interpretation," *American Sociological Review* 43 (1978):623–43; Robert Schlaifer, "The Relay Assembly Test Room: An Alternative Statistical Interpretation," *American Sociological Review* 45 (1980):995–1005; Dana Bramel and Ronald Friend, "Hawthorne, the Myth of the Docile Worker, and Class Bias in Psychology," *American Psychologist* 36 (1981):867–78; Brian L. Pitcher, "The Hawthorne Experiments: Statistical Evidence for Learning Hypothesis," *Social Forces* 60 (1981):133–49; Berkeley Rice, "The Hawthorne Defect: Persistence of a Flawed Theory," *Psychology Today* 16 (Feb. 1982):70–74.

7

Charting Life History: Lewis M. Terman's Study of the Gifted

Henry L. Minton*

University of Windsor

On the ground floor of Stanford University's Jordan Hall, the building that houses the psychology department, is an office that contains about a dozen old-fashioned wooden filing cabinets. Another notable feature of the room is a bust of a fatherly-looking man with a faint, benign smile. The cabinets contain files on a sample of some fifteen hundred individuals who were identified as intellectually gifted children six and a half decades ago. The bust depicts the psychologist who launched this study in 1921, Lewis M. Terman, and is the work of Betty Ford Acquina, one of the subjects in the study who, as an adult, became an accomplished sculptor. This room is not part of an archive, library, or museum. It is the central office for an ongoing research project, the field study that Terman began in 1921. Upon Terman's death in 1956, the directorship of the investigation was taken over by Robert R. Sears, a Stanford psychology professor who was also one of the gifted children, or "Termites," as they have come to be known. Since 1970, two Stanford colleagues have joined Sears as collaborators—Lee J. Cronbach, another Termite, and Pauline S. Sears, Robert's wife.

Initially, Terman intended to follow his gifted youngsters for a period of at least ten years.[1] He was interested in discovering how these children differed from children in general and, by following them into early adulthood, de-

*Research for this chapter was carried out during a sabbatical leave at the Stanford University Archives with the generous support of a Leave Fellowship from the Social Sciences and Humanities Research Council of Canada. I would like to thank Roxanne L. Nilan and her staff at Stanford for their help in obtaining archival materials.

termining whether their early intellectual superiority was maintained. After the first ten-year phase, he arranged for continued follow-ups, in the hopes that his subjects would be studied "as far into adult life as finances and other circumstances would permit."[2] And so what began as a relatively brief follow-up of bright children became a pioneering longitudinal study of the life histories of a select group. My purpose in this chapter is to tell the story of how Terman conceived and carried out his study of the gifted. It is more than just the relating of an ambitious, far-ranging piece of research, however, for Terman's personal background set the stage for his interest in gifted children; and how he conceptualized and shaped his investigation was influenced by the times and the cultural milieu in which he worked. In turn, through his own work he was able to effect change in the social world.

Terman's Scientific Goals

Terman was a man with a mission. As a psychologist, he believed that he could contribute to the making of an American society based on the principle of meritocracy. In such a society, the hierarchical division of labor would reflect the distribution of ability in the population.[3] Terman assumed that ability was primarily the result of heredity. In a meritocratic society, the most responsible positions, therefore, would be held by those individuals who have the highest levels of intellect and are industrious enough to make use of their inherent talent. Individual differences in native ability would thus determine the class structure of inequalities in wealth, power, and status. In essence, each person's place in the social hierarchy would be based on his or her merit.

The idea that the social order should be based on individual merit, rather than any preexisting system of wealth, power, and status, was consistent with the democratic ethos of American society. But it was the growing industrialization of America toward the end of the nineteenth century that made the concept of meritocracy so salient. The developing specialization of the labor market required a system in which individual differences in ability could be identified. Furthermore, those individuals with high ability needed highly specialized training to prepare them for the more responsible occupational positions they would assume. Terman viewed mental tests as the most efficient means of achieving a meritocratic social structure. Such tests would identify native intelligence and, if administered at school age, would appropriately sort pupils into educational tracks according to ability level. Terman was especially committed to the identification of children at the highest level of native intelligence, the gifted. If such children were accurately identified by tests and then provided with special educational opportunities to challenge their intellects, they could assume the positions of leadership necessary for social progress in the emerging age of industrialization. They would also have the moral character to look after the welfare of those individuals at the lower levels of ability.[4]

Terman's concern for a more efficient society was part of his ideology regarding the nature of science. Like most American psychologists of his generation, he advocated application as an inherent component of science.[5] To a certain extent, such a commitment was an outgrowth of the assumption that scientific knowledge was essential for social progress, an idea that was accentuated by the reform spirit of the Progressive era in America in the late nineteenth and early twentieth centuries. Furthermore, American psychologists at this time were, with some notable exceptions such as E. B. Titchener, concerned about legitimizing their fledgling science by demonstrating its practical potential. Terman's scientific ideology was shaped primarily by his mentor, G. Stanley Hall.[6] Terman studied under Hall at Clark University, where he received his doctorate in 1905. Terman also embraced Hall's evolutionary perspective and uncritically accepted Hall's untested belief that heredity was a more significant determining factor than environment.

Terman's interest in the gifted appears to have begun at an early age. He was born in 1877 and raised on an Indiana farm.[7] From his own accounts, he was a precocious student at the one-room school he attended and was sensitive to the fact that he stood apart from his peers intellectually. This early self-awareness, therefore, seems to have been the initial source of his interest in the gifted. He eventually completed his undergraduate studies in psychology at Indiana University and stayed on there for his master's degree. In a senior seminar, Terman was asked to prepare two reports, one on mental deficiency, the other on genius. The reading for these two reports introduced him to the writings of Frances Galton and Alfred Binet. The following year, in his M.A. thesis on leadership among children, he included some of Binet's measures of suggestibility.[8] He concluded that intelligence was one of the most important qualities contributing to leadership.

In 1903, when Terman went to Clark for his doctoral training, he determined to continue his research on individual differences. For his doctoral project, he chose an experimental study of mental tests. Hall disapproved of tests, however, so Terman had to turn to Edmund C. Sanford, Clark's experimental psychologist, as his dissertation adviser. In his research, Terman drew on the existing work on tests, including that of Galton and Binet. Terman saw Galton's work as particularly significant, because, unlike Hall, Galton was both an evolutionist and an advocate of mental testing. By means of mental tests, Terman identified the mental processes that distinguished two groups of schoolboys: a "bright" group and a "dull" group.[9] While his master's and doctoral research gave no pointers to his later longitudinal research efforts, these projects did lay the groundwork for his interest in categorizing people, especially in identifying those who were extraordinary. Moreover, this work sensitized him to the importance of utilizing adequate methods to measure individual differences.

In 1910, after a period of several years' recovery from tuberculosis, Terman received a faculty appointment at Stanford University. He was therefore able to return to the research interests that he had developed in his graduate work. With the encouragement of E. B. Huey, a fellow Clark graduate, Terman began to work with the 1908 Binet-Simon scale of intelligence. H. H. Goddard, another of Hall's students, who had preceded Terman by a few years, had published translations of Binet's original 1905 scale and the subsequent 1908 revision.[10] Terman's first tentative revision of the Binet-Simon scale appeared in 1912,[11] and the finished product, the so-called Stanford-Binet, was published in 1916.[12] An innovative feature of the Stanford-Binet was the inclusion of the "Intelligence Quotient," or IQ—that is, the ratio between mental and chronological ages—a concept first introduced by William Stern, but not used previously in mental tests.

Terman regarded the mental test as an experimental method, no less experimental than the laboratory experiment.[13] It was suited to such problems of intelligence as individual and race differences, the phenomena of mental growth, and the psychology of genius; but it could also be useful in other areas, such as the study of emotion, volition, and temperament. Implied in his thinking about the mental test as a method was the notion that it was a means of identifying "types" of personality qualities (be they of an intellectual or nonintellectual nature) and that these qualities could be expressed in concrete, quantitative form. Furthermore, tests could be used to chart developmental change and therefore had the potential to dispel myths about personal development. They could also provide information about the relative contribution of biological and environmental influences to individual and group differences. Such issues could not be examined by the laboratory experiment. For investigation of the awesome variables of time, heredity, and culture, variables intricately connected with individual and group differences, the mental test was the appropriate experimental method.

In his study of the gifted, Terman incorporated other methods besides the mental test. Among these were questionnaires, ratings, interviews, records of personal accomplishment, and physical and health records. Terman saw all these as examples of experimental methods, and in many cases he had to innovate and design the assessment devices. Because of the real-life, complex nature of the phenomena he was studying, he had to bring the laboratory to the real world.[14] In doing so, he required that his subjects record their own experiences and life accomplishments and also involved significant others, such as the subjects' parents, teachers, physicians, counselors, and eventually even their spouses and offspring, all of whom were asked to reflect on the gifted subjects under study. The magnitude of the project, in both time and scope, required extensive planning, financial support, and personnel. Terman was thus a pioneer in matters of research organization and enterprise. He extended the experimental method to the real world and into the realm of a research industry.

Identifying the Gifted through Mental Tests

With the publication of the Stanford-Binet in 1916, Terman became a highly visible figure. It is therefore not surprising that in the spring of 1917 he was called to serve on a committee that had been assembled at Vineland, New Jersey, to devise mental tests for the army. The committee was chaired by Robert M. Yerkes. The United States had entered World War I, and Yerkes, as president of the American Psychological Association, spearheaded the association in contributing to the war effort.[15] Terman brought with him a new group test of intelligence that had been developed by his doctoral student Arthur S. Otis.[16] The Otis test served as a basis for the development of the army group tests. Although serious questions have been raised about the significance of the psychologists' contributions to the war, there is no doubt that the war provided an enormous boost for the mental testing movement.[17] Approximately 1,750,000 men were tested and on the basis of their test scores given job classifications or screened from further service.

When Terman returned to Stanford in 1919, he seized on the contribution of the army tests to military efficiency and predicted that the tests would soon be universally used in the schools.[18] To this end, in collaboration with Yerkes, he secured a grant from the General Educational Board of the Rockefeller Foundation to adapt the army tests for school use. Working with a National Research Council committee that included Yerkes and Edward L. Thorndike, he had "National Intelligence Tests" for grades 3–8 ready for use by 1920.[19] In 1922 Terman, as chairman of a National Education Association (NEA) committee on the use of intelligence tests in revising elementary education, published with the committee a book that extolled the use of testing for reorganizing schools so that students could be classified into homogeneous ability groups—in other words, for a tracking system.[20]

In July 1923 Terman gave an address to the NEA in which he predicted that within one or two decades tracking would become standard.[21] His prediction was to come true: by 1923 the new group mental tests were generally welcomed in the schools as an expedient tool for sorting pupils into ability groups.[22] After this early rush of enthusiasm, some school officials criticized the use of the tests, pointing to the dangers of labeling and the difficulties of dealing with parents' objections to testing. However, by 1930 intelligence testing and ability grouping were common practices in elementary schools. With an expanding school population, the schools themselves were ready for a differentiated curriculum, and, for the most part, school administrators viewed mental tests as an efficient means for sorting pupils.

Terman saw the widespread use of mental tests in the schools as a reflection of how testing could be of use to American society. It was to be the primary means of achieving his view of a meritocracy, which would of course, have a genetic basis. He presented this vision in a popular article in 1922, arguing as follows:

> *There is nothing about an individual as important as his IQ, except possibly his morals. . . . The great test problem of democracy is how to adjust itself to the large IQ differences which can be demonstrated to exist among the members of any race or nationality group. . . . All the available facts that science has to offer support the Galtonian theory that mental abilities are chiefly a matter of original endowment. . . . It is to the highest 25 per cent. of our population, and more especially to the top 5 per cent., that we must look for the production of leaders who will advance science, art, government, education, and social welfare generally. . . . The least intelligent 15 or 20 per cent. of our population . . . are democracy's ballast, not always useless but always a potential liability. How to make the most of their limited abilities, both for their own welfare and that of society; how to lead them without making them helpless victims of oppression; are perennial questions in any democracy.*[23]

The highest purpose that testing could serve was the identification of children who were intellectually gifted and therefore had the potential to become leaders of society. It was the responsibility of the schools, once these children were identified, to devote the necessary time and effort to cultivating their potential. As Terman commented, "The school's first task is to find its gifted children and to set them tasks more commensurate with their ability."[24] Such a goal was related to the differentiated curriculum he was advocating, and the notion of grouping pupils on the basis of innate ability was perfectly consistent with the ideals of democracy. Every child would have the same opportunity "to make the most of whatever abilities nature has given him."[25] Terman's educational reforms reflected his scientific goals. The changes he advocated were based on sound scientific method, in this case the mental test, and scientific method was being applied as a means of achieving a more efficient, democratic society.

Preliminary Studies of Gifted Children

During the early twenties, Terman was influential in fostering the widespread use of mental tests in schools. However, his chief aim by this time was to demonstrate how schoolchildren with superior IQs would excel in their future scholastic performance. Moreover, in order to dispel the belief commonly held by physicians and educational theorists that child prodigies became neurotic and "burned-out" before they reached their potential, he wanted to show that if gifted children were given the appropriate support and encouragement, they would be well-adjusted and well-rounded in their general development.[26]

In constructing the Stanford-Binet, Terman had begun to collect data on children with high IQs. In 1915 he reported a study of 31 children with IQs above 125.[27] Contrary to his expectations at the time, teachers' ratings indicated that these intellectually precocious children were well-developed in other spheres of functioning. They were not sickly, eccentric, one-sided, or socially inept as he had initially presumed they would be. The following year, with the collaboration of Margaret Hopwood Hubbard, he collected data on a sample of 59 children with IQs above 140.[28] More extensive ratings and information were obtained from teachers than in the previous study, and similar data were supplied by parents. These precocious children also turned out to be emotionally and socially well-adjusted.

In 1919, at Terman's request, Stanford established a ten-year research fellowship for the study of gifted children, which provided further opportunity for revising the preliminary information and rating forms.[29] Moreover, an interest blank was developed for children to fill out about themselves. By the spring of 1921, with the aid of the annual fellowships, complete data were available for 121 children with IQs over 140. The record of good personal adjustment emerging from these cases supported Terman's earlier findings about gifted children. Terman also pointed to social class and ethnic-racial differences. With respect to class differences, he concluded that "heredity is superior," since 50 percent of the fathers belonged to professional groups and not one to the unskilled group. Regarding ethnic distinctions, he reported an "excess of Jewish cases and a deficiency of cases from the Italian, Portuguese, and Mexican groups living in the vicinity of Stanford University."[30]

In addition to gathering test, rating, and questionnaire data, Terman carried out several individual case studies. In 1917 he published an intellectual portrait of Francis Galton's childhood,[31] based on Karl Pearson's biography, which contained letters written by the young Galton describing his intellectual accomplishments. According to Terman, Galton's childhood vocabulary, interests, and scholarly feats suggested that his mental age was approximately double his chronological age—that is, that he had an IQ near 200.[32] Terman also reported a father's account of the training of an infant daughter who by the age of twenty-six months could read as well as the average first-grader.[33] With Jessie Chase Fenton, a recipient of the Stanford Gifted Children Fellowship, Terman described the case of a nine-year-old girl who was an accomplished poet.[34] Five of her poems, as rated by Stanford students in advanced English classes, compared favorably with poems by well-known authors.

By 1921 Terman was ready to go beyond the preliminary data he had collected. His goal was to obtain a sample of a thousand cases so that he could claim a reasonably representative sample of intellectually gifted children. In this venture he was supported by the Commonwealth Fund of New York with a grant of $20,300, which was supplemented the following year by $14,000 plus an additional $8,000 from Stanford.[35] As spelled out in his grant application, Terman intended to obtain at least two intelligence tests for each of the thousand subjects, as well as measures of school achievement, trait ratings, and social data. He also intended a follow-up of the subjects for a period of at least ten years.

In launching his study of the gifted, Terman began the first psychological investigation involving a longitudinal research design, in which a sample of subjects were followed over the course of several years. The only precedents were brief longitudinal single-case studies based on baby diaries.[36] (During the 1920s, several other longitudinal studies of children were begun.) Terman's study was also innovative in its scope. Since his aim was to gather as complete an assessment of his subjects as possible, he made use of a wide variety of methods. Since he was often attempting to measure characteristics not previously assessed, he had to devise many of the instruments he used. For example, as part of the study, the first achievement test battery (the Stanford Achievement Test) was constructed. Another instrument to emerge from the study was the first measure of masculinity-femininity (the Terman-Miles scale).

The Search for a Thousand Gifted Children

Upon receipt of the Commonwealth Fund grant, Terman devoted three months to finalizing plans, tests, and information blanks, as well as to securing the necessary research collaborators and assistants.[37] Stanford colleague Truman L. Kelley was enlisted as assistant director and essentially served in the capacity of a statistical consultant. Giles M. Ruch, who was completing his dissertation under Terman, served as an administrative assistant and also took on the major responsibility of developing the achievement and general information tests.[38] In addition, Terman hired four full-time field assistants: Florence Fuller, Florence L. Goodenough, Helen Marshall, and Dorothy M. Yates.

The data to be collected for each child in the first year of the study included two intelligence tests (the Stanford-Binet and National-Form B), an achievement test (the Stanford Achievement Test), a test of general information (science, history, literature, and the arts), a test of knowledge of and interest in play activities, games, and amusements, an interest blank, and a two-month reading record kept by the children. In addition, reflecting his effort to make the real world part of his laboratory, Terman enlisted the aid of parents and teachers. He had previously made use of such "lay-experimenters" in his preliminary studies of gifted children, and he now expanded their data input. The parents filled out a home information blank, which asked for a developmental case history, a report on home training, and ratings on twenty-five traits; and the teachers filled out a school information blank, which covered school health records, quality of schoolwork, social adjustment, and the same twenty-five traits that the parents were given.

The fieldwork began in September 1921. The original intention was to identify the highest 1 percent (IQs above 140) of all California schoolchildren. However, due to financial limitations, only the larger and medium-sized urban areas were canvassed, and, as it turned out, the 1 percent cutoff was set at an IQ of 135.[39] Goodenough and Fuller were assigned to Los Angeles, Marshall to San Francisco, and Yates to the East Bay (Oakland and Berkeley). Volunteer assistants took responsibility for covering smaller cities such as Santa Barbara, Fresno, San Jose, and Santa Ana.

In the various cities, the field-workers attempted to canvass all the elementary schools (grades 3–8), and in the larger cities, the high schools as well. For standardization in selecting the sample, the following procedure was adopted in the elementary schools: in each classroom, the teacher was asked to fill out a blank calling for the name of the brightest child in the class, the second brightest, the third brightest, and the youngest.[40] The teacher was also asked to give the name of the brightest child he or she had had the previous year. All the nominated children in a given school were then given a group intelligence test (National-Form B). Those who scored high on this test were given an abbreviated Stanford-Binet, and those scoring high on this short version were in turn given a complete Stanford-Binet.[41] To check on the efficiency of this search method, the entire population of three schools (which had already been canvassed for teacher nominations) was tested. The results revealed that the search procedure was identifying close to 90 percent of all who would have qualified if each pupil had been given the Stanford-Binet. However, there were difficulties in trying to cover all the schools, particularly in the larger cities. Goodenough wrote to Terman about the difficulties in Los Angeles and questioned whether it was worthwhile covering fourteen special schools that handled children who had been found guilty of minor offenses.[42] Terman responded that she should use her own judgment, voicing concern about taking extra time to cover "side lines that do not promise reasonably well."[43] It is likely that these special schools, which apparently did not get included, had a disproportionate share of children from lower social-class backgrounds; it is also likely that social-class bias (in favor of the higher levels) would have generally influenced teacher nominations. Terman did not appear to be sensitive to these possible sources of bias, which would have worked to the exclusion of lower-class children. His tendency to attribute class differences primarily to heredity would account for his relative neglect of cultural factors that might influence the selection of subjects.

Among the various categories of teacher nominations, the youngest child proved to be the most fruitful in terms of qualifying for the IQ cutoff of 135, followed closely by the brightest child. The systematic search yielded a total of 661 subjects, 354 boys and 307 girls, from an elementary-school population of about 160,000. This group, designated the "Main Experimental Group," was compared with a control group consisting of a random sample of children of comparable age.[44] A second Binet-tested group of 365 elementary school-children, 197 boys and 168 girls, was also included. Some of these children had been tested and followed up prior to 1921; others were discovered with the help of volunteer testers in smaller California communities not covered by the main survey. A third group, made up primarily of junior and senior high-school children, was included in the study on the basis of group intelligence tests. This group consisted of 444 subjects, 273 boys and 171 girls. The total gifted group added up to 1,470 cases, 824 boys and 646 girls.[45] It would seem that through the various nomination and "discovery" procedures, a sex bias in favor of boys may also have been operating.[46]

The remaining data were collected during the year 1922–23.[47] In an attempt to dispel the popular notion already mentioned that gifted children were underdeveloped in nonintellectual areas, Terman included medical and physical assessments, as well as measures of personality, character, and interests. The medical examinations of the gifted children (87 percent of the sample was examined) were carried out by two physicians. Anthropometric measurements, including height, weight, breathing capacity, grip, and body-part dimensions, were obtained for most of the children identified through the systematic search procedure carried out by the field assistants. These physical measures were supervised by Bird T. Baldwin, a psychologist with expertise in this area and director of the Child Welfare Research Station at the University of Iowa. His assistant, Beth L. Wellman, made the actual measurements. Finally, character and personality tests (constructed by A. S. Raubenheimer, a graduate student of Terman's) and a test of intellectual, social, and activity interests (constructed by Jennie Benson Wyman, another of Terman's graduate students) were administered.

The data amounted to close to a hundred pages for each gifted child, two-thirds of which were test and measurement material, the other third, questionnaire items. The IQs for the pre-high-school subjects ranged from 135 to 200, with a mean Stanford-Binet IQ of 151.[48] The IQs for the high-school subjects ranged from 135 to 169, with a mean IQ of 143 on the Terman group test. In terms of the racial-ethnic origin of the gifted sample, it was estimated that by comparison with the general population of the cities concerned there was about a 100 percent excess of Jewish ancestry, a 25 percent excess of native-born parentage, and an underrepresentation of Italian, Portuguese, Mexican, and Negro ancestry.[49] The social-class breakdown in terms of father's occupation revealed a preponderance of professional, semiprofessional, and business categories (81.4 percent). It was concluded that the typical gifted child was the product of "superior parentage," from the standpoint of both cultural-educational background and heredity, the latter gleaned from genealogical data. This combined advantage was judged to account for the slightly better "physical specimen" among the gifted sample as compared with the average child. Such a comparison was based on the anthropometric measurements, health histories, and medical examinations.

Educationally, the average gifted child was accelerated when compared with his or her age-group. With respect to mastery of subject matter, this acceleration was about 44 percent, much higher than the 14 percent acceleration in grade placement, leading Terman to conclude that the gifted pupils were kept at school tasks two or three grades below their actual level of achievement. The interests of gifted children were seen as many-sided and self-initiated. They learned to read easily and read more than the average child. Their play preferences showed a degree of maturity two or three years beyond the norm for their age. On character tests, the gifted were above average on qualities such as trustworthiness, emotional stability, and "wholesome" social attitudes. Trait ratings by teachers and parents confirmed this character portrait.

Terman pointed to two "facts" that stood out in the composite picture:

> (1) The deviation of the gifted subjects from the generality is in the upward direction for nearly all traits. . . . There is no law of compensation whereby the intellectual superiority of the gifted is sure to be offset by inferiorities along nonintellectual lines. (2) The amount of upward deviation is not the same in all traits. It is greatest in those aspects of behavior most closely related to intelligence, such as originality, intellectual interests, and ability to score high in achievement tests.[50]

Terman cautioned that this composite portrait reflected central tendencies. He noted that one could find individual examples of almost any personality defect, social maladjustment, behavior problem, or physical frailty. He concluded, however, that among gifted children the incidence of such deviations was lower than in the general population. For Terman's purposes, this last point was most significant for two reasons. First, it demonstrated that gifted children did not conform to the commonly held belief (in the 1920s) that such children were often one-sided and neurotic. Second, it suggested that gifted children had the kinds of well-rounded personalities and skills that, given the opportunity, could be harnessed for leadership roles in Terman's meritocratic society. Terman acknowledged that the purpose of his study was to identify and describe gifted children and eventually to follow up the development of these children. He had no specific recommendations about the educational methods that should be adopted to meet the needs of intellectually superior children.[51] However, he strongly advocated a differentiated school curriculum that would place gifted children in special classrooms where they could accelerate educationally according to their ability, rather than their age (as in the traditional curriculum).

One other aspect of the second year of the study needs to be noted. Grant money was also used to support a parallel study conducted by Catharine M. Cox (her dissertation) under Terman's supervision. This was an ambitious extension of Terman's method of estimating Galton's IQ to a representative group of 300 eminent individuals throughout history. Here was a situation in which history was being used as an experimental laboratory of sorts. The completed study was published as the second volume of the monograph series on the gifted.[52] Terman described the purpose of the study as to determine whether the childhood traits of individuals who later achieved eminence paralleled the traits that he had discovered among his sample of gifted children.[53] In essence, he concluded that this was indeed the case. As he stated, "We are justified in believing that geniuses, so called, are not only characterized in childhood by a superior IQ, but also by traits of interest, energy, will, and character that preshadow later performance. The ancient saying that 'the child is father to the man' probably expresses a truth far more profound than anyone has hitherto suspected."[54]

The Promise of Youth

In 1927 Terman received a grant of $10,800 from the Commonwealth Fund to carry out his planned follow-up of the gifted children;[55] this was supplemented by financial support from Stanford, as well as from his own funds. During 1927–28 three field assistants retested the children and interviewed parents and teachers, using the same kinds of tests and ratings as were used in collecting the original data, for the most part. The follow-up sample consisted of the majority (91.7 percent) of the main experimental group of the initial study.[56] The major finding of the follow-up was that, for the group as a whole, the composite picture "did not greatly change" over the six-year interval.[57] The intellectually gifted children (some now adolescents and college students) continued to show high academic achievement, varied interests, good personality adjustment, and better-than-average health and physique. The results thus supported Terman's expectations about "the promise of youth" within a group of gifted children.

There were also some new findings of note, among which were the results of a specially constructed measure of masculinity-femininity.[58] This was another example of Terman's attempt to demonstrate that the gifted were well adjusted in nonintellectual areas of functioning; in this instance, appropriate gender identification. In the original survey, masculine and feminine interests were derived from questionnaire preferences regarding play activities, games, and amusements. Among the gifted sample, a high masculinity index reflected preference for activities that were frequently elected by boys in the control group and infrequently by girls, and likewise the femininity index. The 1921–22 results showed that the gifted sample was similar in its gender orientation to the control sample. Terman had secured a National Research Council grant in 1925 to investigate sex differences in nonintellectual traits. With the help of Catharine Cox Miles (who had married Walter Miles in 1927), a masculinity-femininity (M-F) test was devised and was ready for use in the 1927–28 survey. This multiple-choice test consisted of a variety of items. There were word associations, for example, consisting of a stimulus word and four response choices from which the subject had to choose one. Based on a normative sample of high-school and college students, the response words were categorized as masculine or feminine. An illustration of this type of item was the stimulus word *jealous*. If the subject chose *lover* or *women*, he or she received a masculine score; if *angry* or *green* were chosen, the subject received a feminine score. Another type of item dealt with general information: for example, "Eggs are best for us when," followed by four responses. The masculine responses were "fried" and "hard-boiled"; the feminine, "deviled" and "soft-boiled". Other types of items included preferences for books, objects, and activities, and responses to situations that might arouse emotions, such as anger or fear. [59]

The results showed that gifted girls as a group were significantly more "masculine" than the normative sample of female students. On the other hand, gifted boys were generally similar to the male-student norms. Terman and his coauthors suggested that the "masculine" tendency demonstrated by the gifted girls was a desirable deviation from the norm, citing the historical examples of Queen Elizabeth (the First) and George Sand. They also pointed out that these results lent some truth to Cesare Lombroso's opinion that "there are no women of genius; the women of genius are all men." [60] Yet the authors did express some concern about the future adjustment of gifted subjects who showed extreme gender inversion, such as Roberta, who liked to dress up in a boy scout outfit and a naval officer's uniform, and Renwick, a boy organist who played with dolls and amused himself by designing feminine garments and acting out feminine operatic roles. [61]

The question of gender also appeared in the reported finding of the sex ratio among the gifted. In the first volume of the monograph series, it was stated that there was a higher proportion of boys, and this sex difference was even more noticeable at the high-school level. According to Terman and his coauthors, the follow-up study indicated that the larger excess of boys, at least at the upper age levels, was due to the fact that "gifted girls do not maintain their intellectual superiority in adolescence as well as boys do." [62] To account for this, it was suggested that boys have a somewhat greater variability in IQ scores and that girls have an "earlier cessation of mental growth." No mention was made of the social pressures that gifted female adolescents might be subject to if they continued to excel intellectually. In this regard, it is of interest that Leta Hollingworth, another major investigator of intellectually superior children, was very sensitive to the selective biases and social pressures working against gifted girls and shared her concerns with Terman, concerns that he did not assimilate into his thinking.[63]

Included among Terman's conclusions was a discussion of the sociopolitical implications of studying and identifying the intellectually gifted.[64] He continued to advocate a meritocratic society, arguing that "genius" was even more important now than it had been historically, because of the increasing complexity of civilization and of science. He spelled out this notion as follows:

> That important scientific discoveries are sometimes made by fairly commonplace intellects may be freely admitted. . . . It is more reasonable to believe that the mounting quantity and growing complexity of knowledge call more insistently for the masterful genius today than ever before. Disrupted social and economic orders, from England to Japan and from Canada to the Argentine, are calling almost in vain for statesmen of genius and vision. . . . Lawmaking in most countries, and perhaps nowhere more than in the United States, is chiefly the product of fourth-rate minds.[65]

In completing the first follow-up of his gifted sample, Terman demonstrated his skills as a scientific manager. He was successful in obtaining the necessary financial support for his ambitious project, as well as in efficiently directing a research staff, many of whom were his graduate students, who in turn carried out their own research in areas related to the study. In reporting his results, he was able in general to confirm the expectations he had started with. Indeed, he did have confirmatory evidence, but his interpretations contained biases, most notably with regard to class and sex. His hereditarian assumptions led him to neglect the intricate ways in which culture worked. Thus, he seemed insensitive to conditions that might exclude lower-class youngsters from a study of gifted children. Furthermore, as we have already seen, he failed to consider the kinds of social pressures that might impede bright adolescent girls from excelling in the same way as their male peers.

The Gifted Child Grows Up

In 1947 Terman, in collaboration with Melita Oden, reported a twenty-five-year follow-up of the gifted group.[66] This monograph also contained reports of follow-ups that had been conducted in 1936 and 1940. The 1936 survey was limited to a mailing of two questionnaires: the first, an information blank to be filled in by the subjects regarding educational and occupational history, avocational interests, general health, and marital status; the second, a home information blank to be filled in by the parents that included personality ratings of the subject and the parents' own accomplishments and activities. These items of information were what had previously been recorded in the 1921 and 1928 surveys. This mail follow-up was more successful than had been anticipated, for about 90 percent of the subjects were located.

In 1939 a grant of $20,000 was obtained from the Carnegie Corporation. Other supplemental grants were added, so that by 1945 a total of about $49,000 was available for the collection of new material. During 1939–40 the subjects were both interviewed (for the purpose of updating the case histories) and given a battery of tests and information blanks. The questionnaires included an extended information blank, a specially constructed personality test, the Strong Vocational Interest Blank, the Concept Mastery Test (a specially constructed measure of abstract intelligence), and a marriage blank designed to yield a numerical index of marital happiness. Approximately 98 percent (a total of 1,434) of living subjects were included in the 1940 survey, an unusually high rate of subject cooperation. The average age of the sample was thirty. In 1945 a follow-up information blank was mailed out, and the returns showed only a small attrition, the sample totaling 1,418 subjects.

The data showed that the intellectual level of the group continued to be within the upper 1 percent of the general population.[67] Vocational achievement was well above the average of college graduates. Furthermore, as the earlier reports had indicated, personal adjustment for the group was good. There were several demonstrations of this. Such "serious maladjustments" as insanity, delinquency, alcoholism, and homosexuality showed a normal or below-normal incidence. Marital adjustment was equal or superior to that of groups less highly selected for intelligence. The sexual adjustment of married subjects was as normal as that found in a less gifted and less educated group of married couples.

There were also some interesting findings derived from comparisons of subgroups within the gifted sample. Those gifted children who tested above 170 IQ were more rapidly promoted in school, did better schoolwork, attained more education, and were more successful in their later careers than lower-testing members of the group. Jewish subjects differed very little from non-Jewish subjects in ability and personality traits but displayed a stronger drive to achieve, formed more stable marriages, and were a little more liberal in their political and social attitudes.

In another comparison, the male sample (in 1940, when the men were twenty-five years old or older) was divided into three groups based on a rating of "life success." The criterion of success was defined as "the extent to which a subject had made use of his superior ability."[68] The three groups constituted approximately the highest fifth, the middle three-fifths, and the lowest fifth.[69] The highest and lowest groups, designated A and C, each consisted of 150 men of comparable mean age and range of age who were almost equally successful during the elementary-school years. However, in high school the two groups began to draw apart as the C group's grades began to drop. During college the grades of the C group were strikingly lower. By 1940 this group showed increasing social maladjustment (fewer marriages, higher incidence of divorce) and a poor employment record (frequent unemployment and job turnover). What appeared to account for the sharp differences between the A and C groups was the stronger tradition of education in the families of the A group. Three times as many A fathers as C fathers had graduated from college, and more than twice as many A fathers were in the professional classes. Another difference was the lower emotional stability and poorer social adjustment of the C group when rated as children in the initial survey. It was concluded that environmental factors and personality adjustment were significant determinants of the extent to which "potential genius" would be successfully expressed. In reaching this conclusion, Terman seemed to be giving more weight to the role of environment than one would have expected based on his initial assumption regarding the genetic foundation of intellectual superiority and the consequent importance of the early identification of giftedness. While not refuting these assumptions, he acknowledged on the basis of his follow-up data that "intellect and achievement are far from perfectly correlated."[70] It thus became important to understand how environment could facilitate or stifle the expression of giftedness.

Various grants from the Carnegie Corporation, the Rockefeller Corporation, and the Office of Naval Research supported the next follow-up, which ran from 1950 to 1952 and was reported in the fifth volume of the study, published in 1959.[71] Although this appeared three years after Terman's death, Terman had written initial drafts of some of the chapters, and Oden completed the manuscript. The subjects were again given the Concept Mastery Test (slightly revised from the previous follow-up), an abbreviated version of the marital happiness test, and information blanks about themselves, their spouses, and their children. Those living in California were interviewed, and their offspring of appropriate age were given a Stanford-Binet (the testing of offspring had begun in the 1940 follow-up). In 1955 an information blank was mailed out to obtain updated data. At this time, the average age of the subjects was about forty-five, and the total sample was somewhat over 1,300 (93 percent of those living).

The gifted group at mid-life were found to have maintained their intellectual superiority and, at least in the case of the men, to have attained a high level of career success.[72] Some of the men had achieved notable distinctions in their fields; for example, somewhat over a hundred were listed in such prestigious biographical sources as *American Men of Science*, the *Directory of American Scholars*, and *Who's Who in America*. The career situation for the women was quite different. For the most part they were housewives, though some had achieved career distinction. But as Terman and Oden pointed out, even for women with a career, decisions were based more on external factors like gender-role conformity and job discrimination than on talent, training, or interest.

The mid-life survey also contained a question about what the subjects perceived life success to be. Vocational achievement was frequently listed, but other indices frequently mentioned included a happy marriage and family, contributions to the welfare of others, and emotional maturity. As in the previous follow-up, the gifted sample as a whole continued to portray a well-rounded picture of personal satisfaction and effectiveness.[73]

Terman's involvement in the study included more than overseeing data collection and writing up results. He was interested in disseminating information about his research on the gifted, and over the years he granted several interviews to journalists.[74] In 1947 he made a guest appearance on the radio show the *Quiz Kids*. His appearance on the show coincided with the publication of the fourth volume of his series of reports, the one devoted to the twenty-five year follow-up. In introducing Terman, the program director gave his new book a plug.[75] Terman was very interested in the program because he believed it performed a major function in informing the public that highly gifted children were well-adjusted and versatile.[76]

> *I have devoted a good part of my life to research on children of high IQ. . . . But despite all my investigations, and those of others, many people continued to think of the brainy child as a freak—physically stunted, mentally lop-sided, nonsocial, and neurotic. Then came the Quiz Kid program, featuring living specimens of highly gifted youngsters who were obviously healthy, wholesome, well-adjusted, socially minded, full of fun, and versatile beyond belief. . . . Result: the program has done more to correct popular misconceptions about bright children than all the books ever written.*[77]

Terman's efforts to reach out to the general public—in effect to popularize his work—represent interesting examples of the interconnectedness of science and social context. His research was both shaped by, and helped to shape, social thought.

An aspect of the work with the gifted that Terman found especially satisfying was the opportunity for personal contact with many of the subjects under study. He kept up a correspondence with many of them over the years and in some instances received them as guests in his home. Thus, to many of the gifted children who "grew up" (and came to be identified as Termites),

Terman was a benevolent father figure and psychological counselor. After pouring over the files of the gifted subjects, one comes away with the image of Terman as someone who was deeply concerned with and personally interested in the lives of the gifted men and women he studied.[78] For some, his personal interest had a significant impact on the direction of their lives. Part of the psychological dynamic underlying Terman's personal involvement seems to have been his own identification with them.[79] Early in his career, he was sensitive to the need for early identification and encouragement of gifted children. In the era and the agrarian environment in which he grew up, such identification and encouragement were not available (though in his own case he credited his family with supporting his desire for more schooling). Terman, in his interactions with the gifted in his study, was able to provide the personal guidance and encouragement that he had, for the most part, missed when he was growing up. Moreover, through his role as "guardian angel," he attempted to effect the outcomes he sought to achieve in his study—that is, to foster the expression of potential giftedness.

Conclusions

Terman deserves to be credited with pioneering a most ambitious and thorough study of children with high ability. In terms of the amount of data generated, the sample size, the financial and staff support, and the fact that its sixty-year span represents the longest developmental investigation ever attempted, it ranks as a seminal longitudinal study. It also stands as a testament to Terman's tenacity and dedication in carrying through what he defined as his primary mission in life: to change the public's negative image of gifted children and to demonstrate how significant their contributions to society could be when they became adults. Indeed, the public attention and the largely confirmatory conclusions that derived from his study appeared to contribute to attitudinal changes. By 1947 he was satisfied that prejudicial myths about the gifted, such as "early ripe, early rot," were far less common than they had been half a century before.[80] On a related note, it appears that the gifted subjects themselves were generally positive about being a part of the study.[81]

In carrying through his mission, Terman was very sensitive to the need not only to detect intellectual giftedness at an early age, but once identified, to provide proper encouragment for its development. He was therefore highly critical of the tendency of some parents to exploit their gifted children by seeking publicity and putting them on display. As far as he was concerned, such practices contributed to the negative image of child prodigies and "burned" them out before they could reach their potential. One of the most publicized examples of this kind of burn-out was the case of William James Sidis, son of a Harvard psychology professor (Boris Sidis), who at four could write French and English on a typewriter.[82] He had a nervous breakdown at twelve and, although a Harvard law graduate, ended up as a clerk with a passion for collecting trolley-car transfers and committed suicide in 1944 at the age of forty-six. At the time, Terman commented to a *Time* magazine reporter: "I think the boy was very largely ruined by his father, giving him so much bad publicity."[83]

The study must also be appraised in terms of Terman's aim that it be a demonstration project for a meritocratic society. When his Stanford-Binet test was published in 1916, he stated: "The future welfare of the country hinges in no small degree upon the right education of . . . superior children. Whether civilization moves on and up depends on the advances made by creative thinkers and leaders in science, politics, art, morality, and religion. Moderate ability can follow, or imitate, but genius must show the way."[84] Terman also consistently supported the view that "mental abilities are chiefly a matter of original endowment."[85] Thus individuals endowed with superior ability and given the appropriate educational environment had the potential to be leaders in society.

Was Terman able to validate such a model of meritocracy? The answer is essentially negative, largely because his basic assumption that superior intellect was innate was never tested. Indeed, he uncovered evidence that environmental opportunities made a difference in achievement. Among the men, success was related to being exposed to intellectual stimulation and to emotional support. Such facilitative conditions for achievement were generally not available to the women because, as Terman acknowledged, they were constrained by the force of the traditional feminine role. However, while acknowledging the role of environment in fostering or impeding the realization of potential of the gifted to excel, he appeared to maintain his view that intellect itself, as assessed by mental tests, was primarily genetic in origin. As a result, he failed to consider the ways in which the environment could influence test performance and consequently IQ scores. This neglect is especially significant for the interpretation of his study, because an IQ cutoff was used to determine the composition of the sample. Environmental opportunities worked in favor of including children from middle- and upper-class homes. These were the children best prepared to be evaluated in test situations, as well as the ones most familiar with the kinds of materials included in the mental tests. Consequently, this was the group most likely to be represented in the sample Terman was constructing. His study is therefore best interpreted as an investigation of giftedness among a group of relatively privileged children.[86]

The merits and limitations of Terman's study aside, it provides insight into the cultural influences that shaped American psychology in its formative years, as well as into the impact of psychology in producing social change. Terman was committed to the advancement of psychology as a science, and a central aim of this project was to demonstrate the applicability of psychology to the social progress of America. Like so many psychologists of his generation, he was swept up by the promise of applied psychology as demonstrated by the army mental testing program of World War I. Terman had played a leading role in the development of the army tests, and during the 1920s he successfully contributed to the establishment of mass intelligence testing programs in American schools. Terman saw testing as providing the means for appropriately classifying schoolchildren according to their native ability. In this way a meritocratic society could be developed, with everyone contributing within the limits of his or her potential. The testing movement, as guided by Terman and others, thus provided the basis for an efficient, ordered society. "Prediction and control," "human engineering," and "social efficiency" were catch phrases for postwar American psychology. Furthermore, American society was receptive. Efficiency and order had been themes of the Progressive era reform movement of 1890–1920.[87]

Emerging from the interplay of scientific development and social context, Terman's study was part of an innovative trend of extending the psychology laboratory to the real world. Spurred by the ambitious involvement of the discipline in World War I, psychologists in the postwar years looked increasingly to education, business, the family, and other social domains as laboratory settings. Terman's study of the gifted, with its emphasis on longitudinal stability and the development of observational and measurement techniques to assess the external environment, represents one of the most successful examples of American psychology's movement toward the real-world experiment.

Notes

1. Lewis M. Terman et al., *Genetic Studies of Genius*, vol. 1, *Mental and Physical Traits of a Thousand Gifted Children* (Stanford, Calif.: Stanford University Press, 1925), p. 6.
2. Lewis M. Terman and Melita H. Oden, *Genetic Studies of Genius*, vol. 4, *The Gifted Child Grows Up: Twenty-Five Years' Follow-up of a Superior Group* (Stanford, Calif.: Stanford University Press, 1947), p. 3.
3. For discussions of the concept of meritocracy, see Samuel Bowles and Herbert Gintis, *Schooling in Capitalist America* (New York: Basic Books, 1976), pp. 102–24; and Jeffrey M. Blum, *Pseudoscience and Mental Ability: The Origins and Fallacies of the IQ Controversy* (New York: Monthly Review Press, 1978), pp. 161–81.
4. Terman expressed his ideas about a meritocratic society in various places. For a particularly good example, see Lewis M. Terman, "Were We Born That Way?", *World's Work* 44 (1922):655–60.
5. See Lewis M. Terman, "The Status of Applied Psychology in the United States," *Journal of Applied Psychology* 5 (1921):1–4.

 6. See Lewis M. Terman, "Trails to Psychology," in A *History of Psychology in Autobiography*, vol. 2, ed. Carl Murchison (Worcester, Mass.: Clark University Press, 1932), pp. 297–331.
 7. Ibid., p. 298.
 8. Lewis M. Terman, "A Preliminary Study in the Psychology and Pedagogy of Leadership," *Pedagogical Seminary* 11 (1904):413–51.
 9. Lewis M. Terman, "Genius and Stupidity: A Study of the Intellectual Processes of Seven 'Bright' and Seven 'Stupid' Boys," *Pedagogical Seminary* 13 (1906): 307–73.
10. H. H. Goddard, "The Binet and Simon Tests of Intellectual Capacity," *The Training School* 5 (1908):3–9; and idem, "A Measuring Scale for Intelligence," *The Training School* 6 (1910):146–55.
11. Lewis M. Terman and H. G. Childs, "A Tentative Revision and Extension of the Binet-Simon Measuring Scale of Intelligence," *Journal of Educational Psychology* 3 (1912):61–74, 133–43, 198–208, 277–89.
12. Lewis M. Terman, *The Measurement of Intelligence* (Boston: Houghton Mifflin, 1916).
13. See Lewis M. Terman, "The Mental Test as a Psychological Method," *Psychological Review* 31 (1924):93–117.
14. For a discussion of the interplay between the research laboratory and the real world, see Bruno Latour, "Give Me a Laboratory and I will Raise the World," in *Science Observed: Perspectives in the Social Study of Science*, ed. Karin D. Knorr-Cetina and Michael Mulkay (Beverly Hills, Calif.: Sage, 1983), pp. 141–70.
15. See Robert M. Yerkes, "Psychology in Relation to the War," *Psychological Review* 25 (1918):85–115.
16. Clarence S. Yoakum and Robert M. Yerkes, *Army Mental Tests* (New York: Holt, 1920), p. 2.
17. See Daniel J. Kevles, "Testing the Army's Intelligence: Psychologists and the Military in World War I," *Journal of American History* 55 (1968):565–81; and Franz Samelson, "Putting Psychology on the Map: Ideology and Intelligence Testing," in *Psychology in Social Context*, ed. Allan R. Buss (New York: Irvington, 1979), pp. 103–68.
18. Lewis M. Terman, *The Intelligence of School Children* (Boston: Houghton Mifflin, 1919), p. xiv.
19. Terman also developed a comparable test at the high-school level—the Terman Group Test of Mental Ability for grades 7–12.
20. Lewis M. Terman, Virgil E. Dickson, A. H. Sutherland, Raymond H. Franzen, C. R. Tupper, and Grace Fernald, *Intelligence Tests and School Reorganization* (Yonkers, N.Y.: World Book Company, 1922).
21. Lewis M. Terman, "The Conservation of Talent," *School and Society* 19 (1924):359–64.
22. See David B. Tyack, *The One Best System: A History of American Urban Education* (Cambridge, Mass.: Harvard University Press, 1974), pp. 198–216; and Paul D. Chapman, "Schools as Sorters: Lewis M. Terman and the Intelligence

Testing Movement, 1890–1930" (Ph.D. diss., Stanford University, 1980); Ann Arbor, Mich.: University Microfilms, no. 80-11615.

23. Terman, "Were We Born That Way?", pp. 657–59.

24. See Lewis M. Terman, "The Problem," in Terman et al., *Intelligence Tests and School Reorganization*, pp. 1–31, quote on p. 3.

25. Lewis M. Terman, Introduction to *Mental Tests and the Classroom Teacher*, by Virgil E. Dickson (Yonkers, N.Y.: World Book Company, 1923), pp. xiv–xv, quote on p. xv. This monograph describes demonstration tracking plans in the schools in Oakland and Berkeley, California.

26. Terman and Oden, *Genetic Studies of Genius*, vol. 4, pp. 1–2. In an earlier publication Terman had generally supported the thesis that precocious giftedness was associated with psychopathology; see Lewis M. Terman, "A Study in Precocity and Prematuration," *American Journal of Psychology* 16 (1905):145–83.

27. Lewis M. Terman, "The Mental Hygiene of Exceptional Children," *Pedagogical Seminary* 22 (1915):529–37.

28. Terman, *Intelligence of School Children*, pp. 165–267.

29. Terman et al., *Genetic Studies*, vol. 1, p. 4.

30. Ibid.

31. Lewis M. Terman, "The Intelligence Quotient of Francis Galton in Childhood," *American Journal of Psychology* 28 (1917):209–15.

32. Galton's early intellectual prowess did not prepare him particularly well for academic success. Once he left the tutelage of his family, his academic record was rather mediocre. See Raymond E. Fancher, "Biographical Origins of Francis Galton's Psychology," *Isis* 74 (1983):227–33.

33. Lewis M. Terman, "An Experiment in Infant Education," *Journal of Applied Psychology* 2 (1918):219–28.

34. Lewis M. Terman and Jessie C. Fenton, "Preliminary Report on a Gifted Juvenile Author," *Journal of Applied Psychology* 5 (1921):163–78.

35. Terman et al., *Genetic Studies*, vol. 1, pp. 5–6.

36. For histories of child development and longitudinal studies, see John E. Anderson, "Child Development: An Historical Perspective," *Child Development* 27 (1956):181–96; and Robert R. Sears, "Your Ancients Revisited: A History of Child Development," in *Review of Child Development Research*, vol. 5, ed. E. Mavis Hetherington (Chicago: University of Chicago Press, 1975), pp. 1–73.

37. Terman et al., *Genetic Studies*, vol. 1, pp. 5–17.

38. Ruch's work in developing the achievement test was related to the development of the Stanford Achievement Test, coauthored with Kelley and Terman.

39. In following up the gifted sample since 1970, Robert Sears and his collaborators discovered some errors in the original scoring of the Stanford-Binet tests. In fact, a few of the subjects had IQs a little below the 135 cutoff point for the group. See Lewis M. Terman, Robert R. Sears, Lee J. Cronbach, and Pauline S. Sears, *Terman Life Cycle Study of Children of High Ability, 1922–1982* (Ann Arbor, Mich.: Inter-University Consortium for Political and Social Research, 1983), p. 1.

40. Terman et al., *Genetic Studies*, vol. 1, pp. 19–37.

41. Grades 1 and 2 were initially canvassed using only the Stanford-Binet. However, to make the work of the field assistants manageable, these grades were subsequently eliminated from the survey, in November 1921 (ibid., p. 8).

42. Florence L. Goodenough to Lewis M. Terman, 22 Jan. 1922, Lewis M. Terman Papers, Stanford University Archives, Stanford University Libraries, Stanford, California.

43. Terman to Goodenough, 27 Jan. 1922, Terman Papers.

44. There were actually several control groups, each drawn primarily from the population of California schoolchildren. For the Stanford-Binet and the Stanford Achievement Test, the control groups were the students used in developing the tests. For instruments constructed specially for the study of the gifted, the control groups were drawn largely from the schools that contributed to the gifted sample. See Terman et al., *Genetic Studies*, vol. 1, pp. 45, 177, 291, 393, 445, 461.

45. Terman and Oden, *Genetic Studies*, vol. 4, p. 7. These figures were corrected from those reported in earlier volumes.

46. Terman acknowledged this possibility but felt that it was not a factor, since the vast majority of nominations were made by women teachers. He also pointed out that the sex ratio among those who actually qualified was higher than that among the original nominations. Nevertheless, these points do not address the possible bias in favor of boys in both the nomination and the testing situations. For Terman's discussion, see Terman et al., *Genetic Studies*, vol. 1, pp. 50–51.

47. Ibid., p. 12. Data collection during the second year of the study was supported by an additional Commonwealth Fund grant.

48. The summary results are taken from the updated description in Terman and Oden, *Genetic Studies*, vol. 4, pp. 11–57.

49. No estimates were made regarding Chinese and Japanese children, due to the fact that, for the most part, they attended segregated schools, and these schools were not canvassed.

50. Terman and Oden, *Genetic Studies*, vol. 4, p. 57.

51. Terman et al., *Genetic Studies*, vol. 1, pp. 639–40.

52. Catharine M. Cox, *Genetic Studies of Genius*, vol. 2, *The Early Mental Traits of Three Hundred Geniuses* (Stanford, Calif.: Stanford University Press, 1926).

53. Lewis M. Terman, Preface to ibid., p. vi.

54. Ibid., pp. viii–ix.

55. Published as Barbara S. Burks, Dortha W. Jensen, and Lewis M. Terman, *Genetic Studies of Genius*, vol. 3, *The Promise of Youth: Follow-up Studies of a Thousand Gifted Children* (Stanford, Calif.: Stanford University Press, 1930).

56. Ibid., p. 22.

57. Ibid., p. 475.

58. Ibid., pp. 153–61.

59. The final version of the M-F test is contained in Lewis M. Terman and Catharine Cox Miles, *Sex and Personality: Studies in Masculinity and Femininity* (New York: McGraw-Hill, 1936), pp. 482–530.

60. Burks, Jensen, and Terman, *Genetic Studies*, vol. 3, p. 161.

61. Ibid., pp. 328–31.
62. Ibid., pp. 471–72.
63. Leta S. Hollingworth to Terman, 3 Jan. 1921, Terman Papers.
64. Burks, Jensen, and Terman, *Genetic Studies*, vol. 3, pp. 467–69. This section appeared in the last chapter, which was written by Terman.
65. Ibid., p. 468.
66. Terman and Oden, *Genetic Studies*, vol. 4.
67. A summary of these results is provided in Lewis M. Terman and Melita H. Oden, *Genetic Studies of Genius*, vol. 5, *The Gifted Group at Mid-Life: Thirty-five Years' Follow-up of the Superior Child* (Stanford, Calif.: Stanford University Press, 1959), pp. 21–22.
68. Terman and Oden, *Genetic Studies*, vol. 4, p. 349. This investigation was limited to men, because it was felt that the achievement of women would be difficult to estimate due to a lack of adequate norms.
69. Ibid., pp. 349–52.
70. Ibid., p. 352.
71. Terman and Oden, *Genetic Studies*, vol. 5.
72. Ibid., pp. 143–52. See also Lewis M. Terman, "Scientists and Nonscientists in a Group of 800 Gifted Men," *Psychological Monographs* 68 (1954): no. 7 (whole no. 378).
73. Rounding out the overall pattern were data obtained from spouses and children. The spouses had high educational achievement and were generally of high intellectual calibre. The IQ testing of the offspring also revealed superior intellectual functioning. See Terman and Oden, *Genetic Studies*, vol. 5, pp. 136–42.
74. The most extensive was a two-day interview with A. E. Wiggam, a journalist who specialized in popularizing scientific research. This interview was written up and included in A. E. Wiggam, *Exploring Your Mind with the Psychologists* (New York: Blue Ribbon Books, 1928), pp. 213–72.
75. Terman to John Llewellen, 16 Dec. 1947, Terman Papers.
76. Terman to Eliza Merrill Hickok, 27 Mar. 1947, Terman Papers.
77. Lewis M. Terman, typescript of radio address for the Quiz Kid program 7 Dec. 1947, Terman Papers.
78. These files, which are confidential, are part of the Terman Papers and are located in Stanford's psychology department.
79. Terman, "Trails to Psychology," pp. 298–05.
80. Terman and Oden, *Genetic Studies*, vol. 4, pp. 1–2. Also by this time, organizations such as the American Association for Gifted Children and the National Association for Gifted Children played active roles in promoting the interests of the gifted. Terman was an honorary vice-president of the former and a member of the board of the latter.
81. Robert R. Sears (interviewed 16 Mar. 1984) and Lee J. Cronbach (interviewed 29 Mar. 1984) have each indicated how being a subject in the study benefited their own educational and career development. There are also many instances of this kind in the files on the gifted subjects. On the other hand, Cronbach also reported that, as a subject, he felt the pressures associated with achievement,

especially because the label "genius" was attached to the study. He feels that this label created a sense of inadequacy among many subjects because of the high expectations connected with being in a study of genius so-called.

82. "Prodigious Failure," *Time*, 31 July 1944, pp. 60, 62.
83. Ibid., p. 62.
84. Terman, *The Measurement of Intelligence*, p. 12.
85. Terman, "Were We Born That Way?", p. 658.
86. Another limitation of Terman's study is the fact that none of the control groups were followed up. For the gifted children in the study, the fact that they were so identified had an impact on their future development. Robert Sears points out that it would have been helpful to have had a random sample from the same communities as the gifted group, as well as a comparable gifted group subject to different treatment. Cohorts from later periods would also have added to the usefulness of the study. See Sears, "Your Ancients Revisited," p. 55.
87. See Samuel Haber, *Efficiency and Uplift: Scientific Management in the Progressive Era, 1890–1920* (Chicago: University of Chicago Press, 1964); and Robert H. Weibe, *The Search for Order: 1877–1920* (New York: Hill and Wang, 1967).

8

Concerns about
Artifacts in
Psychological
Experiments

Jerry M. Suls
State University of New
York at Albany
Ralph L. Rosnow
Temple University

Much of the complexity of the human behavior described by psychological experimenters lies in the nature of the human organism. However, some of it derives from the social nature of psychological experiments and from the experimenting psychologist's model of human behavior, the research subject. That is, some of it resides in the fact that participants often know perfectly well that they are research subjects and that they are expected to play a certain role in interaction with another human being, the experimenter. Our purpose in this chapter is to describe the rise of concerns about this threat to validity, which takes the form of a class of systematic errors often referred to as "experimental artifacts,"[1] and the reaction of psychologists to these concerns.

Early Concerns

Since the late nineteenth century, when psychology emerged as a formal discipline, psychologists have relied on the experiment as a major tool with which to conduct research. Early experimental psychologists grappled with one aspect of the artifact problem, even as behaviorism became dominant in the first decades of this century. Agitation about the biases of introspection led, in turn, to concerns about the validity of laboratory procedures, expressed by such questions as: Does a particular manipulation adequately correspond to a hypothetical construct? Have confounding variables been eliminated so that unambiguous inferences may be drawn from the data? Such concerns notwithstanding, early psychologists generally avoided the more fundamental problem of the interdependence of the intentionally imposed treatment conditions and the experimental artifacts that might unintentionally result from the type of role consciously enacted by their subjects.

Hindsight suggests at least three instances during the early part of this century—and there are others—that could conceivably have sparked interest in isolating, measuring, and possibly eliminating or circumventing experimental artifacts. Foremost among these is the case of Clever Hans, a horse known throughout Europe for his remarkable "intellectual" feats. Hans could tap out the answers to mathematical problems or the date of any day mentioned, aided ostensibly by a code table in front of him. Visitors from all over Europe came to examine Hans. One visitor, the psychologist Oskar Pfungst, discovered (through careful observations made over a six-month period) that Hans was responding to unintentional cues from his questioners.[2] For example, someone would ask Hans an arithmetic question that required a long tapping response, and then the questioner would lean forward as if settling in for a long wait. Hans would respond to the questioner's forward movement, not to the actual question, and would keep tapping until the questioner unwittingly, perhaps by suddenly straightening up, communicated the expectancy that Hans would stop.

Pfungst's unraveling of the mystery of Clever Hans dramatically demonstrated the potentially contaminating influence of unconscious cues deriving from questioners' expectations. Given this influence on animal subjects, might not the same principle hold for human research subjects interacting with an experimenter oriented by his own theoretical expectations and hypotheses? Though Pfungst's efforts were published and cited, the wider methodological implications of his discovery did not strike a resonant chord in psychology during this period. To be sure, a number of leading researchers voiced their suspicion that experimenters might unwittingly influence their subjects.[3] However, their concerns, along with the wider methodological implications of Pfungst's discovery, went largely unheeded for several decades.

In the 1920s, the results of a series of experiments conducted in a factory raised the artifact question somewhat more directly. We refer to the Hawthorne study conducted by Elton Mayo and his colleagues, which was designed to examine how workers' productivity and job satisfaction were affected by workplace conditions (lighting, temperature, rest periods, and so on).[4] The striking result, which was repeated by historians and textbook writers, for many of whom the "Hawthorne effect" became synonymous with the placebo effect as a tag label for the power of suggestion in experimental research, was that the workers' production increased or remained stable whatever changes in working conditions were implemented by the researchers. Whether illumination was increased or decreased, whether rest periods were lengthened or shortened, worker production never slackened. Further, these results were obtained not because of the particular nature of the experimental manipulations, but reportedly because the workers were "flattered" to have been selected as research participants and were eager to perform well. Since the interpretations (and misinterpretations) of this seminal study are discussed in chapter 6, it will suffice to say here that, as in the case of Clever Hans, the official account of the Hawthorne experiments, as echoed by researchers and textbook-writers, failed to spark any systematic research on the experimental artifact problem.

This is not to say, however, that psychologists were, without exception, complacent about the wider theoretical implications of the data-collection situation. The third in our trilogy of instances took place in 1933. Saul Rosenzweig (a young psychologist who had just completed his Ph.D. at Harvard) published what, with hindsight, is generally regarded as a landmark paper, in which he argued that the experimental situation is a psychological problem in its own right.[5] Rosenzweig contended that subjects might try to guess the purpose of the experiment and then give the answers they thought were desired by the experimenter. Further, the experimenter might unwittingly influence the results (not unlike the questioners of Clever Hans). Rosenzweig suggested that these concerns might be profitably investigated and that ways should be found to avoid or minimize the problems. It is yet to be understood what led Rosenzweig to this perceptive analysis and why he did not actively pursue its implications. In any case, his paper was largely ignored, only to be rediscovered by researchers working in the social psychology of the experiment four decades later.[6]

Early Resistance to Artifacts

In light of Pfungst's dramatic discovery, the Hawthorne study, and Rosenzweig's prescient analysis, it might have been expected that research on experimental artifacts would have been high on psychologists' agendas. However, the rise of sustained theoretical interest in, and systematic research on, the experimental artifact problem did not begin in earnest until the 1950s. But why did early psychologists tend to ignore or fail to appreciate what, in retrospect, were clearly serious issues? We can think of three plausible explanations.

First, the phenomenon of artifacts stemming from playing a subject role presupposes the active influence of conscious cognitions. Such a presupposition was largely inconsistent with behaviorist tenets at the time, which emphasized the use of only observable responses as data and dismissed cognition as a variable of less than scientific significance.[7]

Second, concerns about pervasive biases that may be part and parcel of the laboratory experiment were possibly viewed as likely to impede the emergence and making influence of experimental psychology due to its status as a "science" in the United States. There was a tremendous growth in academic psychology departments and an increasing role for psychologists in government, the military, and industry because of widespread optimism as to the likely benefits of scientific psychology. Voicing concerns about possible weaknesses of laboratory research, on which major psychological facts and theories were based, might promote doubts about the field and undermine its influence.

Third, owing in large part to its scientific aspirations, psychology in its formative stages was strongly influenced by ideas gleaned from physics and biology—for example, by covering-law models rooted in simple mechanistic tenets related to the Cartesian conception.[8] By the 1930s, psychologists were finding support for the major assumptions of the mechanistic approach in objectivist assertions of the logical positivist view.[9] This approach placed great faith in the impartiality of experimental research, yet the case of Clever Hans and the Hawthorne study raised, by implication, the possibility that impartiality was an illusion. Is it any surprise that psychologists were resistant to concerns that, if taken seriously, would seem to erode what many viewed as a fundamental verity of modern science?

We submit that, for these three reasons, early psychologists were not prepared to take the methodological implications of Pfungst's study of Clever Hans, the Hawthorne effect, or Rosenzweig's conceptual analysis as seriously as they might have, had the historical period been more conducive to a questioning of fundamental verities. The situation began to change in the late 1950s, as positivist and logical empiricist tenets began to lose their hold on psychologists with the rise of cognitive psychology and the sprouting of a more liberalized idea of scientific psychology. By the 1960s, scientists in all fields were talking about the critical limits of scientific inquiry, instead of still treating science as an endless frontier. In almost every field, from physics and mathematics to philosophy, biomedicine, and sociology, there seemed to be a crisis of confidence brewing, at the center of which was an erosion of trust in traditional postulates.

Contemporary Artifact Researchers

Martin T. Orne was one of the first wave of contemporary artifact researchers to initiate a program of empirical investigation into the social psychology of the psychological experiment. Orne came to realize the need for systematic research on this subject as a consequence of observations made in the course of his research on hypnosis. His experiments of the 1950s suggested that the trance manifestations exhibited by volunteer subjects on entering hypnosis might be primarily determined by the subjects' motivation to "act out" the role of a hypnotized person. Both the subject's preconceptions of how a hypnotized person ought to act and cues communicated by the hypnotist were observed to be determinants of the subject's conception of how this role was to be enacted.[10]

Orne theorized that if subjects participating in hypnosis research wanted to give the hypnotist what he or she was looking for, then subjects in other kinds of psychological research might be doing the same thing. Orne argued that research participants typically are sensitive to any task-orienting cues that are unwittingly communicated to them via campus scuttlebutt, the experimenter's instructions, the research setting, and other aspects of the experimental situation, and that they are prone to act out the role of the "good subject" by giving experimenters what they think they want. Orne coined the term "demand characteristics of the experimental situation" to refer to the mixture of hints and cues that govern a subject's perceptions of his or her role and of the experimenter's hypothesis.[11]

One representative study of the effects of demand characteristics tested the hypothesis that subjects under experimental hypnosis will behave in whatever ways they are led to believe are characteristic of hypnotized subjects.[12] Orne first concocted a novel characteristic of hypnosis, "catalepsy of the dominant hand," which he demonstrated, using volunteers, to a large college class in a lecture on hypnosis. The volunteers were given the post-hypnotic suggestion that on entering a trance they would manifest catalepsy of the dominant hand. The class was instructed that catalepsy of the dominant hand was a classic reaction of the hypnotized subject, and attention was called to the fact that the right-handed subject exhibited catalepsy of the right hand and the left-handed subject exhibited catalepsy of the left hand. In another lecture section, designed to serve as a control condition, a demonstration of hypnosis was also given, but there was no discussion or display of catalepsy of the dominant hand. A few weeks later, students from both classes were invited to serve as research subjects in a study of hypnosis. Catalepsy of the dominant hand was exhibited by almost all the subjects who had attended the lecture and demonstration where it had been asserted that the response was characteristic of the hypnotized state, but by none of the subjects in the control section. Orne concluded that the typical subject is attentive to demand characteristics and attempts to be a "good subject" by confirming what he or she believes to be the experimenter's scientific hypothesis.

Studies by Orne and other artifact researchers have demonstrated that research participants will comply with demand characteristics in diverse kinds of experiments, including attitude-change experiments,[13] figure-ground perception studies,[14] and classical conditioning experiments.[15] In research on sensory deprivation, for example, Orne and Scheibe found that control subjects vicariously exposed to the accoutrements of this research but not actually deprived of sensory stimulation reported the same dramatic hallucinations as did sensorily deprived subjects.[16] In other words, it appeared that the (unwitting) manipulation of demand characteristics could produce effects that would normally be ascribed to manipulation of the independent variable (in this case, sensory deprivation).

Expectations of Experimenters

At the same time that Orne and his associates were exploring the role of demand characteristics, Robert Rosenthal was studying experimenter-expectancy bias, which subsequently became known as the "Rosenthal effect." The bias consists in the experimenter hypothesizing a certain experimental outcome and then unintentionally behaving in such a way as to make the prophesied event more likely to occur. As in the case of Orne's research on demand characteristics, Rosenthal was serendipitously led to this artifact in the pursuit of other research interests. In his dissertation research, he attempted to demonstrate the psychoanalytic mechanism of projection, but he found scant evidence.[17] However, he did discover through some secondary analyses evidence that "unconscious experimenter bias" may have influenced his results. This led him to turn his attention to the demonstration of unconscious experimenter bias. In a long series of experimental studies, beginning with work in which he collaborated with Kermit L. Fode (for which they were awarded the 1960–61 Sociopsychological Prize of the American Association for the Advancement of Science), he undertook a systematic examination of this form of bias.

In one experiment, Rosenthal and Fode informed a group of student experimenters that their rats were "maze bright" and another group that their rats were "maze dull."[18] The students were instructed to run the animals through a set of learning trials in a T-maze. Whenever the rat ran to the correct side of the maze, it was rewarded with food. From the first day and continuing through the trials, animals believed to be bright showed daily improvement in performance, whereas those believed to be dull improved at the beginning but then showed a worsening in performance. Subsequent research along similar lines reported experimenter-expectancy effects for operant acquisition, stimulus discrimination, and behavioral chaining in rats.[19] Rosenthal postulated the reason for such findings: experimenters who believed that their rats had been bred for brightness handled their animals more gently and more often than did those expecting poor performance from their "dull" rats. The "brighter" rats were also watched more closely, which in the operant learning situation, may have led to more rapid, appropriate reinforcement of the desired responses.

Rosenthal and his co-workers also examined the role of experimenter expectancy in research on human subjects. In another early study, Rosenthal and Fode had student experimenters instruct subjects to rate a series of portrait snapshots of people on a continuum of perceived failure to perceived success (rated from -10 to $+10$).[20] Though all the faces had been selected because independent judges had rated them as neutral on the failure-success criterion, one group of experimenters was now led to believe that their subjects would average a -5 rating and another group that their subjects would average a $+5$ rating. Rosenthal and Fode's finding was that subjects run by experimenters who had been led to expect a positive rating responded more positively than subjects run by experimenters who had been led to expect a negative rating.

Several hundred studies have probed for these and other such experimenter-expectancy effects, with relatively impressive degrees of success.[21] The behavioral mechanism by which all these effects operate is not entirely clear, but they appear to be mediated by kinesic and paralinguistic cues to which subjects are sensitive and responsive in varying degrees.

Evaluation Apprehension

Although Orne theorized that subjects in psychology experiments have a predilection to enact the good-subject role, in the early 1960s, it became clear to a number of artifact researchers, including Orne, that subjects do not always want to fulfill the experimenter's scientific expectations. For example, many subjects become concerned about what the "experimenter is really trying to find out about me"; Milton J. Rosenberg was the first to name and systematically investigate this variable—"evaluation apprehension"—within the conceptual framework of the social psychology of the psychological experiment.[22]

Rosenberg's interest stemmed from an influential experiment performed by Leon Festinger and J. Merrill Carlsmith in the late 1950s.[23] Festinger and Carlsmith reported that college students paid a dollar to argue for a position they did not believe in were subsequently more likely to bring their attitudes into line with their argument than another group of students who were paid twenty dollars to argue for a position they did not believe in. According to Festinger, the subsequent attitude shift was the result of cognitive dissonance: saying something one does not believe for a small incentive produces an uncomfortable psychological state which, presumably, can be reduced by bringing one's attitude into line with one's public behavior. To Rosenberg, Festinger and Carlsmith's results were puzzling, since, according to general reinforcement theory, as Rosenberg interpreted it, a large incentive should produce more attitude change than a small incentive. Rosenberg postulated that an artifact in the Festinger and Carlsmith procedure might actually account for their results, rather than the claimed manipulation of cognitive dissonance, and he set about to prove his point.

Rosenberg designed a replication experiment in which the counterattitudinal statement was made to appear as part of one study and the measurement of attitude was made to appear as part of another.[24] He reasoned that the subjects in Festinger and Carlsmith's experiment who were offered an incentive for expressing a counterattitudinal statement might have become suspicious as to the purpose of the study, in particular as to whether they were being evaluated on some important personality dimension. That is, Rosenberg conjectured, Festinger and Carlsmith's subjects thought, "The experimenter probably wants to see whether getting paid so much will affect my own attitude, whether I am the kind of person whose views can be changed by buying them off."[25] As a result, subjects paid the larger sum of money would be prone to resist giving evidence of attitude change so as not to be perceived as people who were dishonest or could be bribed. In short, Rosenberg theorized that in Festinger and Carlsmith's high-incentive condition, subjects felt evaluation apprehension, concern about being observed and judged while in the laboratory setting. Rosenberg thought that it should be possible to avoid this potentially confounding variable in his own replication experiment by separating the counterattitudinal statement from the attitude measurement. Presumably, under the conditions operating in his own study, subjects would experience no evaluation apprehension associated with expressing their attitudes, and hence they would show more attitude change after receiving a large reward than a small reward (just as reinforcement theory predicted).

Rosenberg found the result he expected, which he interpreted as indicating that evaluation apprehension (not dissonance reduction) was responsible for the outcome of Festinger and Carlsmith's study. Rosenberg's challenging conclusion immediately began to arouse consternation among psychological experimenters, particularly those working in the area of attitude change. But his thesis also caused uneasiness among researchers working in other areas, since the possible confounding influence of evaluation apprehension bias was suspected in a wide range of areas. It was recognized that subjects experiencing evaluation apprehension might develop hypotheses as to how to win positive evaluation and avoid negative evaluation. Of course, if this effect were merely to increase error variance, as opposed to introducing some systematic bias in experimental responses, it would not be of such interest to researchers. But Rosenberg's work, like that of Orne and Rosenthal, raised the possibility that such tendencies "may exert systematic biases upon experimental responding . . . and generate significant findings that happen also to be illusory ones."[26]

Note that sometimes the "apprehensive subject" role may conflict with the "good subject" role. In some experimental settings the motives of "looking good" and "confirming the hypothesis" may be pitted against each other. In other settings (the more usual ones, to be sure), the two roles complement one another. For example, another team of investigators performed an experiment in which the subjects were asked to read a personality sketch of a fictitious character named Jim.[27] The subjects were instructed to rate Jim on a series of scales as friendly or unfriendly, forward or shy, and so forth. An actor then interrupted the experimenter while the test booklets were being distributed. In one treatment condition, the actor said that he had heard from a friend that the experimenter was trying to prove that "only people with really high IQs are able to come up with the correct impression of someone from a short paragraph." To the actor's question of whether this was the actual aim of the study, the experimenter replied that he would answer later, when the experiment had been completed. In this condition, complying with demand characteristics would presumably be perceived as congruent with the desire to project a favorable image. In another treatment condition, the actor said that he had heard that the purpose of the experiment was to prove that "only people with really low IQs would even attempt to form impressions of a person just from a short description." In this condition, complying with demand characteristics would presumably be perceived as incongruent with the desire to present a favorable image. The results indicated that subjects, given a choice between "doing good" and "looking good," opted to look good rather than comply with demand characteristics.

There is also the possibility that subjects may in some cases be "negativistic" and act in ways that are antagonistic toward the experimenter because of previous frustrating experiences or negative feelings about psychologists. As a result, such subjects may deliberately respond counter to perceived task-orienting cues. Research has not indicated this to be a dominant motive among subjects, but instances have been reported, nonetheless.[28]

Volunteer Selection Effects

As if experimenter expectancy, the good-subject effect, and evaluation apprehension were not problems enough, another artifact problem also surfaced during the 1960s: volunteer-subject bias. For some time it had been recognized by psychologists that most people who participated as subjects for research were college students enrolled in lower-level psychology courses. For example, it was reported that the percentage of research subjects who were college students in studies published in the *Journal of Personality and Social Psychology* increased from 20 percent in 1949 to 49 percent in 1959 and 53 percent in 1969.[29] An often quoted remark made by Quinn McNemar in 1946 was that "the existing science of human behavior is largely the science of the behavior of the college sophomore."[30] However, in a review of research comparing persons who volunteered to participate in experiments with those who did not, Rosenthal and Rosnow noted that even volunteering sophomores were not entirely representative of sophomores in general.[31] This literature revealed a number of procedures found useful in comparing characteristics of those more likely and those less likely to find their way into the role of data-producer for the psychological experimenter. For example, an investigator might begin with an archive containing for each person all the information desired for a comparison between volunteers and nonvolunteers. Requests for volunteers would be made some time later, and those who volunteered would be compared with those who did not volunteer on all the items in which the investigator was interested. Rosenthal and Rosnow reported that volunteers, as compared with nonvolunteers, tended to be higher in social class, more intelligent, more sociable, more approval-motivated, and so on. To the extent that experimenters routinely employed volunteer subjects as research participants, it followed that their experimental findings might not be readily generalizable to the population as a whole, Rosenthal and Rosnow concluded.

Of course, this is a problem of external validity—that is, the approximate validity with which conclusions are drawn about the generalizability of a causal relationship. Researchers, including Rosenthal and Rosnow, also observed that volunteer bias might affect internal validity—the validity of statements made about whether X causes Y—and construct validity—whether the psychological qualities contributing to the relationship between X and Y are properly named. In one representative study, researchers had volunteers and nonvolunteers (identified by their earlier interest or lack of interest in serving as research subjects) participate in a standard attitude-change experiment employing the Solomon four-group design.[32] The purpose of this design (named after its developer, Richard L. Solomon) is to assess initial performance without contaminating it by pretesting; it also allows researchers to determine the interaction between pretesting and the treatment. Some of the volunteers and nonvolunteers were pretested with a questionnaire measuring attitudes toward large-scale nuclear research. Half the participants were then given a persuasive communication that was represented as an excerpt from a *New York Times* editorial on the scientific and social implications of the discovery of a new element called "galaxium" which might be used in large-scale nuclear research. The remaining subjects received a control communication, also represented as an excerpt from the *New York Times*, on the subject of sexual promiscuity among college students. All the subjects were then tested using the original questionnaire. Consistent with earlier findings, no simple pretest-treatment interaction effects were found, though as hypothesized by the researchers, second-order interactions with volunteer status revealed that the pretested volunteers "overreacted" to the treatment and the pretested nonvolunteers "underreacted" to it. One implication drawn by the researchers was that in this kind of research situation, type I errors (which reject the null hypothesis when it is true) may prevail when the subjects are willing participants and type II errors (which fail to reject the null hypothesis when it is false) may be more likely when the subjects are captive or coerced "nonvolunteers." The researchers also contended that, besides possibly magnifying or eradicating the effects of the treatment, pretesting may in some circumstances distort the relationships that emerge between independent and dependent variables when the research participants are volunteer subjects (who are sensitive and accommodating to demand characteristics).

Coping with Artifacts

Thus, by the 1950s and 1960s, evidence had begun to accumulate which was interpreted as suggesting that certain sources of systematic error, or artifact, were inherent in the experimental situation because of the reactive nature of the relationship between the experimenter and the subject. The implications of the Clever Hans case, the Hawthorne study, and Rosenzweig's conceptual analysis were finally receiving more than lip service. By the late 1960s, numerous scholarly papers and several definitive texts on artifacts in experimental research had appeared, written by a small, but highly visible, group of researchers (experimenters themselves) whose major interest was the social psychology of the experiment.

The next question was: What could experimenting psychologists do to minimize the confounding effects of experimenter expectancy, demand characteristics, evaluation apprehensions, and volunteer-subject bias? A number of proposals were advanced by artifact researchers. As a way of detecting experimental demand cues, for example, Orne proposed the use of "quasi-control subjects."[33] A group of participants drawn from the population from which the research subjects were recruited would be treated as "co-investigators," rather than subjects to be manipulated experimentally. After being informed of all the significant details of the experiment, the quasi-control subjects would be asked to predict how they might behave if they were actual subjects. Similarity between the data from the quasi-control subjects and that from the actual subjects would imply that the experimental results could have been affected by the actual subjects' guesses about how they ought to respond, rather than by the experimental manipulation.

Another alternative described by Orne involved using a "sacrifice group" of subjects. At different points during the course of an experiment the participation of some subjects would be terminated, and they would then be questioned about their perceptions of the experiment up to that point.[34] Of course, these and alternative proposals were recommended as supplementary control procedures, to be administered along with the standard experimental controls that were requisite. Presumably, the vital information gleaned by means of these supplementary procedures would inform the experimenter that a subterfuge was possibly needed to disguise the true nature and purpose of the experiment from the research subjects.

Rosenthal proposed a number of ways of circumventing experimenter-expectancy effects.[35] One possibility was to keep experimenters "blind" as to the hypothesis being tested. This procedure is not foolproof, however; for, even if not informed by the experimenter as to the nature of the hypothesis, hired assistants might formulate their own hypotheses. Another way of controlling for experimenter-expectancy effects was to administer the experimental manipulation in writing or to use an automated treatment of some kind so as to avoid a sustained interaction between the experimenter and the subject. Still another possibility proposed by Rosenthal was to test directly for expectancy effects by employing an "expectancy-control design." That is, a given experiment would be repeated by several experimenters, some of whom would be led to expect a certain effect and some of whom would not. If both groups of experimenters obtained the same size of effect, one could be fairly sure that the effect was "real" and not the consequence of some bias introduced by the theoretical orientation or expectancies of the experimenters. However, if the experimenters who expected to find the particular effect did so, and those who did not expect to find it did not, then one could conclude that the effect was probably due to the expectations of the experimenters as much as to any "real effect."

Another solution designed to minimize subject reactivity was to perform research in natural settings (rather than in the laboratory), without subjects being aware that they were participating in an experiment. When unobtrusive measures are employed in natural settings, this obviates the possibility of participants playing the good-subject role (or some other role) in response to their conscious awareness of being in a psychological experiment. Field studies using a captive population avoid the volunteer-bias problem, but they do not necessarily minimize experimenter-expectancy bias. Experimenters may still unwittingly behave in ways that favor the outcomes they expect. Another problem is that unobtrusive measures (which are often poorly validated) are frequently less reliable than more direct measures, because there is only one observation per subject.

To minimize the volunteer-bias problem in laboratory experiments, Rosenthal and Rosnow recommended a number of techniques for encouraging more nonvolunteers to enter the sampling pool.[36] For instance, they suggested that the appeal for volunteers be made as interesting as possible to the target population. They also recommended that it be made as nonthreatening as possible, so that potential recruits would not be put off by unwarranted fears of unfavorable evaluation. Rosenthal and Rosnow urged researchers not to exert undue pressures on nonvolunteers to participate, however, since that would infringe on the subjects' right to privacy and free choice.

These (and other) procedures, while obviously unable to circumvent the artifact problem entirely, were advanced as ways of making psychological research less vulnerable to artifacts. An attempt was also made to generate a theoretical model to facilitate choice of a particular coping procedure in any given situation.[37] In the next section we consider to what extent such proposals were taken on board by psychologists.

Reaction to the Artifact Threat

There is little question that work on the social psychology of the experiment entered the consciousness and vocabulary of psychologists in the 1960s and 1970s. But to what extent did experimental practices really change? How did the psychological community respond to the artifact threat?

The findings of the artifact researchers were themselves scrutinized for artifacts of various kinds (a point to which we shall return in a moment). In a major critical review, one psychologist stated his impression thus: "Quite apart from any systematic inquiry is the remarkable readiness with which the speculative critique of the experiment has been taken up by the community of social scientists and has affected its methodological attitudes."[38] On the other hand, a survey of the attitudes of psychologists regarding the pervasiveness of experimenter-expectancy bias found that experimenters working in the areas of verbal learning, animal behavior, and physiological psychology viewed experimenter-expectancy effects as being more germane to social, clinical, and applied psychology than to their own research areas.[39] To be sure, another lesson of social psychology is that a change in attitude does not automatically make for a change in behavior. Was this also true of methodological attitudes and behaviors?

To assess whether any substantive changes of note had occurred, Jerry Suls and John Gastorf did a content analysis of all articles reporting laboratory or field experiments published during 1960 in the *Journal of Abnormal and Social Psychology* and *Sociometry* and during 1968 and 1976 in the *Journal of Personality and Social Psychology*, the *Journal of Experimental Social Psychology*, and *Sociometry*.[40] Nineteen sixty was chosen as a baseline since it preceded publication of the bulk of the work of artifact researchers, and 1968 and 1976 were chosen as the second and third periods so as to be able to assess the immediate and the long-term effects of the artifact work. Only social psychology and personality research were surveyed, since these areas were viewed as being the prime focus of the artifact critique, and if there were procedural modifications of note, they should show up most prominently in the journals chosen.

Suls and Gastorf found that 620 articles reporting 757 studies involved field or laboratory experimentation. These studies were analyzed for content and coded in terms of whether they used a written treatment, an automated treatment, or some other experimenter-expectancy control; whether the experimenters were blind to the hypothesis or blind to the treatment; and whether multiple experimenters were used. The results are displayed in figure 8.1, which shows the percentage of studies employing each of these procedures in 1960, 1968, and 1976. The most substantial change was in the use of written treatments. However, this may be a coincidence, rather than a reflection of a methodological advance adopted to control for experimenter bias. The 1960s and 1970s witnessed an increase in interest in social perception, particularly in attribution theory, which frequently lends itself to written procedures. Whether written materials were purposely adopted to minimize expectancy bias or not, they often have that effect. In general, with the exception of the automated treatment category, figure 8.1 shows that there was an increase in the use of these artifact-control procedures from 1960 to 1968 to 1976. All the experiments that were coded as having used a written or an automated

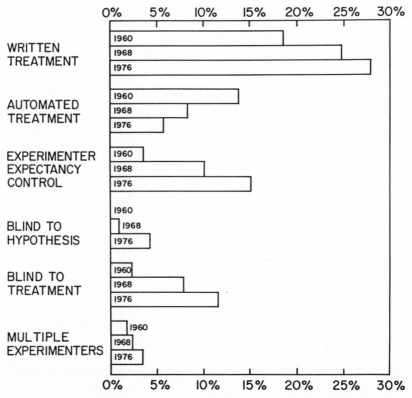

Fig. 8.1. Use of selected artifact control procedures in experiments published during 1960 in the *Journal of Abnormal and Social Psychology* and *Sociometry* and during 1968 and 1976 in the *Journal of Personality and Social Psychology*, the *Journal of Experimental Social Psychology*, and *Sociometry*

treatment or some other expectancy control were counted only once in these three categories. Thus, if a study was coded as having employed an experimenter-expectancy control, it was not eligible to be coded in terms of whether a written or an automated treatment was used as well. Addition of the respective percentages corresponding to these three categories provides an estimate of the general employment of artifact-control procedures in this area of psychology. In sum, artifacts were better controlled in 1976, when almost half the experiments published in these leading journals (48.9 percent) controlled for artifacts in one way or another, than in 1960 (36.1 percent).

Two additional procedures (alluded to previously) for minimizing artifacts are the use of deception and the use of field experiments in which subjects are unaware of their participation. While not coded in the Suls-Gastorf study, surveys indicate that both these procedures are gaining acceptance. For example, Alan E. Gross and India Fleming sampled research articles published in four major social psychological journals during 1959, 1969, and 1978–79 and found that the percentage of studies using deception rose from 1959 to 1969 and did not decrease from 1969 to 1979.[41] Robert J. Menges surveyed studies published in the *Journal of Personality and Social Psychology* in 1971 and found that nearly half employed deception of some kind.[42] Presumably, to the extent that the subject is distracted from the true nature and purpose of the experiment, the biasing effects of demand cues and the experimenter's hypothesis will be attenuated. Interestingly, in the late 1960s, a number of prominent social psychologists criticized the field's reliance on deception techniques,[43] although with little impact, judging from the data reported by Gross and Fleming and by Menges.

As regards the impact of the artifact critique on the use of field (rather than laboratory) settings, Leonard Bickman and Thomas Henchy in 1972 reported an increasing trend toward conducting research in natural settings.[44] Nevertheless, the laboratory setting was apparently still the most common milieu for obtaining scientific information in some major areas of psychological research. David W. Wilson and Robert B. Schafer, in a survey of social psychologists reported in 1978, noted that laboratory experiments were used in 46 percent of instances, field experiments in 12 percent, and nonexperimental field studies in 12 percent, with the remainder divided among archival studies and surveys and so on.[45] The trend noted by Bickman and Henchy toward more studies in field settings may have come about in part because of agitation about experimental artifacts. However, concerns about social relevance no doubt also contributed to this.[46]

One proposition of the sociology of science is that the number of times a work is cited in scientific journals is a good index of its influence.[47] So, as another way to assess reaction to artifact research, we examined citations of four major works over a period of twenty years. The works were: Orne's 1962

American Psychologist article,[48] Rosenthal's book *Experimenter Effects in Be-havioral Research* (published in 1966 and reissued in 1976),[49] Rosenthal and Rosnow's 1969 book *Artifact in Behavioral Research*,[50] and Rosenberg's 1965 *Journal of Personality and Social Psychology* article.[51] The results, culled from the *Social Sciences Citation Index (SSCI)* from 1964 to 1984, are shown in figure 8.2. The frequencies plotted in this figure should be taken as estimates, rather than precise counts, since the points representing the period 1976–80 are the (unweighted) averages interpolated from a summary *SSCI* index. Also some trivial errors were detected in a few original citations listed in *SSCI*; for example, a reference to *Artifact in Behavioral Research* might cite it as having been published in 1968 or 1970. Nevertheless, the citation counts are impressive (particularly those for Orne's article and the two editions of Rosenthal's book) and, overall, support the impression that artifact research has had a significant impact. Further, the patterns are strikingly similar in all four cases, in that they show a rise in citations in the early 1970s and a decline in the 1980s. While the decline might seem to suggest that the influence of this work has sharply diminished, an alternative interpretation might be that the work has become so much a part of the mainstream of social science that researchers no longer feel it necessary to cite particular seminal works.

The Critical Reaction

As noted, the artifact research was itself scrutinized for artifacts of various kinds. It was asked, for example, whether the Rosenthal effect did not raise questions about the very objectivity of the experimenter-expectancy research.[52] Since Rosenthal's experiments were performed by experimenters who also had their own expectations, might those expectations not have affected the results in the expected direction? To be sure, Rosenthal himself was sensitive to this confounding effect; indeed, he described control procedures that could be used to avoid a "meta-expectancy effect." A skeptic might respond that there is an infinite regression of artifacts in psychological experiments, and that the only realistic procedure is to state one's theoretical biases at the outset, rather than hope to eliminate all the artifacts.

Representative of the litany of criticisms issuing from some quarters were a number of arguments advanced by Arie W. Kruglanski in a chapter of a volume in the *Advances in Experimental Social Psychology* series.[53] Reviewing research on demand characteristics, Kruglanski argued that the direction of bias was inconsistent among different studies, sometimes confirming, sometimes disconfirming Orne's hypothesis. Thus Kruglanski concluded that subjects do not consistently try to confirm the experimenter's hypothesis.[54] Turning to evaluation apprehension research, Kruglanski contended that the results there were also inconsistent. He contested an earlier review by Stephen J.

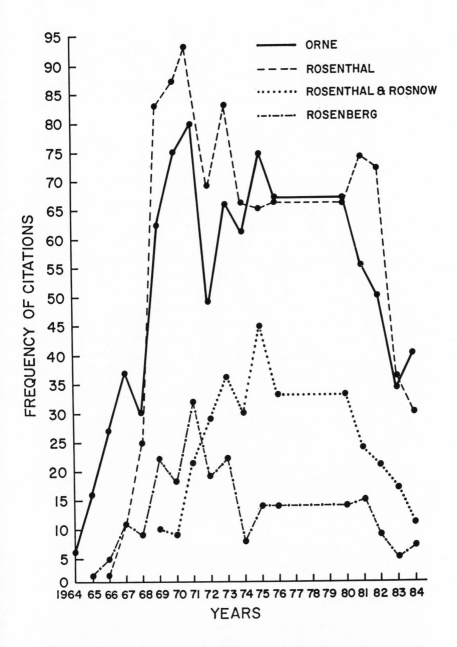

Fig. 8.2. Frequency of citations 1964–84 of Orne's 1962 *American Psychologist* article, Rosenthal's 1966 and 1976 editions of *Experimenter Effects in Behavioral Research,* Rosenthal and Rosnow's 1969 *Artifact in Behavioral Research,* and Roseberg's 1965 *Journal of Personality and Social Psychology* article

Weber and Thomas D. Cook which concluded that subjects were more likely to be apprehensive than cooperative.[55] Kruglanski argued that there was no consistent evidence that either subject role was dominant. The only consistent evidence for bias occurred, he asserted, when the hypothesis was provided to the subject or when subjects were cued as to the nature of the typical or socially desirable response.[56]

Frequently, when a body of research is under attack, one finds the criticism and an invited defense in the same publication. In this instance, however, no rejoinder appeared in *Advances in Experimental Social Psychology*. Kruglanski also reiterated a number of doubts concerning the significance of the volunteer-selection research. He first voiced these criticisms in an article published two years earlier in the *Journal of Personality and Social Psychology* under the title "Much Ado about the 'Volunteer Artifacts.' "[57] A rebuttal by Rosnow and Rosenthal appeared in a subsequent issue of the same journal, and it may be instructive to mention a major criticism of Kruglanski's and Rosnow and Rosenthal's reply in their rebuttal entitled "Taming of the Volunteer Problem: On Coping with Artifacts by Benign Neglect."[58]

In his article, Kruglanski contended that because there were many reasons why a person might volunteer to participate in psychological research, volunteer status, being a "nonunitary construct," was "of little possible interest." In their rejoinder, Rosnow and Rosenthal challenged this argument, on the grounds both that it was traditionally regarded as quite useful to study multiply determined behaviors and that there was a problem of interpretation in Kruglanski's notion of constructs. Rosnow and Rosenthal argued that Kruglanski had confused constructs and measures thought to be related to constructs. Kruglanski asked for internal consistency or reliability of a construct as though one computed KR-20 or Cronbach's alpha for a construct; but one does not compute the reliability of constructs, but of measures, Rosnow and Rosenthal contended. They reported the median reliability of volunteering behavior to be 0.52 with a range from 0.97 to 0.22. As a standard against which to compare these reliability coefficients, they noted that the range of subtest intercorrelations of the Wechsler Adult Intelligence Scale (perhaps the most widely used and carefully developed test of intelligence) went from 0.85 to 0.08 with a median of 0.52.

The Present Situation

Quite apart from specific arguments and counterarguments, it seems clear that the response to the artifact critique has been a combination of acceptance, indicated by citations of artifact work, coverage of this work in standard textbooks, and the various changes in research practices noted by Suls and Gastorf, and skepticism, even resistance from some quarters of the psychological community. For some psychologists, to be sure, the artifact critique constituted a major turning point in their appraisal of the possibilities and limitations of psychology as an experimental discipline. Over the past two decades, the field has borne the brunt of attacks regarding the epistemological assumptions that have in the past constituted an invisible system of presuppositions about psychological experimentation.

A major spokesman in this debate has been Kenneth J. Gergen. In response to Gergen's "social psychology as history" notion—namely, the idea that sociopsychological facts are essentially unrepeatable insofar as they are historical—it has been widely debated whether the evidential status of experimental research in psychology is not like a still photograph of some fleeting event that passes into history at the very moment the picture is taken.[59] Gergen, taking a conventional positivist view of physics and chemistry, has argued that in these fields the past fact can always be observed directly, but that in human subject research there is greater variability and volatility, so that psychological principles are neither definite nor readily verifiable by experimentation. In a similar vein, Jill G. Morawski has argued that conventional experimental social psychology, having "studied conduct through a conceptual lens that regards neither temporal dimensions (history) nor the nuances of language," has stripped social life of its essential context.[60] As a possible way out of the dilemma underscored by Gergen, Morawski, and others and also as a means of circumventing the artifact problem in experimental research, various researchers have turned to the historical narrative or to language as a kind of Rosetta stone which, they argue, will make it possible to decipher the collective individuality of human experience.[61]

At the same time, there has been a growing advocacy of methodological and theoretical pluralism in psychology. A number of variations on the pluralistic, relativistic theme have been propounded under the labels of "transactionalism," "constructivism," "contextualism," and "perspectivism" by researchers and theorists who argue that the essential questions of human nature and human experience are too complex to be the exclusive province of any one methodological or theoretical approach.[62] Briefly, transactionalism stresses the continuity between the knower and the known; constructivism emphasizes that representations of knowledge are developmental and transformative; contextualism focuses on the contexts of understanding, and perspectivism argues for the relative utility (or disutility) of various representations of knowledge from certain perspectives. All proceed from a fallibilistic view of knowledge, accepting the idea that knowledge, while inadequate, is indispensable, nonetheless. Thus it is argued that language, an essential conduit for knowledge, while it is the conventional medium by which we express what we experience, is also limited and thereby imposes limitations on our ability to tell what we know.[63] Restricting psychology to any one methodological

approach—whether quantitative or qualitative, experimental or nonexperimental—automatically cuts psychologists off from experiences that cannot be
easily translated into those terms.

In this chapter we have described the rise of concerns about experimental
artifacts resulting from the social interaction between the experimenter and
the research subject. We have seen that early depictions of problems supposedly
inherent in the laboratory experiment were not fully appreciated until the
1960s. To some extent, the psychological community still responds with a
curious mixture of acceptance and denial. As noted, there has also been a
tendency to redefine the epistemological domain of scientific psychology along
pluralistic and relativistic lines. The effects of this more recent development
have only just begun to reverberate in American and European psychology.
It remains to be seen whether they will result in a further liberalization of
psychology, a new synthesis, or whether they will be subjugated by adherents
of the status quo, only to become the rallying cry for revolutions yet to come.

Notes

1. See Ralph L. Rosnow, "Experimental Artifact," in *The Encyclopedia of Education*, ed. Lee C. Deighton, vol. 3, pp. 483–88 (New York: Free Press and
Macmillan, 1971). By systematic errors are meant uncontrolled variables that
can often be specifically identified but are not self-cancelling; that is, the average
error does not equal zero. Systematic errors can be contrasted with random errors,
which cancel out (on the average) over repeated observations on a single person
or over a group. Though it is an oversimplification, random errors can be thought
of as involving irrelevant variation among individuals, in contrast to systematic
errors, which involve misleading intergroup comparisons. In this discussion we
use the term *artifact* to refer to systematic errors that are attributable specifically
to the role relationship between the experimenter and the subject. See also John
G. Adair, *The Human Subject: The Social Psychology of the Psychological Experiment* (Boston: Little, Brown, 1973); Ralph L. Rosnow, "Social Research:
Artifacts," in *International Encyclopedia of Psychiatry, Psychology, Psychoanalysis,and Neurology*, ed. Benjamin B. Wolman (New York: Van Nostrand
Reinhold, 1977) vol. 10, pp. 328–31; Irwin Silverman, *The Human Subject in
the Psychological Laboratory* (New York: Pergamon, 1977); Robert Rosenthal
and Ralph L. Rosnow, *Essentials of Behavioral Research: Methods and Data
Analysis* (New York: McGraw-Hill, 1984).
2. Oskar Pfungst, *Clever Hans (The Horse of Mr. Von Osten)*, (New York: Henry
Holt, 1911; reissued in 1965 by Holt, Rinehart, and Winston with an introduction
by Robert Rosenthal).
3. See, e.g., Hermann Ebbinghaus, *Memory: A Contribution to Experimental Psychology* (New York: Teachers College, Columbia University, 1913; originally
published in 1885 in a translation by H. A. Ruger and Clara E. Bussenius). See

also Ivan Pavlov, as cited in B. C. Grünberg, *The Story of Evolution* (New York: Van Nostrand, 1929).

4. For a detailed discussion, see Richard Gillespie, "Manufacturing Knowledge: A History of the Hawthorne Experiments" (Ph.D. diss., University of Pennsylvania, 1985); also chap. 6 above.

5. Saul Rosenzweig, "The Experimental Situation as a Psychological Problem," *Psychological Review* 40 (1933):337–54.

6. Generally credited with rediscovering Rosenzweig's work is Irwin Silverman; see, e.g., "The Psychological Subject in the Land of Make-Believe," *Contemporary Psychology* 15 (1970):718–21.

7. See, e.g., John B. Watson, "Psychology as a Behaviorist Views It," *Psychological Review* 20 (1913):158–77. For discussion, see Jerry M. Suls and Ralph L. Rosnow, "The Delicate Balance between Ethics and Artifacts in Behavioral Research," in *New Directions for Methodology of Social and Behavioral Science*, ed. Allan J. Kimmel (San Francisco: Jossey-Bass, 1981), vol. 10, pp. 55–67.

8. For discussion, see Ralph L. Rosnow, *Paradigms in Transition: The Methodology of Social Inquiry* (New York: Oxford University Press, 1981), pp. 17–35. The analogy is based on the assumption that humans are complex pieces of "machinery," in which motion is connected with some outside "stimulus" and the laws of operation can be expressed in exact quantitative terms by functional equations that specify the relations among the parts. It followed that complete prediction was ultimately possible, inasmuch as the ideal case consisted of a sequence of events that, like a universe run with clockwork precision, ran according to invariable laws.

9. For discussion, see Stephen Toulmin and David E. Leary, "The Cult of Empiricism in Psychology, and Beyond," in *A Century of Psychology as a Science: Retrospections and Assessments*, ed. Sigmund Koch and David E. Leary (New York: McGraw-Hill, 1985), pp. 594–617.

10. For discussion and a historical review, see Martin T. Orne, "Hypnosis, Motivation, and the Ecological Validity of the Psychological Experiment," in *Nebraska Symposium on Motivation*, ed. William J. Arnold and Monte M. Page (Lincoln: University of Nebraska Press, 1970), pp. 187–266.

11. See Martin T. Orne, "On the Social Psychology of the Psychological Experiment: With Particular Reference to Demand Characteristics and Their Implications," *American Psychologist* 17 (1962):776–83.

12. Martin T. Orne, "The Nature of Hypnosis: Artifact and Essence," *Journal of Abnormal and Social Psychology* 58 (1959):277–99.

13. Irwin Silverman, "Role-Related Behavior of Subjects in Laboratory Studies of Attitude Change," *Journal of Personality and Social Psychology* 8 (1968):343–48.

14. Monte M. Page, "Modification of Figure-Ground Perception as a Function of Awareness of Demand Characteristics," *Journal of Personality and Social Psychology* 9 (1968):59–66.

15. Monte M. Page, "Social Psychology of a Classical Conditioning of Attitudes Experiment," *Journal of Personality and Social Psychology* 11 (1969):177–86.

16. Martin T. Orne and Karl E. Scheibe, "The Contribution of Nondeprivation

Factors in the Production of Sensory Deprivation Effects: The Psychology of the 'Panic Button,' " *Journal of Abnormal and Social Psychology* 68 (1964):3–12.

17. Robert Rosenthal, "An Attempt at the Experimental Induction of the Defense Mechanism of Projection" (Ph.D. diss., University of California, Los Angeles, 1956).

18. Robert Rosenthal and Kermit L. Fode, "The Effects of Experimenter Bias on the Performance of the Albino Rat," *Behavioral Science* 8 (1963):183–89.

19. Robert Rosenthal and Reed Lawson, "A Longitudinal Study of Experimenter Bias on the Operant Learning of Laboratory Rats," *Journal of Psychiatric Research* 2 (1964):61–72.

20. Robert Rosenthal and Kermit L. Fode, "Psychology of the Scientist: V. Three Experiments in Experimenter Bias," *Psychological Reports* 12 (1963):491–511.

21. The number of experimenter-expectancy studies (N) and the estimated mean effect sizes (σ, in standard deviation units) in eight research areas, reported as of 1977, were: research time studies ($N = 6$, $\sigma = 0.23$), inkblot tests ($N = 9$, $\sigma = 0.84$), animal learning studies ($N = 14$, $\sigma = 1.78$), laboratory interviews ($N = 22$, $\sigma = 0.27$), psychophysical judgments ($N = 23$, $\sigma = 1.31$), learning and ability ($N = 33$, $\sigma = 0.72$), person perception ($N = 114$, $\sigma = 0.51$), and everyday situations ($N = 96$, $\sigma = 1.44$). For discussion, see Robert Rosenthal, "Biasing Effects of Experimenters," *Et Cetera* 34 (1977):253–64. For other review papers, see Robert Rosenthal, "Interpersonal Expectations: Effects of the Experimenter's Hypothesis," in *Artifact in Behavioral Research*, ed. Robert Rosenthal and Ralph L. Rosnow (New York: Academic Press, 1969) pp. 181–277; and Robert Rosenthal and Donald B. Rubin, "Interpersonal Expectancy Effects: The First 345 Studies," *Brain and Behavioral Sciences* 3 (1978):377–86.

22. For an overview, see Milton J. Rosenberg, "The Conditions and Consequences of Evaluation Apprehension," in *Artifact in Behavioral Research*, pp. 280–350.

23. Leon Festinger and J. Merrill Carlsmith, "Cognitive Consequences of Forced Compliance," *Journal of Abnormal and Social Psychology* 58 (1959):203–10.

24. Milton J. Rosenberg, "When Dissonance Fails: On Eliminating Evaluation Apprehension from Attitude Measurement," *Journal of Personality and Social Psychology* 1 (1965):18–42; for further discussion, see idem, "Some Limits of Dissonance: Toward a Differentiated View of Counterattitudinal Performance," in *Cognitive Consistency*, ed. Shel Feldman (New York: Academic Press, 1966), pp. 135–70.

25. Quote from Rosenberg, "Conditions and Consequences of Evaluation Apprehension," p. 286.

26. Ibid., p. 283.

27. Ralph L. Rosnow, Barry E. Goodstadt, Jerry M. Suls, and A. George Gitter, "More on the Social Psychology of the Experiment: When Compliance Turns to Self-Defense," *Journal of Personality and Social Psychology* 27 (1973):337–43.

28. See Philip A. Goldberg, "Expectancy, Choice, and the Other Person," *Journal of Personality and Social Psychology* 2 (1965):895–97; Irwin Silverman and Dale Kleinman, "A Response Deviance Interpretation of the Effects of Experimentally Induced Frustration on Prejudice," *Journal of Experimental Research in Personality* 2 (1967):150–53.

29. Kenneth L. Higbee and M. Gawain Wells, "Some Research Trends in Social Psychology during the 1960s," *American Psychologist* 27 (1972):963–66. For other relevant findings, see Duane P. Schultz, "The Human Subject in Psychological Research," *Psychological Bulletin* 72 (1974):214–28; R. Evans and E. Donnerstein, "Some Implications for Psychological Research of Early versus Late Term Participation by College Students," *Journal of Research in Personality* 8 (1974):102–09.

30. Quinn McNemar, "Opinion-Attitude Methodology," *Psychological Bulletin* 43 (1946):289–374.

31. Robert Rosenthal and Ralph L. Rosnow, "The Volunteer Subject," in *Artifact in Behavioral Research*, pp. 61–120; idem, *The Volunteer Subject* (New York: Wiley, 1975).

32. Ralph L. Rosnow and Jerry M. Suls, "Reactive Effects of Pretesting in Attitude Research," *Journal of Personality and Social Psychology* 15 (1970):338–43.

33. For a general discussion of these controls, see Martin T. Orne, "Demand Characteristics and the Concept of Quasi-Controls," in *Artifact in Behavioral Research*, pp. 161–63.

34. Orne, "Hypnosis, Motivation."

35. Robert Rosenthal, *Experimenter Effects in Behavioral Research* (New York: Appleton-Century-Crofts, 1966); for discussion of other strategies, see Rosenthal and Rosnow, *Essentials of Behavioral Research*.

36. Rosenthal and Rosnow, *The Volunteer Subject*, pp. 117–120; for a summary of this work, see idem, "The Volunteer Subject Revisited," *Australian Journal of Psychology* 28 (1976):97–108.

37. See Ralph L. Rosnow and Leona S. Aiken, "Mediation of Artifacts in Behavioral Research," *Journal of Experimental Social Psychology* 9 (1973):181–201; Ralph L. Rosnow and Daniel J. Davis, "Demand Characteristics and the Psychological Experiment," *Et Cetera* 34 (1977):301–13.

38. Arie W. Kruglanski, "The Human Subject in the Psychology Experiment: Fact and Artifact," in *Advances in Experimental Social Psychology*, vol. 8, ed. Leonard Berkowitz (New York: Academic Press, 1975), p. 102.

39. Stewart Page and Elizabeth Yates, "Attitudes of Psychologists Toward Experimenter Controls," *Canadian Psychologist* 14 (1973):202–08.

40. Jerry M. Suls and John Gastorf, "Has the Social Psychology of the Experiment Influenced how Research is Conducted?", *European Journal of Social Psychology* 10 (1980):291–94.

41. Alan E. Gross and India Fleming, "Twenty Years of Deception in Social Psychology," *Personality and Social Psychology Bulletin* 8 (1982):402–08.

42. Robert J. Menges, "Openness and Honesty versus Coercion and Deception in Psychological Research," *American Psychologist* 28 (1973):103–34.

43. See, e.g., Herbert C. Kelman, *A Time to Speak* (San Francisco: Jossey-Bass, 1968). For other references to the critique of deception, see Ralph L. Rosnow, *Paradigms in Transition*, pp. 55–71.

44. Leonard Bickman and Thomas Henchy, *Beyond the Laboratory: Field Research in Social Psychology* (New York: McGraw-Hill, 1972).

45. David W. Wilson and Robert B. Schafer, "Is Social Psychology Interdisciplinary?", *Personality and Social Psychology Bulletin* 4 (1978):548–52.

46. For a historical discussion of the "relevance crises" in American psychology, see Ralph L. Rosnow, *Paradigms in Transition*.

47. Jonathan R. Cole and Stephen Cole, *Social Stratification in Science* (Chicago: University of Chicago Press, 1973).

48. Orne, "On the Social Psychology of the Psychological Experiment."

49. Rosenthal, *Experimenter Effects in Behavioral Research*.

50. Robert Rosenthal and Ralph L. Rosnow, eds., *Artifact in Behavioral Research*.

51. Rosenberg, "When Dissonance Fails."

52. See Michael Martin, "The Philosophical Importance of the Rosenthal Effect," *Journal for the Theory of Social Behaviour* 7 (1977):81–97.

53. Kruglanski, "The Human Subject in the Psychology Experiment."

54. For examples of this, see Harold Sigall, Elliot Aronson, and Thomas Van Hoose, "The Cooperative Subject: Myth or Reality?", *Journal of Experimental Social Psychology* 6 (1970):1–10; John G. Adair and B. S. Schachter, "To Cooperate or To Look Good: The Subjects' and Experimenters' Perceptions of Each Others' Intentions," *Journal of Experimental Social Psychology* 8 (1972):74–85.

55. Stephen J. Weber and Thomas D. Cook, "Subject Effects in Laboratory Research: An Examination of Subject Roles, Demand Characteristics, and Valid Inference," *Psychological Bulletin* 77 (1972):273–95.

56. Kruglanski, "Human Subject in the Psychology Experiment."

57. Arie W. Kruglanski, "Much Ado about the 'Volunteer Artifact,' " *Journal of Personality and Social Psychology* 28 (1973):348–54.

58. Ralph L. Rosnow and Robert Rosenthal, "Taming of the Volunteer Problem: On Coping with Artifacts by Benign Neglect," *Journal of Personality and Social Psychology* 30 (1974):188–90.

59. See Kenneth J. Gergen, "Social Psychology as History," *Journal of Personality and Social Psychology* 26 (1973):309–20; see also idem, "Experimentation in Social Psychology: A Reappraisal," *European Journal of Social Psychology* 8 (1978):507–27.

60. Jill G. Morawski, "Contextual Discipline: The Unmaking and Making of Sociality," in *Contextualism and Understanding in Behavioral Science: Implications for Research and Theory*, ed. Ralph L. Rosnow and Marianthi Georgoudi (New York: Praeger, 1986), pp. 47–66.

61. See, e.g., John Shotter, *Social Accountability and Selfhood* (Oxford: Blackwell, 1984); Kenneth J. Gergen and Mary M. Gergen, "Narrative Form and the Construction of Psychological Science," in *Narrative Psychology: The Storied Nature of Human Conduct*, ed. Theodore R. Sarbin (New York: Praeger, 1985), pp. 22–44.

62. See, e.g., Irwin Altman and B. Rogoff, "World Views in Psychology: Trait, Interactional, Organismic, and Transactionalist Perspectives," in *Handbook of Environmental Psychology*, ed. David Stokols and Irwin Altman (New York: Wiley, 1985), pp. 25–62; Karin Knorr-Cetina, *The Manufacture of Knowledge: An Essay on the Constructivist and Contextual Nature of Science* (New York: Pergamon, 1981); Theodore R. Sarbin, "Contextualism: A World View for Modern Psychology," in *Nebraska Symposium on Motivation 1976: Personal*

Construct Psychology, ed. J. K. Cole and A. W. Landfield (Lincoln: Nebraska University Press, 1977), pp. 1–42; Marianthi Georgoudi and Ralph L. Rosnow, "Notes toward a Contextualist Understanding of Social Psychology," *Personality and Social Psychology Bulletin* 11 (1985):5–22; William J. McGuire, "A Perspectivist Looks at Contextualism and the Future of Behavioral Science," in *Contextualism and Understanding in Behavioral Science*, pp. 271–301.

63. See, e.g., Ralph L. Rosnow, "Shotter, Vico, and Fallibilistic Indeterminacy," *British Journal of Social Psychology* 25 (1986):215–16.

9

Key Words:
A History of
Debriefing in
Social Psychology

Benjamin Harris*

University of

Wisconsin

The history of a word is never solely a matter of etymology: the need for a new word is socially determined, right at the start, and any subsequent changes of denotation, as well as the cluster of connotations surrounding it, are also in response to demands from society. The word cannot be isolated from its historical background; indeed some key words offer a concise and suggestive clue to the historian or sociologist.
— Sydney Ross, *Annals of Science* 18

In the contemporary usage of English-speaking psychologists there exists the curious word *debrief*. Military in origin,[1] it is used today as a transitive verb, as in the assertion that "a proper experimenter should always debrief his subjects." Found most commonly in the North American dialect of experimental social psychology, *debrief* refers to any of three types of interaction that psychologists have with participants, or "subjects," at the conclusion of a research session. At that time, a psychologist may debrief participants by eliciting their attitudes and beliefs concerning the research, revealing the ex-

*I am grateful to my research assistants, Lynette Hand and Philip Fisher, for their surveys of psychological and popular sources for the terminology of debriefing. Thanks also go to Rebecca Mitchell and J. G. Morawski for their sound editorial advice and to the many colleagues who commented on earlier incarnations of this paper, including that which I presented at the 1984 meeting of the Cheiron Society.

periment's true purpose and methods, or removing any harmful residual effects of the experimental procedures.

Ubiquitous today, such debriefing is of surprisingly recent origin. Even among social psychologists whose experiments have long produced distress and relied on deception, debriefing is a recent development, both as a procedure and as a terminology. Twenty years ago most researchers did not carry out such a procedure; and if they did, it was usually called something else.[2] Even ten years ago, when textbook authors described ethical responsibilities and experimental procedures, the terms *debrief* and *debriefing* were often absent.

Today, by contrast, debriefing has become a universally accepted procedure and methodological descriptor. In textbooks of social psychology it is presented as a necessary part of any research that involves the temporary deception of participants or that might cause them distress.[3] In experimental and clinical psychology, authors have recommended universal adoption of debriefing and its mention in all published psychological research.[4] Even in education, researchers recommend its use as a method of curriculum development, suggesting that students be regularly debriefed about their experience in the classroom.[5]

My purpose in this chapter is to describe the development of debriefing, both as a procedure and as a terminology, from a historical and sociological perspective. Debriefing is interesting historically because it became accepted in psychology quickly, at the time of the rapid change of social psychology into a primarily experimental discipline. It is interesting sociologically because of its contradictory associations with humanism, militarism, and bureaucratism.

In *practice*, debriefing seems humane, since it allows research subjects to discuss their experience with the experimenter—an advance over traditional researchers' indifference to subjects' ignorance or distress. In contrast to this humanism, however, is the set of antihumanist connotations—militarist and bureaucratic—that debriefing *as terminology* brings with it to the laboratory. Thus the social meaning of debriefing's entry into psychology is paradoxical; it appears to be the adoption of a military metaphor for an ethical *desideratum*, that of reducing the distress and ignorance of a fellow human being.

I shall begin with a history of the terminology of debriefing in press accounts and nonpsychological sources, from World War II to the United States space program and contemporary foreign relations. After this will come a history of debriefing in social psychology, from Stanley Milgram's compliance research down to the present day.

To complement this history, I will present an analysis of the evolution of debriefing from the perspective of the sociology of science. The language of debriefing, I will argue, has developed as a technical jargon within the new subdiscipline of experimental social psychology, where it serves to socialize newcomers, foster unity, and exclude the uninitiated. Because of its grammatical properties and connotations, the language of debriefing also helps to maintain the authority of psychological experimenters over their laboratory subjects.[6]

A History of Nonpsychological Uses

Two decades before its entry into the psychological literature, the word *debrief* first appeared as British military jargon. Used most prominently to describe Royal Air Force (RAF) procedures, it referred to the process of interrogating pilots who had returned from bombing missions. Thus a pilot was said to be "briefed" on his mission beforehand and "debriefed" afterwards.[7]

As the words *debrief* and *debriefing* entered popular usage, at least one wartime commentator objected to their unusual grammatical quality.[8] *Debrief*, it was noted, involves unnecessary use of the passive voice, making potential actors into subjects of action. Specifically, using it to describe the interrogation of a pilot after a flight denies the pilot an active role, makes him the object of an action, and obscures the source of that action.

By the end of World War II, *debriefing* had become a permanent element of military jargon, particularly in regard to the handling of airplane pilots. In press accounts, it next appeared in coverage of United States actions in the Korean and Vietnam wars.[9] In those wars, pilots continued to be debriefed, although the Press rarely reported the process or called it by name. In the case of the Korean War, this was in part because the tactics used were different from those used in World War II; in the case of the Vietnam War, in part because of the secrecy surrounding the bombing of noncombatant countries such as Laos and Cambodia. More relevant to a psycholinguistic understanding of debriefing is another reason applicable to both Korea and Vietnam: the passive voice of "Pilot X was debriefed" was inappropriate to United States war propaganda. This propaganda used the symbolism of the brave, individualistic American hero who was fighting a mass of emotionless Asian automatons. Such a hero, it seems, should not passively accept debriefing—that is, routine interrogation by his own side's intelligence officers. To do so would acknowledge the domination of an impersonal military discipline over the individual soldier; it would also portray him as more the subject of others' actions than an actor himself.

In accounts of the Korean and Vietnam wars, this tension between individual heroism and the passivity of being debriefed was resolved by altering either the syntax or the semantics of debriefing. In one case *Life* magazine described an American pilot in Korea as going to a "debriefing shed" to make a routine report, thereby preserving the active voice. In another, a heroic account of an American pilot in Vietnam, included a scene in which the injured flyer "continued to debrief an intelligence officer as he [the pilot] lay on the operating table."[10]

Much more than the Korean or Vietnam wars, the United States manned space program introduced *debrief* to the public through its press releases, the language of which was adopted by journalists eager for engineering and scientific terminology.

In retrospect, *debrief* appears to have been a term that served the needs of both competing ideologies in the space program: engineering control versus human bravery and initiative ("the right stuff").[11] Initially, the term seemed like another piece of jargon from the military bureaucracy, ill-suited to astronauts like Gus Grissom, who impressed the audience at his postflight press conference by his ability to give a "calm, methodical and often humorous report" of what he had done. Grissom appeared not as a redundant human component, but as a crew-cut "fighter pilot giving a matter-of-fact briefing to intelligence officers on a just-completed mission."[12]

Such an individualistic image of the astronaut could not be sustained for long, however. It had to be modified to fit a program that required astronauts to act more as technicians than pilots. To those who followed space flights on television or in the press, this bureaucratic aspect of the space program was most noticeable at the end of each astronaut's flight. Then, instead of being immediately released to the public, astronauts underwent medical tests and extensive interviews before their missions (so-called) were considered complete. As space flights became longer and more complex, these postflight interviews became correspondingly longer and more elaborate, coming to resemble engineering conventions or extended employee interviews more than the postflight telling of tales by fighter pilots.

Calling such sessions "debriefings" was one way of preserving the astronaut's image as a pilot just returned from an important adventure. Although it made him seem more like a team-player than a fighter pilot in Korea, this was necessary to justify days of questioning by engineers and NASA executives. Thus the impersonality of "being debriefed" helped to maintain the identity of the astronaut; like a World War II bomber pilot, he was someone submitting to a bureaucratic procedure that was necessary for the achievement of a larger, heroic goal.[13]

Debriefing in Psychological Research

Within the field of psychology, the terminology of debriefing was first used in the mid-1960s, at the time of the United States space program and the Vietnam War. Its use grew more widespread in the 1970s and attained almost universal acceptance by the mid-1980s, by which time it had become popularly associated with counterintelligence operations, hostage releases, and other foreign relations activities.[14] Between 1964 and 1984, psychologists did not simply add *debrief* to their vocabulary. At the same time their view of the nature of psychological research, including the relationship of experimenter to subject, was changing. Thus the semantics of debriefing in psychology is inextricable from the history of experimentation with human subjects since World War II.

In tracing this history, two events constitute useful chronological mileposts. The first is the initial published use of the term *debrief* by Stanley Milgram in 1964. The second is the inclusion of debriefing terminology in the first modern edition of the *Handbook of Social Psychology*, published in 1968. These mileposts, interesting in their own right, also serve to demarcate three historical periods: from World War II until the controversy over Milgram's obedience research, from Milgram's defense of his research until the modern *Handbook of Social Psychology*, and from the *Handbook*'s publication until today. In relation to the language of debriefing, those periods can be characterized as prehistory, early development, and institutionalization.

Experimental Procedures Prior to 1964

In the years between World War II and 1964, psychologists' research reports never once used the terminology of debriefing. During that period, psychologists rarely practiced debriefing in any of its three modern meanings. That is, psychologists often deceived subjects, without subsequently revealing their deception; that they often placed subjects under stress without later mitigating its effects; and that they failed to assess subject perceptions of the research being conducted.[15]

Although such debriefing practices are assumed to be necessary by researchers today, they are based on a particular awareness of the human research participant—namely, that he or she is a hypothesis-forming being who might be alienated or harmed by psychological manipulations, and who has individual rights that are not secondary to the demands of science. This awareness, common today, was slow in developing. First came an awareness of subjects' rights, then a concern that experimenters might actually be placing subjects at risk. Finally, subjects began to be seen as social beings who could help or harm the experimenter and whose favor should be cultivated.

Before 1953, the American Psychological Association (APA) had not taken any action in direct support of the rights of human subjects in psychological research. It had been assumed, apparently, that psychologists would obey a scientific version of the Hippocratic oath in dealings with all nonprofessionals (that is, patients and experimental subjects).[16] After World War II, however, this assumption was challenged by two developments. The first was internal to the discipline: the unification of applied and academic psychologists within the APA, which resulted in a greater attention to professional issues by that organization (for example, licensing, ethical standards, and interprofessional relations).[17] Second were the revelations during the Nuremberg trials of Nazi atrocities in the form of medical experiments supervised by leading German physicians. These revelations decreased public confidence in the ability of professions such as medicine to police themselves; in the United States the professions responded by codifying their ethical standards and attempting to show evidence of enforcement.

In 1953, in an attempt to project an image of a morally informed, publicly responsive organization, the APA revised its statement of members' ethical responsibilities. That document, *Ethical Standards of Psychologists*, was amended to include for the first time a section on "The Psychologist's Relation to His Research Subjects." Using a combination of stated ethical principles and case studies from psychologists' practice, this section covered the topics of experimentally produced emotional stress, harmful aftereffects of research procedures, and the use of deception by experimenters.[18]

According to the APA guidelines, experimentally induced distress was to be removed by the end of an experiment. Further, if an experiment might create harmful effects, subjects were to be informed of that possibility in advance and should be allowed to withdraw if they wished. The use of deception should be restricted to experiments that could not otherwise be performed.

Through these standards, the APA was announcing that subjects should not be harmed by psychological research. It was also announcing its agreement with the legal concept of informed consent—namely, that an action can be voluntary only if the actor knows of its potential consequence. Although this elevated research subjects to the status of citizens with legal rights, it is based on what by today's standards is a curiously nonpsychological view of psychological research and its participants. Researchers were not expected to routinely educate their subjects about the nature of the research at the end of a session, and there was no suggestion that the perceptions and informal reactions of participants should be elicited. Thus, of the three modern procedures commonly termed *debriefing*, only one was recommended by the APA in 1953, namely, the reduction of personal distress by the end of an experiment.

In the ten years following the APA's publication of its *Ethical Standards*, the actual practice of psychologists was sometimes more conscientious than what had been recommended, sometimes less so. Many experimenters whose research required that subjects suffer distress (for example, in order to study defense mechanisms) worked effectively to reduce anxiety and guilt at the end of each research session.[19] Others revealed to subjects the minor deceptions that had been practiced on them, even when no adverse effects were anticipated.[20]

Most researchers showed no evidence of having revealed their deceptions, however, even when such information might have prevented psychological distress, as when subjects were persuaded to deliver what they thought were painful shocks to fellow students.[21] Further, textbooks of social psychology often failed to cover the topic of the ethical responsibilities of experimenters in any form.[22]

Language Prior to 1964

Prior to 1964, most research reports made no mention of how participants were treated at the conclusion of an experimental session—whether they were calmed, interviewed, or informed of the researcher's purpose.[23] When reference *was* made to various post-experimental procedures, the language was specific to the procedure being discussed (for example, calming the subject) and differed from author to author.

When the author was the APA's committee on ethical standards, the language of post-experimental responsibilities was managerial (that is, authoritative, simple, yet not always direct). According to *Ethical Standards*, psychologists who exposed research subjects to emotional stress "should be prepared to remove . . . the possible harmful aftereffects . . . as soon as permitted by the design of the experiment."[24] Since the APA did not recommend the routine revealing of deception to subjects, its standards were silent on that aspect of debriefing. Likewise, interviewing subjects to assess their perceptions was not discussed.

In the decade following the APA's statement, individual psychologists adopted a variety of verbal conventions in their writing to describe the three tasks that today are called "debriefing." Alleviation of subjects' experimentally induced distress, when performed, was often not mentioned directly in research reports. For example, in his 1960 report of a deception study, William McGuire merely makes passing reference to a "postexperimental 'catharsis' session" before he begins to detail his treatment of research subjects. No direct reference is made to it in the report's section on procedures; instead, that section simply ends with the statement that "the true nature of the experiment was then explained to the S's."[25]

Those authors who did describe their distress-reducing procedures generally used mildly psychodynamic language.[26] Thus two textbook authors recommended offering "an opportunity for subject catharsis" after particularly unpleasant procedures, including (if necessary) a "semitherapeutic interview."[27] Similarly, in addressing researchers who use deception to induce stress, Arnold Buss urged that they end their sessions by telling subjects the truth and arranging for them to "ventilate any feelings [they] may have about being tricked."[28] Dana Bramel used similar language to reassure readers that his research sessions did not end "until the subjects seemed quite restored and satisfied."[29]

The general task of supplying information to previously deceived subjects was described less metaphorically, using phrases such as "The experimenter explained the true purpose of the experiment," "The true purpose and design of the study were revealed," and "The experimental manipulation was explained."[30] This prosaic language helped experimenters avoid the pejorative connotations of the words *deception* and *deceive*, although anyone who explained a deception study's true purpose was obviously revealing the deception at the same time.[31]

One notable exception to this trend was Stanley Milgram's description in 1963 of a session of post-experimental "Interview and Dehoaxing."[32] Also, in defending the ethics of his research the following year, Milgram provided the first published use of a less sarcastic-sounding term for the same procedure: *debriefing*.

From the Milgram Experiment to the new *Handbook of Social Psychology*

The next significant period in the history of debriefing was the four years between Stanley Milgram's 1964 defense of his obedience research and the appearance of Aronson and Carlsmith's chapter on methodology in the *Handbook of Social Psychology*. This was a period of rapid growth for experimental social psychology, as signified by the founding of two new journals dedicated to experimental work *(The Journal of Personality and Social Psychology* and the *Journal of Experimental Social Psychology)*. This growth brought with it changes in research methods, debates over the ethics and validity of various methods, and a new vocabulary for those debates. It was in this context of professional expansion and methodological change that debriefing, as a practice and a terminology, first gained widespread acceptance.

The Ethics of Deception and Distress

Of all the controversies over psychological methodology in the mid-1960s, the most visible was that over the ethics of experiments in which participants were purposely deceived about what was taking place. Prior to Stanley Milgram's research on obedience, the experimental use of deception and distress had evoked little concern or public commentary by psychologists. In psychology journals the only note of concern seems to have been that voiced by the social psychologist Edgar Vinacke, who in 1954 cautioned that deception might adversely affect the public's confidence in psychologists.[33] The sole response to that warning was a colleague's published reassurance that at his campus, students showed no animosity toward experimenters who had deceived them.[34] After that, objections to the practice of deception virtually disappeared from the psychological literature and did not reappear until 1964, when the first critique of Milgram's obedience research was published.

What made Milgram's work so objectionable to some was also what made it memorable to all: Milgram's ability to produce dramatic amounts of emotional distress in his subjects and to induce them to undertake acts of cruelty. He did this through the use of social influence and deception, orchestrated in what is now a familiar scenario to students of social psychology.

In Milgram's study each participant began the experiment paired with a stranger whom he believed to be another volunteer, but who was in fact an accomplice of the experimenter. The experiment was billed as a study of learning, in which one subject (the accomplice) attempted to memorize a list of word pairs. With the accomplice out of sight but audible over an intercom, the naive participant was then ordered to give what he believed to be increasingly painful shocks to the accomplice, using equipment that was in reality harmless.

Milgram's surprising finding was that the great majority of subjects were fully obedient to the orders given them by an authority figure—a high-school biology teacher whom Milgram outfitted in a white laboratory coat and passed off as a research psychologist. However, many of the participants showed dramatic signs of emotional distress during the experiment, such as nervous tics and uncontrollable laughter.[35]

Critics of Milgram's study, most prominently the psychologist Diana Baumrind, disliked both its effects on participants and its methods. With regard to the latter, Milgram was seen as subverting the social relations of psychological research, since his success depended on manipulation of the initial trust of the experimental subject both toward the experimenter as an individual and toward the institutionally sanctioned roles of experimenter and subject.[36] To the extent that Milgram's subjects accepted those roles in the staged experiment, Baumrind reasoned, they followed the experimental script and pushed the shock-levers on cue.

Although this acceptance produced dramatic behavior, including distress over the prescribed actions, Milgram's study was criticized as being not a true study of obedience to personal authority, but rather, a study of the strength of subjects' beliefs in the prescribed roles of scientific research. Thus it was seen not just as ethically compromised, but also as methodologically confounded, since an aspect of the research *setting* had become part of the research.

Countering such criticism, Milgram emphasized his compliance with traditional ethical norms and revealed that none of his subjects had suffered permanent harm. He explained that he had arranged a "friendly reconciliation" between each subject and the accomplice he had been paired with, at which time Milgram had convincingly explained the importance of research on obedience. Further, he had used both an interview and a follow-up questionnaire to verify subjects' positive opinion of the research. All these "debriefing and assessment procedures," Milgram noted, "were carried out as a matter of course."[37]

In response to Baumrind's charge that his research had confounded social context and individual authority, Milgram pleaded guilty. But such confounding, he asserted, gave his study ecological validity, since obedience most often occurs in institutional settings. In the case of his study, the setting had been the "social institution called the psychology experiment."[38] As long as subjects were educated, rather than harmed, by their experience, Milgram said, using such an institution to produce obedience was not wrong.

Following the exchange between Milgram and Baumrind, sides were drawn on the issue of whether deception research was inherently flawed and should be avoided. Most prominent among those who agreed with Baumrind was Herbert Kelman, who believed that deception research was ethically questionable if it created distress or manipulated the subject's trust in the researcher. Such manipulation was also shortsighted, since it undermined the public's confidence in psychologists and made it increasingly difficult to find naive research subjects.[39]

Most active researchers seem to have viewed the ethical issues more narrowly, however, focusing on the importance of doing no lasting harm to subjects. To them, what was most important was convincing subjects of the falsity of any negative self-perceptions that had been induced and providing a social setting in which they could rid themselves of their distress. Also important was publicizing the ethical soundness of social psychological research. Thus, in the period immediately following the Milgram-Baumrind debate, published research reports included increasingly explicit descriptions of experimenters' humane post-experimental treatment of subjects. One experimenter, for example, specified that her post-experimental interviews had each lasted half an hour and had included the opportunity for subjects to express their feelings regarding their research participation.[40] Another noted that in some cases "special apologies were given [to subjects] for the necessity of shocking them."[41] And the well-known psychologist Elliot Aronson detailed subjects' reactions to learning of his deception; happily, they "left the interview room in good spirits."[42]

The Experimental Subject as a Source of Error

At the same time as the ethics of deception were being debated, another controversy arose concerning the "human factor" in social psychological research. In this case, however, the debate was methodological. What was in dispute was whether the perceptions and response biases of subjects were an uncontrolled source of error, contaminating experimental research.

This issue was brought to the attention of most psychologists by Martin Orne in an influential article in the *American Psychologist* in 1962.[43] In describing the experimental subject as an active, hypothesis-forming creature, rather than passive, as previously assumed, Orne's purpose was twofold. First, he was continuing an earlier debate over the validity of hypnotic states, which he had argued could be an intensified version of normal subjects' desire to cooperate with experimenters' demands. Second, and more generally, he was alerting researchers to the possibility that subjects were affected not just by experimental variables, but by their perceptions of experimenters' expectations (which he called "demand characteristics"). This argument was applied to a variety of areas in psychology by Orne, Robert Rosenthal, and others, who found research subjects ranging from planaria to human sixth-graders being influenced by subtle cues from experimenters.[44]

In social psychology, a related debate began in the mid-1960s between supporters and critics of cognitive dissonance theory. What was under dispute was the validity of a standard finding in dissonance research, that paying subjects to write essays that contradicted their personal beliefs resulted in more change in attitude if the pay were low.[45]

Critics of this finding alleged that it was not due to the arousal of cognitive dissonance in the lower-paid essay writers, but rather, that subjects who were overpaid became suspicious of the arrangement and refused to acknowledge a change in attitude that they had actually experienced. The error of dissonance researchers, these critics charged, was their failure to detect subjects' suspiciousness, a first step in eliminating its effects from their laboratory work. If, after careful post-experimental interviewing, suspicious subjects were eliminated, it was alleged, replications of traditional studies would refute the predictions of cognitive dissonance theory.[46]

For the history of debriefing, the significance of this debate was not its eventual outcome—dissonance theory, in modified form, survived[47]—but rather that it sensitized social psychologists to the problem of subject suspiciousness. In response to this problem, changes occurred both in laboratory practice and in the reporting of research. One change was the initiation of research on suspiciousness itself; Brock and Becker, for example, studied whether students became generally more suspicious (and less useful as research subjects) after they had been informed of an experimental deception.[48] Another response was that some individual psychologists withheld information from research participants, to prevent them from passing it on to other, "naive" subjects. Thus Philip Zimbardo did not reveal an experimental deception to student subjects at the end of a 1965 study because their school had no honor code.[49]

A third, more modal response was the demonstration by individual researchers of their awareness of the problem of suspiciousness. They did this, first by introducing more elaborate interviewing procedures at the conclusion of their experimental sessions, which included eliciting "private impressions" by questionnaire, transcribing subjects' verbal interview responses, and in some cases, having students "interrogated."[50] Authors also included more information concerning post-experimental interviewing in their research reports, such as the length of time spent with subjects,[51] the goals of the interviews,[52] and whether they were verbal, by questionnaire, or both.[53] Increasingly, such accounts were demarcated from those of other procedures by a separate subheading in the text of the report.[54] Frequently, too, they referred to one or another aspect of this interviewing as "debriefing."[55]

The Institutionalization of Debriefing

Following Milgram's initial use of the terminology of debriefing in 1964, it gradually became acceptable usage for authors in psychology. A major step in this process of acceptance occurred in 1967 and 1968, when debriefing received the sanction of being used in a major social psychology text and in the new *Handbook of Social Psychology.*

The text was *Foundations of Social Psychology* by Edward E. Jones and Harold Gerard, published at a time when the rapid growth of social psychology had outstripped the coverage and nonexperimental orientation of earlier texts. *Foundations* thus served to introduce a new generation of students to social psychology and to inform older colleagues of current trends in an increasingly experimental field.

In contrast to earlier authors, Jones and Gerard recommended that researchers end each experimental session by discovering what each subject thought of the experiment, rather than simply by telling the subject what had happened or dismissing the subject with no discussion. Such questioning of subjects, together with the tasks of informing subjects and removing any distress, were what Jones and Gerard termed "debriefing"—a "critical step in the experimental process, and [one] that requires considerable skill and careful training."[56] They saw eliciting subjects' impressions as a necessary part of interpreting the results of an experiment; thus, they presented the "debriefing discussion" as an integral part of the psychology experiment and placed it last in their flowchart of experimental tasks to be performed. This stood in contrast to previous texts, in which a final interview with subjects, if mentioned at all, was presented as a post-experimental task—that is, one that fulfilled ethical, rather than methodological, requirements.

A year after the publication of Jones and Gerard's text, the language of debriefing achieved further recognition by its inclusion in the new *Handbook of Social Psychology,* in the chapter reviewing laboratory experimentation in social psychology written by Elliot Aronson and J. M. Carlsmith.[57]

The previous edition of the *Handbook* had been published in 1954, at a time when social psychological research was more eclectic, both in theory and in methods. A quarter-century later, however, experimentalism had come to dominate the research journals, at the same time that the overlap between social psychology and other subfields had decreased.

One of the most striking changes between the old and the new *Handbook* was the changed attitude toward research participants and the participants' relationship to the experimenters. In 1954, the chapter on experimentation made no reference to ethical concerns, deception, or experimenter effects. Compared with the 1968 edition, it read like an undergraduate physics text, concentrating on statistics, design, and reliability of instruments for measurement. Human research participants were portrayed analogously to non-human subjects, as passive sources of information. The brief discussion of subject error attributed it to the demography of the subject population and assumed that with randomization it could be held constant across situations. The author thus denied that different experimental treatments might interact with subjects' biases or awareness of the researcher's intent.[58]

Aronson and Carlsmith's treatment of experimentation in 1968 differed from that of the previous *Handbook* both in tone and in content. The tone was purposely informal, the authors noting that "we will be addressing the reader in much the same way that we address our own graduate students." The content was also unorthodox. Rather than offering encyclopedic coverage of experimental designs, the chapter focused on "the more mundane and less explicit aspects" of research, including the relationship between experimenter and subject and techniques by which "an experimenter handles human subjects."[59]

In this informal discussion of psychological research, the ethical and procedural consequences of deception were emphasized. Aronson and Carlsmith explained that an experimenter was ethically responsible for "debriefing" a previously deceived subject in a manner that would both reveal the true state of affairs and allow for the reduction of distress, restoring the subject to a pre-experimental degree of self-esteem and health.

Methodologically, these authors emphasized, the "debriefing process" should be a gradual one that allows subjects to voice their biases and subjective perceptions of the experimental manipulations. Using such procedures, the experimenter could transform the potentially withholding and resentful subject into an ally and source of further information. Also, a gently inquiring style was well suited to the job of discussing with subjects the true goals of the research—a noncoercive method of convincing them of its merit.

Thus, by 1968, the most authoritative statement of social psychological procedures had adopted the term *debriefing* to refer to the general process of so-called post-experimental interviewing. As used by Aronson and Carlsmith, this language was both informal and imprecise in a manner that suited the authors' needs. To them, it referred to the combined methodological and ethical tasks made necessary by increasing reliance on deception research and by growing awareness of subjects as an independent factor in the most carefully designed laboratory experiments.

Further Acceptance of Debriefing, 1969–Present

In the almost two decades since the appearance of the new *Handbook*, the terminology and practice of debriefing have continued to increase in popularity.[60] This occurred initially amid an ongoing debate over the ethics and methodological effectiveness of post-experimental interviewing, dehoaxing, and the removal of distress.

Ethics

In the realm of ethics, a major development in the early 1970s was the APA's change in attitude toward the dehoaxing and educating of experimental subjects. Throughout the previous decade, the APA's guidelines for research with humans were contained in the 1953 edition of *Ethical Principles* mentioned above. Those principles allowed deception if it were judged necessary for the research problem and if any distress it induced were subsequently removed. Deception that was methodologically necessary that did not produce distress was not considered an ethical issue; thus, experimenters were not instructed to routinely inform all experimental subjects of the tricks that had been played on them.

This view of the ethics of deception changed when the APA drew up separate guidelines for research with human participants. Those new principles, drafted in 1971 and published two years later, considered all deception and passive withholding of information to be of ethical concern. Experimenters engaged in such practices, *Ethical Principles* stated, must subsequently explain the nature of their research to all participants, and "remove any misconceptions that may have arisen."[61]

An additional concern of the APA ethics committee was subjects' acceptance of experimenters' post-experimental explanations. Some subjects might be so strongly affected by a deception, the commentary section of the *Principles* suggested, that they would perceive later explanations as further attempts at deception. To allay such suspicions, it was recommended that post-experimental discussions with subjects include an opportunity for them to ask questions, which should then be answered honestly and convincingly. If subjects' doubts persisted during such "debriefings," the commentary stated, perhaps the initial deception was too strong and should not be used in future.[62]

Thus, by 1973, the APA had adopted the position that all experiments should be followed by a session of education concerning the experimental methods and purposes. Further, when a significant amount of deception had been employed, subjects should be interviewed as a means of removing lingering doubts and mistrust. These ethical principles not only recommended removal of experimentally induced stress, but also mandated a post-experimental discussion with three purposes: dehoaxing, catharsis, and assessment of subject perceptions.[63]

Methodology

To those concerned with the effectiveness of experimental methods, the late 1960s marked a new phase in the discussion of subject bias and experimenter effects. As in the discussion that Orne, Rosenthal, and Rosenberg had begun earlier, a key issue was the effectiveness of post-experimental interviews.

Earlier, social psychologists had become sensitized to the possibility that subjects' perceptions and suspiciousness were biasing the results of certain types of experiments (for example, in cognitive dissonance). The response of researchers was to interview subjects at the conclusion of experiments more carefully and to attempt to remove any residual effects of deception. Although such methodological changes were felt by most to be sufficient to ensure the validity of experimental research, skepticism persisted and became focused on the issue of the effects of repeated research participation. What evidence was there, skeptics asked, that post-experimental discussions had a restorative effect on subjects? If subjects' confidence in experimenters was not restored, it was argued, then the entire subject population would eventually become contaminated by suspiciousness.[64]

This question had been raised earlier by Kelman in his appeal for decreased use of deception in order to preserve the effectiveness of social research. Soon it was being tested empirically by experimenters who devised ingenious methods for first deceiving subjects, then dehoaxing them, and finally assessing whether they truly accepted the dehoaxing information. In one study, for example, college students were first led to believe (falsely) that they had been judged socially inadequate; they were then told that this was not true and that they had been lied to. The students' true feelings about their social adequacy were then assessed, to see whether the initial deception was still having an effect.[65]

As is often the case with controversial issues, both sides found support in the research which tested the effectiveness of dehoaxing. Initially, experimenters found that the effects of deception persisted past the post-experimental interview. Such effects, however, were of the sort to be of more ethical than methodological concern, taking the form of lowered self-esteem (resulting from false, negative feedback) or continued belief in minor deceit about experimental procedures.

The more methodologically significant effect had been predicted to be a spreading contamination of research by suspicious subjects, whose cynicism would increase with each participation in an experiment, and whose responses would then become untrustworthy. General suspiciousness, it was shown, may have been produced in repeatedly deceived and debriefed subjects; but such suspiciousness was not found to significantly influence their behavior in other experiments. The most widely accepted conclusion from research on debriefing was that deception might alienate some individuals from psychology as a profession, but that it did not decrease the internal validity of most experimental research.[66]

Language Use

In published research reports, textbooks, and commentaries, the terminology of debriefing became standard in the decade following Aronson and Carlsmith's chapter in the *Handbook*. Earlier, the three tasks of post-experimental discussions were more often referred to by other terms, such as *dehoax, catharsis,* and *inquiry*. Gradually, however, authors began to substitute *debrief* for one or more of these words.

In research articles, sections on methodology commonly ended with reports of subjects being interviewed and debriefed, or simply (and ambiguously) debriefed. In textbooks, the word *debriefing* first appeared in quotation marks or preceded by the qualifier "so-called."[67] By the late 1970s, however, *debriefing* was in use without such qualification, to describe what had become a standard procedure of experimental research. This change is most visible in the widely selling social psychology text by Robert Baron and Donn Byrne, which in 1974 (with W. Griffith) contained none of the language of debriefing, but in 1977 had adopted it as synonymous with all three tasks of post-experimental interviewing. To emphasize the importance of this procedure, the authors included a photo of the "thorough debriefing" of a student by an experimenter which was said to be "an essential safeguard in social research."[68]

Debriefing, Technical Jargon, and Scientific Legitimation

In reviewing the history of debriefing, it is tempting to see it as simply the gradual adoption of a useful procedural innovation. Debriefing, one might argue, has developed in response to two needs of psychologists over the last twenty years: first, the need for a procedural modification that would maintain public confidence in the psychological experiment as an ethically sound institution; second, the need for a technique to prevent contamination of research data by subject biases. Debriefing procedures, one could say, became popular because they uniquely met these two pressing needs; and the terminology of debriefing was adopted because it succinctly described these new procedures.

The strength of such an analysis is its recognition that social psychology is an experimental discipline with rapidly changing methods which is influenced by extrascientific factors—for example, public concern over deception research. Its weakness is the assumption that changes in terminology naturally follow and accurately describe changes in scientific procedures. Debriefing, it assumes, was adopted in response to a changed set of experimental procedures. As those procedures became institutionalized, so did the terminology that best represented them.

Examination of the history of debriefing shows the relation of language and practice to be more complex. The term *debriefing*, for example, is not the most accurate term for what occurs at the end of a particular social psychology experiment, since it fails to distinguish among three distinct activities— the dehoaxing, interrogating, and desensitizing of participants.[69] It is also not the best term with which to reassure the public that psychologists are humanists, since it is popularly associated with returned astronauts, bomber pilots, and CIA operatives.

An alternative view of the language of debriefing is that its adoption has been related only indirectly to changing practice of social psychologists. Rather than a simple reflection of new procedures, debriefing may best be seen as fulfilling a pair of sometimes contradictory needs. This language serves, first, as technical jargon in the relatively new subfield of experimental social psychology. It also serves the larger field of social psychology as part of that discipline's legitimizing ideology. Specifically, it legitimizes a social science that increasingly excludes social factors from its consideration.

Debriefing as Technical Jargon

The simplest explanation for the rise of debriefing is the first, that it is part of the technical jargon of *experimental* social psychology, a subfield that gained hegemony over its parent discipline in the years 1960–80. According to sociolinguists, if *debrief* were such a jargon or language code, it could be expected to perform both pragmatic and semantic functions. Pragmatically, codes establish a relationship between users and separate users from nonusers. Semantically, codes allow for the expression of complex ideas in simple form.[70]

The language of debriefing, when related to the recent history of social psychology, fits such a sociolinguistic model well. The term first appeared in the mid-1960s, at the time when social psychologists who specialized in laboratory research first achieved dominance over their nonexperimental colleagues. That dominance was facilitated by the perfection of experimental techniques—most noticeably deception—that allowed social processes to be modeled in the laboratory. But using these techniques necessitated new forms of communication. Novices had to be instructed in the new social psychology of the experimenter-subject relationship, or what Aronson and Carlsmith called "how an experimenter handles human subjects."[71] Newcomers also needed to be socialized into the professional group of experimentalists (with their own journals, research topics, and philosophical assumptions),[72] and the morale and unity of this group had to be maintained.

Many authors have found the term *debriefing* well suited to the instructional role, since its interrogatory connotations remind the reader that subject perceptions and attitudes need to be assessed.[73] It can also be used synonymously with either *dehoaxing* or *catharsis*, making it easier to refer to two or more of these processes in a single research report. In addition to its educative functions, the language of debriefing fosters unity and esprit de corps. Like the phrase "We just ran our subjects [through the procedure]," the statement "I debriefed my subjects" is insiders' talk.[74] It may be heard in the laboratory or at psychologists' conventions or may be read in technical journals. However, since it would never be found in statements to outsiders (for example, in the formal parts of the APA's *Ethical Principles*), its use serves to unify, to create a boundary between experimental social psychologists and all outsiders.[75]

It also helps establish an identity for those who use it. Like the phrase "running subjects," "debriefing" has an informal, antiliterary, but also unemotional ring to it. It is well suited to the self-image of experimental social psychologists as tough-minded, hard-working laboratory types, who resemble their colleagues in general experimental psychology more than sociologists and personality theorists.[76]

Debriefing and the Syntax of Bureaucracy

In addition to its semantic and intraprofessional uses, the language of debriefing serves yet another function: that of reinforcing bureaucratic social relations. This comes, I assert, from its ability to recast actors into the role of manipulated objects, while disguising the process of manipulation.

As mentioned at the beginning of the chapter, *debriefing* was coined as a term that transformed the active into the impersonal passive. Instead of saying "The pilot reported," "The pilot briefed the intelligence officer," or even "The pilot was interrogated by the colonel," the military would say, "The pilot was debriefed. "Thus the pilot is never allowed to become someone of special status (either high or low) because of something that he has done.[77] Instead, the pilot is someone who proceeds through (that is, "is processed by") the system.

Within the field of social psychology, an analogous transformation occurs. Individuals who participate in an experiment and provide information to a researcher are debriefed. They are cast in neither the active role of contributor nor the passive role of an organism being blatantly manipulated by an experimenter. Instead, they are simply "debriefed subjects," individuals subjected to an impersonal procedure.

Relevant to this process is the timing of debriefing's ascendance in social psychology. During the decade 1965–75, as debriefing was becoming dominant, groups of critics concerned with ethics and with methodology challenged the traditional ways in which experimenters treated their subjects. As noted earlier, the first group campaigned against deception and induced distress in research with humans. The second group urged that subjects' biases be taken into account by experimenters, who were accused of aping the physical sciences in their disdain for subjective factors in laboratory work. As an alternative to current practices, members of both these groups called for the greater empowerment of research subjects. In the ethics debate, opponents of repeated deception urged that the subject-experimenter relationship be restored to one of trust and mutual respect. In the discussion of subject biases, some critics argued for the adoption of a social-constructionist view of research subjects that would recognize them as intentional, account-generating beings who act as both observers and those observed, speakers and listeners.[78]

Today, these challenges to the traditional social relations of the psychology laboratory have been rebuffed. This has been accomplished, however, through cooptation rather than confrontation, aided by both the procedure and the language of debriefing. As the preceding history indicates, the 1960s and 1970s saw experimenters alter their practice to include the debriefing of most subjects. Specifically, they listened to subjects in order to assess the effectiveness of the experiment's deceptions and to judge any distress that might have been caused. Experimenters then explained the deceptions that had been perpetrated and attempted to remove any distress that remained.

But such debriefing, although seemingly more humane than failing to dehoax subjects, was incapable of doing what critics called for: namely, empowering subjects. For after eliciting subject perceptions, contemporary experimenters cannot change their past behavior or the experiment. Instead, they continue the debriefing by imposing a purportedly scientific reality on the individuals who have just volunteered their (mistaken) view of the research. Rather than being empowered, the experimental subject receives another lesson in the importance of looking to the experimenter for the correct view of things.[79]

This is not to deny that debriefing is done with the best of intentions. It is only to say that such procedures have had the opposite effect from that which many critics intended; they have made research less social and more like the physical sciences than ever before.[80] Although experimenters pay much more attention to subjects as cognitive beings, their goal is to strip the psychology laboratory of all naturally occurring social cues and then create the ones necessary to elicit the effect they desire. Thus the laboratory has become a setting in which every perception, reaction, and speculation of each subject is thoroughly controlled by the experimenter. Such control is deemed preferable to subjects' developing idiosyncratic, private hypotheses of the experimenter's intent, thereby biasing the subject's reaction. Experimental control is also believed to be necessary to prevent temporarily stressful manipulations from getting out of hand and having an unanticipated, lasting effect. The cost of such control, however, is to further reduce the subject's contribution as a being with the capacity for social understanding; for social understanding is not possible in an intentionally artificial world.

It is this preprocessed, overcontrolled, benevolently bureaucratic setting that the language of debriefing connotes. "The subjects were debriefed" expresses well the fact that a set of important procedures were performed on subjects at the end of their visit to the social psychology laboratory. Although the exact nature of the actions is not always conveyed (for example, whether the subjects were dehoaxed or desensitized), what is made clear is that the necessary operations were carried out, and that it is now safe for the subject to be released from the experimenter's control. As in the case of stories of returning military and diplomatic personnel, it is something of a relief to hear that the debriefing has been completed. It is an assurance that the procedures of education, interrogation, and emotional restoration have been smoothly—albeit impersonally—performed.

Notes

1. George Lloyd Rule, "The Special Vocabulary of the United States Air Force" (Master's thesis, Stanford University, 1957), p. 47; Elizabeth Christensen, "Debrief," *American Speech* 25, no. 1 (Feb. 1950):74; *A Supplement to the Oxford English Dictionary* (Oxford: Clarendon Press, 1972), p. 747.
2. Robert J. Menges, "Openness and Honesty versus Coercion and Deception in Psychological Research," *American Psychologist* 28 (1973):1030–34; Lisa B. Perry and Paul R. Abramson, "Debriefing: A Gratuitous Procedure?", *American Psychologist* 35 (1980):298–99; Daniel Ullman and Thomas T. Jackson, "Researchers' Ethical Conscience: Debriefing from 1960 to 1980," *American Psychologist* 9 (1982):972–73.
3. Robert A. Baron and Donn Byrne, *Social Psychology*, 4th ed. (Boston: Allyn and Bacon, 1984).
4. Perry and Abramson, "Debriefing," p. 299.
5. E.g., Daniel L. Duke, "Debriefing: A Tool for Curriculum Research and Course Improvement," *Curriculum Studies* 9 (1977):157–63. Closer to home I note that my university has a body named the "Freshman Seminar Implementation Committee," which has scheduled a "debriefing session" (apparently for the faculty whom it supervises). See Secretary of the Faculty, University of Wisconsin-Parkside, "Meetings and Announcements," 12–19 Dec. 1986.
6. For background on the authority relations of modern experimental psychology, see Kurt Danziger, *The Historical Construction of Social Roles in the Psychological Experiment*, York University Department of Psychology Reports, no. 123 (1982).
7. Rule, "Special Vocabulary"; *Supplement to the O.E.D.* first usage; Christensen, "Debrief."

8. *Supplement to the O.E.D.*, second usage.
9. John Dille, "Two Jets Carry a Third at 30,000 Feet," *Life* 31 (17 Dec. 1951): 30–31; *Supplement to the O.E.D.*, third usage; James R. McCarthy and George B. Allison, *Linebacker II: A View from the Rock* (Maxwell Air Force Base, Ala.: Airpower Research Institute, 1979), p. 145.
10. Donald K. Schneider, *Air Force Heroes in Vietnam* (Maxwell Air Force Base, Ala.: Airpower Research Institute, 1979), p. 11.
11. Tom Wolfe, *The Right Stuff* (New York: Farrar Straus, 1979).
12. John W. Finney, "Grissom Receives Medal for Flight," *New York Times*, 23 June 1961, p. 61.
13. John Noble Wilford, "Astronauts Flown to Cape for Debriefing on Mission," *New York Times*, 7 June 1966, p. 1; Evert Clark, "Two Astronauts End 8-Day Flight Tired but in 'Wonderful Shape'; Johnson Hails U.S. Space Gains," *New York Times*, 29 Aug. 1965, p. 1; "Apollo 7 Crewmen Brief 20 Comrades," *New York Times*, 25 Oct. 1968, p. 42.
14. Thomas Powers, *The Man who Kept the Secrets* (New York: Knopf, 1970), p. 70; Charles Fenyvesi and Walter Shapiro, "Debrief Encounter," *New Republic*, 2 Aug. 1982, pp. 12–13; Alex Brummer, "Castro Rescues Jackson by Freeing 26 Political Prisoners," *Guardian*, 15 July 1984; Thomas A. Sancton, "Smoothing the Way," *Time*, (17 Nov. 1980), p. 79. See also Ralph Blumenthal, "An Upstate Murder in 1983 is Reported Linked to Iran Arms Smuggling," *New York Times*, 2 Dec. 1986, p. 5; Flora Lewis, "Moscow's Memory Hole," *New York Times*, (18 Nov. 1986), p. 27; Ralph Blumenthal, "New Technology Helps in Fight against the Mafia," *New York Times*, 24 Nov. 1986, p. 30B; Frances FitzGerald, "Rajneeshpuram—Part II," *New Yorker*, (29 Sept. 1986), p. 125.
15. Ullman and Jackson, "Researchers' Ethical Conscience"; Menges, "Openness and Honesty." A notable exception was Solomon Asch in his research on conformity in groups; see Solomon E. Asch, "Effects of Group Pressure upon the Modification and Distortion of Judgments," in *Groups, Leadership and Men*, ed. Harold Guetzkow (Pittsburg, Pa.: Carnegie Press, 1951), pp. 177–90.
16. Irwin A. Berg, "The Use of Human Subjects in Psychological Research," *American Psychologist* 9 (1954):108–11.
17. Donald S. Napoli, *Architects of Adjustment: The History of the Psychological Profession in the United States* (Port Washington, N.Y.: Kennikat Press, 1981).
18. American Psychological Association, *Ethical Standards of Psychologists* (Washington, D.C.: APA, 1953).
19. Dana Bramel, "A Dissonance Theory Approach to Defensive Projection," *Journal of Abnormal and Social Psychology* 64 (1962):121–29; Arnold H. Buss, *The Psychology of Aggression* (New York: Wiley, 1961), pp. 1–307.
20. Albert Pepitone and Chester Wilpizeski, "Some Consequences of Experimental Rejection," *Journal of Abnormal and Social Psychology* 60 (1960):359–64.; Philip Zimbardo, "Involvement and Communication Discrepancy as Determinants of Opinion Conformity," *Journal of Abnormal and Social Psychology* 60 (1960):89.
21. Timothy C. Brock and Arnold H. Buss, "Dissonance, Aggression, and Evaluation of Pain," *Journal of Abnormal and Social Psychology* 65 (1962):197–202; Jack E. Hokanson. "The Effects of Frustration and Anxiety on Overt Aggression," *Journal of Abnormal and Social Psychology* 62 (1961):346–51.

22. Allen L. Edwards, "Experiments: Their Planning and Execution," in *Handbook of Social Psychology*, vol. 1, ed. Gardner Lindzey (Cambridge, Mass.: Addison-Wesley, 1954); David Krech, Richard S. Crutchfield, and Egerton L. Ballachey, *Individual in Society; A Textbook in Social Psychology* (New York: McGraw-Hill, 1962); Paul F. Secord and Carl W. Backman, *Social Psychology* (New York: McGraw-Hill, 1964); Stephen Stansfeld Sargent and Robert C. Williamson, *Social Psychology*, 3d ed. (New York: Ronald Press, 1966). It should be noted that such texts also included much less information on experimental methodology than those published ten years later.

23. For an example, see Leonard Berkowitz, "Manifest Hostility Level and Hostile Behavior," *Journal of Social Psychology* 52 (1960):165–71. See also Ullman and Jackson, "Researchers' Ethical Conscience," for a survey of post-experimental practices.

24. APA, *Ethical Standards*, 1953 ed., p. 122.

25. William J. McGuire, "Direct and Indirect Persuasive Effect of Dissonance Producing Images," *Journal of Abnormal and Social Psychology* 60 (1960):354.

26. Exceptions to this style were the occasional uses of behaviorist terminology to describe post-experimental procedures; e.g.: "The experimental manipulation was explained to him and he was given a chance to verbalize his reaction to the experiment" (Philip S. Gallo and Charles G. McClintock, "Behavioral, Attitudinal, and Perceptual Differences between Leaders and Non-Leaders in Situations of Group Support and Non-Support," *Journal of Social Psychology* 56 [1962]:126).

27. W. A. Scott and Michael Wertheimer, *Introduction to Psychological Research* (New York: Wiley, 1962), p. 293.

28. Buss, "Psychology of Aggression," p. 42.

29. Bramel, "A Dissonance Theory," p. 124.

30. Elliot Aronson and J. Merrill Carlsmith, "Performance Expectancy as a Determinant of Actual Performance," *Journal of Abnormal and Social Psychology* 65 (1962):180; Zimbardo, "Involvement and Communication," p. 89; Gallo and McClintock, "Behavioral, Attitudinal." Exceptions to this practice of using prosaic language include "unveiling the deception" and "revealed the deception" (Bramel, "A Dissonance Theory," p. 124, and Harold B. Gerard and Jacob M. Rabbie, "Fear and Social Comparison," *Journal of Abnormal and Social Psychology* 62 [1961]:588, respectively).

31. A further alternative was to refer to deception by a euphemism. Thus Pepitone and Wilpizeski state that "E informed S of the nature of the experiment, exposed the dissimulation . . ." ("Some Consequences," p. 360).

32. Stanley Milgram, "Behavioral Study of Obedience," *Journal of Abnormal and Social Psychology* 67 (1963):371–78.

33. W. Edgar Vinacke, "Deceiving Experimental Subjects," *American Psychologist* 9 (1954):155.

34. Arthur C. MacKinney, "Deceiving Experimental Subjects," *American Psychologist* 10 (1955):133.

35. Milgram, "Behavioral study." I use masculine pronouns here because all Milgram's participants and accomplices were male.

36. Diana Baumrind, "Some Thoughts on Ethics of Research: After Reading Mil-

gram's 'Behavioral Study of Obedience'," *American Psychologist* 19 (1964):421–23.

37. Stanley Milgram, "Issues in the Study of Obedience: A Reply to Baumrind," *American Psychologist* 19 (1964):849.

38. Ibid., p. 850.

39. Herbert Kelman, "Human Use of Human Subjects: The Problem of Deception in Social Psychological Experiments," *Psychological Bulletin* 67 (1967):1–11.

40. Claire G. Fishman, "Need for Approval and the Expression of Aggression under varying Conditions of Frustration," *Journal of Personality and Social Psychology* 2 (1965):809–16.

41. Larry Rabinowitz, Harold H. Kelley, and Robert M. Rosenblatt, "Effects of Different Types of Interdependence and Response Conditions in the Minimal Social Situation," *Journal of Experimental Social Psychology* 2 (1966):187.

42. Elliot Aronson and Darwyn Linder, "Gain and Loss of Esteem as Determinants of Interpersonal Attractiveness," *Journal of Experimental Social Psychology* 1 (1965):156–71.

43. Martin T. Orne, "On the Social Psychology of the Psychological Experiment: With Particular Reference to Demand Characteristics and their Implications," *American Psychologist* 17 (1962):776–83.

44. See Robert Rosenthal and Ralph L. Rosnow, eds., *Artifact in Behavioral Research* (New York: Academic Press, 1969).

45. Jack W. Brehm and Arthur R. Cohen, *Explorations in Cognitive Dissonance* (New York: Wiley, 1962). See also chap. 8 above.

46. Irving L. Janis and J. B. Gilmore, "The Influence of Incentive Conditions on the Success of Role Playing in Modifying Attitudes," *Journal of Personality and Social Psychology* 1 (1965):17–27; Milton J. Rosenberg, "When Dissonance Fails: On Eliminating Evaluation Apprehension from Attitude Measurement," *Journal of Personality and Social Psychology* 1 (1965):28–43.

47. William J. McGuire, "Suspiciousness of Experimenter's Intent," in *Artifact in Behavioral Research*, pp. 13–60; Edward E. Jones and Harold B. Gerard, *Foundations of Social Psychology* (New York: Wiley, 1967), pp. 485–97.

48. Timothy C. Brock and Lee Alan Becker, " 'Debriefing' and Susceptibility to Subsequent Experimental Manipulations," *Journal of Experimental Social Psychology* 2 (1966):314–23. See also Elliot Aronson, "Avoidance of Inter-Subject Communication," *Psychological Reports* 19 (1966):238.

49. Philip G. Zimbardo, "The Effect of Effort and Improvisation on Self-persuasion Produced by Role-playing," *Journal of Experimental Social Psychology* 1 (1965):103–20.

50. Edward E. Jones, Kenneth J. Gergen, Peter Gumpert, and John W. Thibaut, "Some Conditions Affecting the Use of Ingratiation to Influence Performance Evaluation," *Journal of Personality and Social Psychology* 1 (1965):613–25; Rosenberg, "When Dissonance Fails"; James C. Baxter, Melvin J. Lerner, and Jerome S. Miller, "Identification as a Function of the Reinforcing Qualities of the Model and the Socialization Background of the Subject," *Journal of Personality and Social Psychology* 2 (1965):695.

51. Fishman, "Need for Approval," p. 812.

52. Rosenberg, "When Dissonance Fails," p. 34; Thomas J. D'Zurilla, "Recall Ef-

ficiency and Mediating Cognitive Events in 'Experimental Repression'," *Journal of Personality and Social Psychology* 1 (1965):253–57.

53. James M. Dabbs and Irving L. Janis, "Why Does Eating while Reading Facilitate Opinion Change? An Experimental Inquiry," *Journal of Experimental Social Psychology* 1 (1965):133–44, esp. p. 138.

54. Fishman, "Need for Approval"; Nickolas B. Cottrell and Dennis L. Wack, "Energizing Effects of Cognitive Dissonance upon Dominant and Subordinate Responses," *Journal of Personality and Social Psychology* 6 (1967):132–38.

55. Brock and Becker, " 'Debriefing' "; Aronson, "Avoidance."

56. Jones and Gerard, *Foundations*, p. 62.

57. Elliot Aronson and J. Merrill Carlsmith, "Experimentation in Social Psychology," in *Handbook of Social Psychology*, rev. ed., ed. G. Lindzey and E. Aronson, vol. 2 (Reading, Mass.: Addison-Wesley, 1968), pp. 1–79.

58. Edwards, "Experiments."

59. Aronson and Carlsmith, "Experimentation," p. 29.

60. According to a recent survey of research published in the *Journal of Personality and Social Psychology* in 1979, two-thirds of the studies involving deception reported the subsequent debriefing of participants, and the actual frequency of debriefing overall was much higher than that. Eighty-one percent of all researchers privately acknowledged debriefing their subjects, although deception was used in only 59 percent of their studies. See John G. Adair, Terrance W. Dushenko, and R. C. L. Lindsay, "Ethical Regulations and Their Impact on Research Practice," *American Psychologist* 40 (1985):59–72.

61. American Psychological Association, *Ethical Principles in the Conduct of Research with Human Participants* (Washington, D.C.: APA, 1973), p. 77. It is noteworthy that the most severe penalty that the APA could impose for violation of these principles was removal of the offender from membership.

62. Ibid., p. 80. The word *debriefing*, used only once in this commentary, appears within quotation marks. Apparently this is the authors' way of saying "the so-called debriefing process."

63. A related, less altruistic function was convincing subjects of the futility of protesting their treatment: "cooling the mark out" in the language of confidence games. See Erving Goffman, "On cooling the Mark Out: Some Aspects of Adaptation to Failure," in *Interpersonal Dynamics: Essays and Readings on Human Interaction* ed. Warren G. Bennis, David E. Berlew, Edgar H. Schein, and Fred I. Steele, 3d ed. (Homewood, Ill.: Dorsey Press, 1973), pp. 273–84; Frederick E. Tesch, "Debriefing Research Participants: Though this be Method there is Madness to it," *Journal of Personality and Social Psychology* 35 (1977):217–24.

64. Brock and Becker, " 'Debriefing'."

65. Elaine Walster, Ellen Berscheid, Darcy Abrahams, and Vera Aronson, "Effectiveness of Debriefing following Deception Experiments," *Journal of Personality and Social Psychology* 6 (1967):371–80.

66. Stephen J. Weber and Thomas D. Cook, "Subject Effects in Laboratory Research," *Psychological Bulletin* 77 (1972):273–95; David S. Holmes, "Debriefing after Psychological Experiments," *American Psychologist* 31 (1976):858–67.

67. Jonathan L. Freedman, J. Merrill Carlsmith, and David O. Sears, *Social Psychology* (Englewood Cliffs, N.J.: Prentice-Hall, 1970), p. 438; Clair Sellitz,

Lawrence S. Wrightsman, and Stuart W. Cook, *Research Methods in Social Relations* (New York: Holt, 1976), p. 221; Elliot Aronson, *The Social Animal*, 2d ed. (San Francisco: Freeman, 1972), p. 285.

68. Robert A. Baron and Donn Byrne, *Social Psychology*, 2d ed. (Boston: Allyn and Bacon, 1977), p. 32. Earlier edition by Robert A. Baron, Donn Byrne, and W. Griffith (Boston: Allyn and Bacon, 1974).

69. *Debriefing* was not the first term to be used in a generic manner for all post-experimental tasks. In 1960, one author used the term *catharsis session* to refer to the procedures of revealing the deception, pledging subjects to secrecy, and assessing their suspicions. Since that author was reporting on his dissertation research, it is logical to suppose that this generic use of *catharsis session* was common to a larger group of researchers at the very least those in his graduate program). See Lawrence S. Wrightsman, Jr., "Effects of Waiting with Others on Changes in Level of Felt Anxiety," *Journal of Abnormal and Social Psychology* 61 (1960):216–22.

70. Robin Tolmach Lakoff, "Doubletalk: Sexism in Tech Talk," in *Technological Woman*, ed. Jan Zimmerman (New York: Praeger, 1983), pp. 38–43.

71. Aronson and Carlsmith, "Experimentation," p. 1.

72. In 1965 the APA's *Journal of Abnormal and Social Psychology* divided into the *Journal of Abnormal Psychology* and the experimentally dominated *Journal of Personality and Social Psychology*. At the same time, the *Journal of Experimental Social Psychology* was started.

73. E.g., Edward E. Jones, pers. com., 27 Nov. 1985.

74. The phrase "running subjects" refers to all interactions between experimenter and human subject in the laboratory, as in the exchange: "Where's Diane?"; "She's in her lab running subjects." The metaphorical reference is to psychologists in animal learning and motivation experiments watching rodents run through specially constructed mazes.

75. Studied informality is a characteristic way of socializing new members of the subfield, as exemplified by the *Handbook of Social Psychology*'s methodology chapter, the authors of which address their readers "in much the same way that we address our own graduate students" (Aronson and Carlsmith, "Experimentation," p. 29).

76. It may also qualify as an example of male talk, tending to exclude women by its unemotional quality and its harking back to (mostly male) psychologists' experience collecting and analyzing information for government intelligence organizations during World War II. For a useful case study of male talk within a profession, see Perri Klaus, "Hers," *New York Times*, 4 Oct. 1984, p. C2.

77. At the same time, the pilot maintains some autonomy by not being subjected to a clearly degrading procedure such as interrogation. On the use of *debrief* as a euphemism for *interrogate*, see John Silverlight, "Words," *Observer*, 11 Aug. 1985.

78. Robert M. Farr, "On the Social Significance of Artifacts in Experimenting," *British Journal of Social and Clinical Psychology* 17 (1978):299–306.

79. Tesch, "Debriefing," p. 221.

80. Farr, "On the social significance."

CONTRIBUTORS

KURT DANZIGER is in the Department of Psychology at York University, Toronto, Ontario. In addition to numerous social psychological and historical studies, he is preparing a history of the subject in psychological research.

LAUREL FURUMOTO is in the Department of Psychology at Wellesley College, Wellesley, Massachusetts. Her research in the history of psychology includes a recent book on the history of women psychologists, coauthored with Elizabeth Scarborough.

RICHARD GILLESPIE is in the Department of History and Philosophy of Science at the University of Melbourne, Parkville, Australia. He has completed a comprehensive study of the Hawthorne experiment. His research interests include the history of developing and applying knowledge to monitor human performance.

BENJAMIN HARRIS is in the Department of Psychology, University of Wisconsin at Parkside. His research interests include personality, social psychology, and the history of psychology. He has published numerous articles on the development of twentieth-century psychology.

GAIL A. HORNSTEIN is in the Department of Psychology at Mt. Holyoke College, South Hadley, Massachusetts. She works in the areas of phenomenology and the history of psychology and is completing a book on the history and cultural impact of quantification in psychology.

HENRY L. MINTON is in the Department of Psychology, University of Windsor, Windsor, Ontario. His research examines the history of personality and social psychology. Among his works is a forthcoming biography of Lewis Terman.

JILL G. MORAWSKI is in the Department of Psychology at Wesleyan University, Middletown, Connecticut. Her research includes the construction of new theory in social psychology, particularly feminist theory, and the history of psychology. Her current work focuses on psychologists' discourse.

RALPH L. ROSNOW is in the Department of Psychology at Temple University, Philadelphia. His many books and articles have explored new theory in social psychology. Among them is a recent volume on contextualism in the behavorial sciences, edited with Marianthi Georgoudi.

KARL E. SCHEIBE is in the Department of Psychology, Wesleyan University, Middletown, Connecticut. His interests include dramaturgy, narrative, and the history of psychology. He is currently translating a volume by Wilhem Wundt with Rolf Kroger.

JERRY M. SULS is in the Department of Psychology, State University of New York at Albany. His research interests include the social psychology of self, comparison processes, and health.

INDEX